T0342252

YALE AGRARIAN STUDIES SERIES

JAMES C. SCOTT, SERIES EDITOR

The Agrarian Studies Series at Yale University Press seeks to publish outstanding and original interdisciplinary work on agriculture and rural society—for any period, in any location. Works of daring that question existing paradigms and fill abstract categories with the lived experience of rural people are especially encouraged.

—James C. Scott, *Series Editor*

James C. Scott, *Seeing Like a State: How Certain Schemes to Improve the Human Condition Have Failed*
Steve Striffler, *Chicken: The Dangerous Transformation of America's Favorite Food*
James C. Scott, *The Art of Not Being Governed: An Anarchist History of Upland Southeast Asia*
Edwin C. Hagenstein, Sara M. Gregg, and Brian Donahue, eds., *American Georgics: Writings on Farming, Culture, and the Land*
Timothy Pachirat, *Every Twelve Seconds: Industrialized Slaughter and the Politics of Sight*
Kuntala Lahiri-Dutt and Gopa Samanta, *Dancing with the River: People and Life on the Chars of South Asia*
Alon Tal, *All the Trees of the Forest: Israel's Woodlands from the Bible to the Present*
Felix Wemheuer, *Famine Politics in Maoist China and the Soviet Union*
Jenny Leigh Smith, *Works in Progress: Plans and Realities on Soviet Farms, 1930–1963*
Graeme Auld, *Constructing Private Governance: The Rise and Evolution of Forest, Coffee, and Fisheries Certification*
Jess Gilbert, *Planning Democracy: Agrarian Intellectuals and the Intended New Deal*
Jessica Barnes and Michael R. Dove, eds., *Climate Cultures: Anthropological Perspectives on Climate Change*
Shafqat Hussain, *Remoteness and Modernity: Transformation and Continuity in Northern Pakistan*
Edward Dallam Melillo, *Strangers on Familiar Soil: Rediscovering the Chile-California Connection*
Devra I. Jarvis, Toby Hodgkin, Anthony H. D. Brown, John Tuxill, Isabel López Noriega, Melinda Smale, and Bhuwon Sthapit, *Crop Genetic Diversity in the Field and on the Farm: Principles and Applications in Research Practices*
Nancy J. Jacobs, *Birders of Africa: History of a Network*
Catherine A. Corson, *Corridors of Power: The Politics of U.S. Environmental Aid to Madagascar*
Kathryn M. de Luna, *Collecting Food, Cultivating People: Subsistence and Society in Central Africa through the Seventeenth Century*
Carl Death, *The Green State in Africa*
James C. Scott, *Against the Grain: A Deep History of the First Civilizations*
Loka Ashwood, *For-Profit Democracy: Why the Government Is Losing the Trust of Rural America*
Jonah Steinberg, *A Garland of Bones: Child Runaways in India*
Hannah Holleman, *Dust Bowls of Empire: Imperialism, Environmental Politics, and the Injustice of "Green" Capitalism*

For a complete list of titles in the Yale Agrarian Studies Series, visit yalebooks.com/agrarian.

HANNAH HOLLEMAN

Dust Bowls of Empire

Imperialism, Environmental Politics, and the Injustice of "Green" Capitalism

Yale UNIVERSITY PRESS
NEW HAVEN AND LONDON

Published with assistance from the Mary Cady Tew
Memorial Fund.

Yale University Press books may be purchased in quantity
for educational, business, or promotional use. For
information, please e-mail sales.press@yale.edu (U.S. office)
or sales@yaleup.co.uk (U.K. office).

Set in Janson type by IDS Infotech Ltd., Chandigarh, India.
Printed and bound by CPI Group (UK) Ltd, Croydon, CR0 4YY

Library of Congress Control Number: 2018938166

ISBN 978-0-300-23020-8 (hardcover : alk. paper)

A catalogue record for this book is available from the British
Library.

10 9 8 7 6 5 4 3 2 1

For Lou Ella and Betty Joe

At the end of the Civil War the US Army hardly missed a beat before the war "to win the West" began in full force. As a far more advanced killing machine and with seasoned troops, the army began the slaughter of people, buffalo, and the land itself, destroying natural tall grasses of the Plains and planting short grasses for cattle, eventually leading to the loss of topsoil four decades later.

—Roxanne Dunbar-Ortiz, *An Indigenous People's History of the United States*, 2014

The attitude of capitalism—industrial and pre-industrial—toward the earth was imperial and commercial; none of its ruling values taught environmental humility, reverence, or restraint. This was the cultural impetus that drove Americans into the grassland and determined the way they would use it.

—Donald Worster, *Dust Bowl: The Southern Plains in the 1930s*, 1979

Man-induced soil erosion is taking place today in almost every country inhabited by civilized man, except northwestern Europe. It is a disease to which any civilization founded on the European model seems liable when it attempts to grow outside Europe. . . . The white man's burden in the future will be to come to terms with the soil and plant world, and for many reasons it promises to be a heavier burden than coming to terms with the natives.

—G. V. Jacks and R. O. Whyte, *The Rape of the Earth: A World Survey of Soil Erosion*, 1939

CONTENTS

ACKNOWLEDGMENTS

I thank Jean Thomson Black, my superb editor at Yale University Press, for all her work and insight that helped improve my manuscript. Working with Jean made me feel confident at every step of the way that YUP was the exact right choice of press for me and this book. Also at the press, I thank Michael Deneen, Mary Pasti, Harry Haskell, Jeffrey Schier, and the very helpful reviewers, whose comments in response to my original proposal guided me in important ways as I completed the project. Finally, I thank James C. Scott, faculty editor of the Yale Agrarian Studies Series, for inviting me to include my work in this important scholarly series.

Many, many thanks go to the wonderful members of the Department of Anthropology and Sociology at Amherst College for feedback on earlier versions of this work, as well as encouragement, advice, and friendship throughout the research and writing process. Deborah Gewertz and Frederick Errington deserve special thanks for their friendship, example, and support of my project. They read my work and offered critical feedback, came to my events and talks based on the research presented in this book, invited me into their warm home, introduced me to other scholars, and shared with me their work on a closely related subject. This exchange over the past few years has meant the world to me and contributed to my experiencing a vibrant intellectual life in western Massachusetts. Likewise, my friendship and conversations with Ron Lembo regarding the broader theoretical contours of our work, as well as the major political and social developments in society the past few years and what these mean for us in sociology, have sustained me since my arrival in Massachusetts in ways too numerous to recount. Ron's remarkable capacity for maintaining a deep humanity and care for the work we do in the face of the social distancing that occurs in academic institutions encouraged me in those moments the academy felt perhaps too sterile and removed from the lives of most people to be a space for meaningfully envisioning a just and healthy world. He does not conflate professionalization with disconnection and disinterest, or friendship at work with a series of consciously performed, instrumental interactions. For these reasons he embodies in genuine practice the ideas of "engaged intellectual" and "community" we frequently theorize but often fail to enact. My appreciation for all of this and more is unbounded. Jerome Himmelstein also played a crucial part in my growth as a scholar over the past few years and was a great support to me, especially in his role as department chair, at critical moments during my time as a new faculty member at Amherst College while I developed this project. Leah Schmalzbauer has been since her arrival an incredible force in encouraging me to think about my work in new ways, as well as about our work as sociologists. She helped me so much as I brought this project to completion and has been a wonderful department chair and colleague in sociology. Chris Dole, Vanessa Fong, Danielle Bessett, Karen Graves, and Amy Cox Hall deserve special thanks. I especially appreciate the community Chris and Joy help us keep. I appreciate Vanessa offering to celebrate every step of the way with our work. My gratitude for Eunmi Mun (now at the University of Illinois) and Nusrat Chowdhury is too great to express in words. There are no two people with whom I have spent more time since moving to Massachusetts, and without them my life, and my time writing this book, could not have been as rich, joyful, intellectually satisfying, or fun. Similarly, Jan Dizard and Robin Dizard are responsible for welcoming me in the warmest way into a broader intellectual community in this region and making my life and time spent writing this book intellectually rich and lovely all around. They read and commented on my work, offered advice, shared historical materials, and always had a place at their table for me, as well as many of my friends, where we could talk through a range of events, ideas, and politics while feasting on something delicious. Jan, as my office neighbor and fellow environmental sociologist, frequently offered great insight, introduced me to important work, and shared ideas. Altogether, I cannot imagine a more supportive departmental environment. Their research and example as engaged intellectuals inspires me, and I feel gratitude every day to have them as colleagues and friends.

Special thanks also go to my wonderful colleagues in the new Department of Environmental Studies at Amherst College for their constant support and encouragement, as well as everything I learn from them through conversations and their work. I greatly appreciate Ethan Clotfelter, Jessica Hejny, Rick Lopez, Anna Martini, Joseph Moore, Katharine Sims, Ashwin Ravikumar, and Ethan Temeles. I especially thank Rachel Levin, Jill Miller, Diane Hutton, Jan Dizard, and Edward Melillo for their support, for asking and talking with me about my work, and Ted and Jan for reading an early draft of part of this book and offering important feedback.

At Amherst College, I thank the Dean of Faculty's office for material support for this project, as well as the numerous faculty workshops the office organized so that we could share work, discuss the writing process, and receive advice.

Special thanks to the local participants and organizers at Mt. Holyoke College of the Dust Bowl national traveling exhibit *Dust, Drought, and Dreams Gone Dry*. They invited me to present this research, receive feedback, and learn from other lectures and discussions associated with the exhibit. I am especially grateful for the creativity, work, and participation of Erin Stalberg, Aime DeGrenier, Alan Werner, Serin D. Houston, Mary Glackin, Leslie Fields, and Shiela McCormick.

Thanks also to the University of Massachusetts Sociology Department, as well as to organizers at the University of Calabria, Jiangsu Normal University, China University of Political Science and Law, Johns Hopkins University, the Instituto de Altos Estudios Nacionales, King's College London, the University of Oregon, the University of California, and Connecticut State University, among others, for inviting me to share aspects of my work.

I appreciate all of the helpful questions, comments, conversations, and feedback I've received from fabulous course, workshop, and audience participants—including colleagues, students, activists, and community members—at conferences, Amherst College, and other places I've visited the past few years. Their imprint runs throughout the pages of this book.

And thank you to editor Saturnino M. (Jun) Borras, Jr., and the anonymous reviewers at the *Journal of Peasant Studies*, who offered important feedback on an article related to this project that helped as I completed the book.

Important thanks to the Theory, Environmental Sociology, Comparative Historical, Marxist, and Political Economy of the World System sections of the American Sociological Association, the International Sociological Association (especially RC24, the Environment and Society Research Committee), and the Rural Sociological Society, for intellectual community and recognition of my work.

I thank the entire *Monthly Review* family and my friends, both faculty and graduate students (current and former), of the University of Oregon Sociology Department. I also thank and have a lot of love for my friends, colleagues, and comrades: Ann South, Sandra Lozano, Tania Triana, the entire Massachusetts-based Triana family, Theresa Koford, Carrie Ann Naumoff, Amy Demarest, Helen Scott, Ashley Smith, Michaeline Crichlow, Michael Yates, Ian Angus, Dwaipayan Sen, John Mage, Colleen Woods, Christina Ergas, Martha Camargo, Lorraine Wilson, Misa Joo, Erik Wallenberg, John Simon, Intan Suwandi, Jessie Kindig, Pinky Hota, Vinayak Ramanan, Greg Johnson, Martha Sweezy, Amy (McFalls) Johnson, Sujani Reddy, Paul Matteson, Ron Bashford, Yael Rice, Kiara Vigil, Julia McQuade, Katie Lipsmeyer, Patsy Raney, Samir Amin, Sue Dockstader, Marc Frank, Kate Frank, Steen Mitchell, Margaret Cerullo, Jeffrey Walker, Ken Kiser, Cade Jameson, Ryan Wishart, Wendy Woodson, Jordan Besek, Joe Fracchia, Patrick Joe Holman, Mark Holman, Shannon Bell, Patrick Greiner, Susie Day, Christen Mucher, Robert McChesney, and Julius McGee, who helped through discussion, their supportive friendship, or reading and offering feedback on all or part of this work. I especially appreciate Fred Magdoff and Amy Demarest sharing their home with me for a monthlong writing retreat in 2016, and Helen Scott, Nancy Welch, and Ashley Smith for making that month in Burlington so wonderful even though it was February.

It is most deeply necessary, but utterly insufficient, for me to thank John Bellamy Foster, Fred Magdoff, Brett Clark, Roxanne Dunbar-Ortiz, Richard York, Rebecca Clausen, Stefano Longo, Dorceta E. Taylor, Naomi Klein, Nancy Welch, R. Scott Frey, Matthew R. Sanderson, David Naguib Pellow, Donald Worster, and Kari Marie Norgaard. Without their work, mine would not be possible. These engaged scholars and writers embody what Paul Baran called the necessary "commitment of the intellectual" to truth and courage in the face of "all the fury of dominant interests and against all the assaults of agnosticism, obscurantism, and inhumanity."

Special appreciation goes to Gretchen Gano, Dawn Cadogan, Steven Heim, Fayise Mohamed Ahmed Abrahim, Esperanza Chairez, Jiwoon Choi, Noraida Colón, Zalo Crivelli, Manuel Matos, Thomas Matthew, John (JP) Miller, Paula Peña, Julia Herion-Cruz, Kyra Raines, and Amanda Strickland, for crucial research and library assistance, as well as critical conversation as I developed this project.

I owe a special debt of gratitude to Leena Valge and Nancy E. Doherty. Nancy made every aspect of this book better through her critical edits and questions, suggestions for revision, and so much more. I appreciate forever Leena's incredible assistance with research and manuscript preparation. I could not have finished the book the way I did without their help.

The preceding acknowledgments are not exhaustive, and may inadvertently leave out the names of important people who helped along the way. If your name is missing from where it belongs, please know I thank you, from the bottom of my heart.

I would like to acknowledge Taylor & Francis publishers (www.tandfonline.com) and the *Journal of Peasant Studies* for allowing me to include in my book adapted portions of my 2016 article "Denaturalizing Ecological Disaster: Colonialism, Racism and the Global Dust Bowl of the 1930s" in the *Journal of Peasant Studies* 44, no. 1: 234–260.

In completing the necessary research and finishing a book-length project, you miss a lot. I was sorry to miss a reunion of my classmates after twenty years of not seeing one another together in the same place. We are like family, many of us having known each other since we could walk. There are countless ways the members of the Okmulgee, Oklahoma, class of 1997 and our experiences—how we grew up and learned to think about the world together, the friends we lost too young along the way, our commitment to one another "4-Life"—drove the desire to write about home and do the work represented in this book. Many of the themes that appear in the following pages are themes of our lives in Oklahoma. The people with whom I grew up shaped me as a person and the way I think. I appreciate and love them for remaining close in spirit even as I have been physically far away.

My Oklahoma family makes my whole world go round and gives me more love and inspiration than I can describe. They were very patient with me as I missed many important family occasions because I was writing this book and completing other projects. My immediate family, mom, dad, sister, brothers, my beautiful nieces and nephews, as well as my aunts, uncles, cousins and their lovely children, and our grandmothers and grandfathers—all gave me the energy and the desire to keep going. I have missed them all, but been lifted up by them, while writing every word.

I thank all the Williams family in England, Wales, and beyond, who showed me many kindnesses and provided much support as I worked, especially over the past couple of years, to finish this book.

My heart was broken twice while writing this book as we lost two family members, both too young—my sweet young cousin Luke, and my uncle Steve. I keep these two close to my heart as I work. I miss them. Very much. Life is not the same without them. I devote this work to them and to my dear friend, whom I also miss every day, John Peters.

I live with two people without whom nothing about writing this book would have been the same.

Jeffrey Beckett Humphrey, my best friend from Oklahoma for more than twenty years and currently a housemate, made a lot of room at home for me to write and offered daily encouragement.

Words cannot express the impact Chris Williams had on my writing this book. Let me just say I appreciate everything he did to make it good.

Finally, I wish to thank all the true freedom fighters and earth protectors, including many of the people acknowledged above, as well as our ancestors who knew that a better world was not only possible but necessary to survival. Without the struggles waged and won by our ancestors, as well as those struggles we continue to push forward today, many of us would not be here. Many places would no longer exist. Even more of the earth's air, water, land, and human relationships would be toxic and unfit to support thriving life. We must carry on the historic work of those who came before and who are today on the front lines. There is too much to lose, and everything to gain, from building the movement for total liberation in which solidarity is the principle and love is the practice. As the great artist Marge Piercy ended her poem "The low road,"

> It goes on one at a time,
> it starts when you care
> to act, it starts when you do
> it again after they said no,
> it starts when you say *We*
> and know who you mean, and each
> day you mean one more.

DUST BOWLS OF EMPIRE

INTRODUCTION

It kept gittin' worse and worse and wind blowin' harder and harder and it kept gittin' darker and darker. And the old house was just a-vibratin' like it was gonna blow away. And I started tryin' to see my hand. And I kept bringin' my hand up closer and closer and closer and closer and closer and I finally touched the end of my nose and I still couldn't see my hand. That's how black it was. And we burned kerosene lamps and Dad lit an old kerosene lamp, set it on the kitchen table and it was just across the room from me, about—about 14 feet. And I could just barely see that lamp flame across the room. That's how dark it was and it was six o'clock in the afternoon. It was the 14th of April, 1935. The sun was still up, but it was totally black and that was blackest, worst dust storm, sand storm we had durin' the whole time.

A lot of people died. A lot of children, especially, died of dust pneumonia. They'd take little kids and cover 'em with sheets and sprinkle water on the sheets to filter the dust out. But we had to haul water. We had a team and we had water barrels. We hauled stock water and household water both. And we didn't have the water to use for that, so we just had to suffer through it. And lots of mornin's we'd get up and strain our drinkin' water like people strain milk, through a cloth, to strain the debris out of it. But then, of course, a lotta grit went through and settled to the bottom of the bucket, but you had have drinkin' water. And when you got you a little dipper of water, you drink it. You didn't take a sip and throw it away, because it was a very precious thing to us because we had to haul it. . . .

Some people thought it was an act of God and a punishment for—and possibly in a way it kindly was, because they'd more or less what you'd say raped the land. The way they had done the

> land, 'cause, to me, God didn't create the plains to be farmland. He created it for what He put on it, in grass and cattle. And they come in and completely changed it.
>
> They abused it somethin' terrible. They raped it. They got everything out they could and—but there'd been cycles like that before and there'd been cycles like that since, but not that severe.
>
> —The 1930s Dust Bowl as remembered by Melt White of Dalhart, Texas

Given the horror and human tragedy of the 1930s Dust Bowl, you'd think our society would summon all its forces to avoid repeating such ecological and social devastation. And yet, not only are we repeating the mistakes of the past on a vaster and more terrifying scale, but also people with the power and capital to do so are refining methods of ecological destruction and social immiseration beyond the imagination of Dust Bowl survivors like Melt White. As physicist Joseph Romm explains in the journal *Nature*, we now confront the reality that "dust-bowlification" is an increasingly likely threat in the face of climate change.[1]

Romm defines dust-bowlification as "extended or permanent drought over large parts of currently habitable or arable land—a drastic change in climate that will threaten food security and may be irreversible over centuries."[2] The term *dust-bowlification* is more vividly accurate than *desertification*, because the process about which Romm warns is not a transition from one healthy ecosystem to another. Deserts are resilient, beautiful ecological regions. They are high in biodiversity and have their own fine-tuned ecology, an adapted web of life that includes desert-dwelling humans. Land degradation, unsustainable freshwater use, and aridification do not turn affected areas into deserts; rather, they disrupt and destroy regional ecologies. The 1930s Dust Bowl on the U.S. southern plains is for many the ne plus ultra of historical examples.

There, the ancient grasslands that protected the soil from prairie winds and rains and nourished regional species such as the bison were destroyed within just a few decades, following the violent opening of the plains to white settlement and the global market in the 1800s. Under pressure from the vagaries of the world economy, settlers sheared the land to expand cash-crop agriculture and ranching.[3] Too much of the soil, that "ecstatic skin of the earth," as author William Bryant Logan calls it, was left bare.[4] In the 1930s, as major drought descended on the plains, winds and static electricity lifted the desiccated, exposed topsoil, forming dust storms on an unprecedented scale that wreaked havoc for years.

Such massive loss of soil and continued dry conditions meant the land could no longer support life as it once had. Thousands of families like Melt White's did what they could to survive the maelstrom or left town. Those who had no choice but to remain, or who chose to stay and pray for rain, choked on the very soil that had once lived beneath their feet and provided their livelihoods. Many thought it was the end of the world.

The activist singer, songwriter, poet, and author Woody Guthrie, who grew up in the Oklahoma county next to the one in which I was raised, sang of the farmers' plight in his *Dust Bowl Ballads*. Songs with names like "Dust Pneumonia Blues," "I Ain't Got No Home in This World Anymore," "Dust Bowl Refugee," "Talking Dust Bowl," and "Vigilante Man" told the stories of the poor who—as if the dust weren't enough—had to battle the banks, bosses, large landowners, and the thugs they hired, to evict tenants and discourage, through terror, collective organization for better conditions in the countryside.[5]

By the end of the 1930s tens of thousands of people were displaced.[6] And this was only decades after tens of thousands of people, including the ancestors of contemporary Osage, Sac and Fox, Kiowa, Cheyenne, and Arapaho, along with other indigenous peoples, had been displaced or massacred so the government could seize their land, open it to white settlement, and allow exploitation of the region's land and resources.[7] So when scientists today predict the increasing possibility of Dust Bowl–like conditions, they are signaling a particular kind of extreme ecological *and* social change. The projected changes have extreme consequences. But also extreme are the social forces, historical developments, policies, and practices that produce such massive socio-ecological crises.

The severity and significance of such projections become even clearer when we understand how calamitous the Dust Bowl is considered relative to other disasters. In the United States the Dust Bowl is officially the "drought of record."[8] Environmental scientist William Lockeretz writes, "The dust storms of the 1930s were the worst man-made environmental problem the United States has ever seen, whether measured in physical terms or by their human and economic impact."[9] Historian Donald Worster describes the Dust Bowl as an "event of national, even planetary significance," and refers to ecologist Georg Borgström's ranking of the Dust Bowl as one of the three worst ecological disasters in history, along with the "deforestation of China's uplands about 3000 B.C." and "the destruction of Mediterranean vegetation by livestock."[10] Worster notes, however, that "unlike either of those events . . . the Dust Bowl took only 50 years to accomplish."[11] Geographer William Riebsame suggests that the Dust Bowl serves as a cognitive "anchor against which we compare the magnitude of other events."[12]

In the most cited scholarly account of the Dust Bowl, Worster suggests that a valuable outcome of the disaster, and the reason it is an important historical case study, is its potential to have an "enlarging, critical effect" on our thinking by providing "a model from which we can learn much about the ecological insensitivity of our culture."[13] Today there is indeed a revival of interest in the subject as a case study and warning, because the Dust Bowl is viewed simultaneously as extraordinary and—with dust-bowlification an increasingly likely threat—not extraordinary at all.[14]

Clear parallels between the social and ecological crises of the 1930s and those we confront today mean the Dust Bowl has become a major historical referent of the climate change era. The headlines are hard to miss: "California Could Become a 'Dust Bowl' Like 1930s Oklahoma" (*Time*, April 10, 2015); "The Dust Bowl Returns" (*New York Times*, February 9, 2014); "China's Dust Bowl" (*Time*); "Dust Bowls Aren't Just an 'Interstellar' Thing" (*NPR*, November 14, 2014); "Dust Bowl Days Are

Here Again" (*Scientific American*); "East Africa's Dust Bowl" (*Al Jazeera*, July 17, 2011); "21st Century US 'Dustbowl' Risk Assessed" (*BBC*, February 13, 2016); "NASA Scientists Are Comparing Climate Change to Dust Bowl" (*Business Insider*, October 20, 2015); "NOAA Scientists Study Historic 'Dust Bowl' and Plains Droughts for Triggers" (U.S. National Oceanic and Atmospheric Administration, October 13, 2009); "Lester Brown: 'Vast Dust Bowls Threaten Tens of Millions with Hunger' " (*Guardian*, February 24, 2015); "Farm Policy in Age of Climate Change Creating Another Dust Bowl, Critics Say" (*Inside Climate News*, March 22, 2017); "Dust Bowl-ification of U.S. Southwest Leads to 800% Jump in Valley Fever Cases" (*Think Progress*, June 12, 2017); "Inside the Syrian Dust Bowl" (*Foreign Policy*, September 5, 2016).

Scientists and scholars across disciplines are returning to the Dust Bowl to make sense of our present situation. NASA scientists have conducted a series of studies of the 1930s disaster to better understand the future we now face. In a 2015 press release they warned that as bad as the Dust Bowl was, the drought of the 1930s lasted less than a decade, whereas climate change will bring on similar events, but they are projected to last "at least thirty to thirty-five years."[15] NASA chief scientist Ellen Stofan in her address at the 2015 Rethinking the Future of Food Conference invoked the Dust Bowl to dramatize our need to transform agriculture in the face of a more hostile climatological future.[16]

A group of social scientists reviewing the growing body of scholarly work on the subject note that "the Dust Bowl is recent enough to provide a powerful learning analog" to contemporary ecological and economic crises.[17] In spite of growing interest, the authors suggest that "researchers have only begun to plumb the Dust Bowl experience," and the era "still has much to teach us about preparing for and responding to acute socio-environmental challenges that will continue to arise in our present era of anthropogenic climate change, food and water scarcity, and global economic uncertainty."[18]

Such reviews illustrate that existing literature, spanning a variety of disciplines, draws important lessons from the Dust Bowl on the U.S. southern plains. I contend in this book, however, that the majority of scientists, policymakers, commentators, and activists view the disaster through far too narrow a geographical, historical, theoretical, and philosophical lens, seriously limiting the lessons we can draw from this period and the ways in which the Dust Bowl experience can inform current debates about social and ecological change. Existing narratives may in fact hamper our search for ways to avoid the more devastating sequels to the Dust Bowl projected by scientists.

The most influential analyses of the Dust Bowl focus on the ecological and social disaster as a regional phenomenon, even if influenced by broader cultural and economic factors. Standard accounts begin with the arrival of white settlers and the introduction of the "plow that broke the plains."[19] Some end with the triumph of the pioneer over the land, depicting "a courageous people who were tough and determined to stay, even against the worst odds."[20] Others focus on the "Dust Bowl refugee" problem resulting from the displacement of farmers—whether owners, laborers, or tenants—because of crop failures, market collapse, and bank foreclosures, and the persistent hardship of those who remained to work the degraded land, even with the help of progressive government programs.

Historian William Cronon published an article in 1992 that, in philosopher and historian Carolyn Merchant's words, "caused an earthquake in environmental history."[21] In it Cronon uses the example of the wide range of Dust Bowl narratives to illustrate the point that the same set of facts can be used to tell very different stories about environmental history. He contrasts historian Donald Worster's *Dust Bowl: The Southern Plains in the 1930s* with historian Paul Bonnifield's *The Dust Bowl: Men, Dirt, and Depression.* Both books were published in 1979, and, as Cronon writes, "the two authors dealt with virtually the same subject, had researched many of the same documents, and agreed on most of their facts, and yet their conclusions could hardly have been more different."[22]

These two books not only draw very different conclusions, but also tell very different stories. Bonnifield relates a tale of human resilience in the face of what he treats as mostly a natural disaster. The story ends by celebrating the contribution of those who stayed on in the face of adversity to contribute to the prosperity of the nation as a whole. He writes, "Because they stayed during those hard years and worked the land and tapped her natural resources, millions of people have eaten better, worked in healthier places, and enjoyed warmer homes. Because those determined people did not flee the stricken area during a crisis, the nation today enjoys a better standard of living."[23] In contrast, Worster's Dust Bowl is a manmade disaster with no happy ending. It was, in his assessment, "the inevitable outcome of a culture that deliberately, self-consciously, set itself [the] task of dominating and exploiting the land for all it was worth."[24]

Despite their differences, these two stories have something in common with one another and virtually every other Dust Bowl narrative, in that they emphasize the plight of the land in the U.S. southern plains region and of poor whites, mirroring the focus of globally famous cultural depictions of the Dust Bowl in the cinematography of Pare Lorentz and, more recently, Ken Burns; John Steinbeck's National Book Award– and Pulitzer Prize–winning novel *The Grapes of Wrath*; the music of Woody Guthrie; and the photography of Dorothea Lange.[25] As a result, enduring popular and scholarly images of that period include billowing dust storms, desertscapes dotted with ruins of once verdant wheat and cotton fields, and poor white folks struggling in places like Oklahoma or Texas, or else trudging their way out West.

These images are poignant and important reminders not just of the tragedy, but of the class dynamics and ecological rapaciousness of the ruling "capitalist ethos" that brought what Worster terms "Henry Fordism to the plains" in the form of industrial agriculture and an "all-out dedication to cash."[26] However, as the research presented in this book demonstrates, such images do not capture the broader context within which these changes occurred: the rapid expansion of colonialism and imperialism from which an international crisis of soil erosion emerged by the 1930s—of which the southern plains Dust Bowl was one traumatic instance.

These two critical limitations of existing Dust Bowl narratives—the narrow regional focus and an inattention to the settler colonial context—have led to a whitewashing of the Dust Bowl and to a generalized misunderstanding of its causes and of the extent and enduring ecological and social impact of both the policies and practices that led to the disaster and those adopted in response to it.

Problems of interpretation are compounded by popular and scholarly accounts that suggest the Dust Bowl was unforeseen and therefore unpreventable, but once it was recognized as a crisis, human perseverance and ingenuity resolved it. School textbooks, U.S. policymakers, and scientists continue to repeat this simplistic view. For example, NASA's Ellen Stofan said of the Dust Bowl: "People generally watched it happening, didn't totally understand why it was happening. Eventually scientists came in, helped, the situation was remedied."[27] President Barack Obama, in his 2008 electoral victory speech, said, "When there was despair in the dust bowl and depression across the land, she saw a nation conquer fear itself with a New Deal, new jobs, a new sense of common purpose. Yes we can."[28] Such interpretations imply that society has become all the more resilient and prepared for future crises as a result of living through this period. These views obscure the reality that the real lessons of the Dust Bowl have not been heeded in its wake any more than were the warnings that could have prevented the crisis in the first place.

In the decades preceding the Dust Bowl, Anglo-European and U.S. frontier and colonial officials had ample warning about the growing problem of soil erosion. There were sufficient stores of knowledge and technical know-how to address the growing crisis and known historical examples of societies' erosion-prevention efforts. Furthermore, for decades, a cadre of elites, from U.S. presidents to captains of industry, were part of an international cohort of colonial scientists, businessmen, and officials who were committed conservationists aware of the need for soil conservation on a major scale.

These facts bring up critical questions we need to answer to shed light on how the Dust Bowl could have occurred at all, and what the 1930s have to teach us about our own era. One of the most urgent questions is: What social, economic, and political forces continue to prevent society from applying its cultural-historical, scientific, and ethical knowledge effectively enough to address ecological crises on the scale and at the pace necessary to prevent widespread humanitarian and ecological disasters? This is a central question I address in the chapters that follow.

As social and natural scientists revisit the Dust Bowl period to better understand the present and future, this book contributes an empirical and theoretical reinterpretation of the Dust Bowl that addresses its scope and scale, causes and consequences, and aftermath—bringing the narrative forward to the present day. By necessity this analysis crosses disciplinary boundaries, working at the intersection of sociology, history, political economy, and ecology, while also drawing on relevant work from other fields. The framework I develop here not only allows for a fresh and more comprehensive Dust Bowl story from which new lessons emerge, but presents a fresh set of facts that link the Dust Bowl to the present not as an analog, but as an antecedent.

To place the calamitous event within a broader geographical and historical context than is found in contemporary literature, my argument draws on original research into an underutilized body of government documents, scholarly and scientific literature, conference proceedings, and other periodical sources documenting and commenting on the global crisis of soil erosion before and during the 1930s disaster. I explain how the international, rather than regional, problem of soil erosion of this era constituted what historian David Anderson refers to as the "first global environmental problem," which writers at the time viewed in racial terms as another "white man's burden" on a world scale.[29]

In reinterpreting the Dust Bowl, I argue that the phenomenon was just one dramatic regional manifestation of a global social and ecological crisis generated by the "new imperialism" that began in the 1870s and lasted through the first decades of the twentieth century. The ideology of the new imperialism, which W. E. B. DuBois defines as "the divine right of white people to steal," spurred the developments that made the Dust Bowl possible, including the expansion of white settler colonialism.[30] From this perspective, the Dust Bowl as a case offers critical insights into the links between ecological degradation and social domination that characterize what sociologists and environmentalists refer to as the "ecological rift of capitalism." Understanding the social drivers of the ecological rift helps move us beyond more limited environmental justice perspectives, which often focus on inequalities in terms of outcomes of environmental harm, rather than as drivers of it, and ignore the systemic nature of environmental injustice.

Moreover, this reevaluation of the Dust Bowl helps explain why, despite the transnational circulation of scientific information and warnings about the global problem of soil erosion, the "Great Plow Up" and acceleration of global deforestation persisted—and indeed persists to this day.

Mainstream environmentalism, which developed within the colonial context and dominated the policy response to the Dust Bowl, represented an early version of what we now call "green capitalism" or "ecological modernization" approaches to ecological change. Then, as now, policymakers and mainstream environmentalists attempting to address ecological crises were hamstrung by their commitment to, or uncritical acceptance of, the social status quo and therefore could not resolve the disaster. As a consequence, they helped shift ecological problems technologically, geographically, temporally, or socially, facilitating the continuation of "business as usual." Their efforts offered the illusion of resolution, while the social drivers of the crisis remained intact.

The ideological legacy of the "heyday of imperialism and colonialism," as economist Branko Milanovic describes this earlier period of globalization, helps normalize global inequality today and facilitates the world's most powerful corporations' extraction of resources, labor, and financial wealth from the so-called least-developed regions—assisted by national governments and international financial institutions.[31] The transformation of land and cultures around the world that made the first Dust Bowl era possible also makes possible this continued exploitation. The era heralded a future of deepening ecological crises beginning with World War II.

Scientists refer to the period since 1950 as the "Great Acceleration," an era marked by "fundamental shifts in the state and functioning of the Earth System that are beyond the range of variability of the Holocene and driven by human activities."[32] The Great Acceleration, of which climate change is one aspect, does not represent a parallel to this earlier period of ecological destruction, but a continuation and amplification of it. We face even greater problems today with soil erosion, desertification, and the planetary crisis of climate change, as the world suffers the results of what sociologist John Bellamy Foster refers to as the "accumulation of catastrophe."[33]

For all of us now seeking to understand why we continue to witness an acceleration of ecological crises in spite of the enormous known costs to human communities and thousands of species, our unprecedented scientific and technological sophistication, decades of international negotiations and political reform, ongoing protests, and painful past experience, this analysis has urgent relevance. As the chapters that follow illustrate, the case of the Dust Bowl challenges the claims of proponents of green capitalism or "ecological modernization" that global ecological crises summon into existence "a civilizational community of fate" capable of spurring an adaptive, science-and-technology–based response that is both ecologically restorative and just.[34] This book draws new lessons from the Dust Bowl based on the reinterpretation developed herein and the work of others that sheds light on the barriers we must overcome to break out of the cycle of intergenerational ecological and social violence in which we are enmeshed and work toward genuine ecological and social justice.

We stand at the crossroads now; scientists suggest that "policy decisions made in the next few years to decades will have profound impacts on global climate, ecosystems and human societies—not just for this century, but for the next ten millennia and beyond."[35] While we have reason to hope we can avert further ecological devastation, I argue that hope must be considered in social terms, rather than in technological or scientific ones. Securing a healthy future for humankind and other species on earth will require learning from history, overcoming social divisions, and fundamentally altering social relations between humans to restore a sustainable metabolism between human society and the rest of the biosphere.

The end of this book is not the end of the story, because multiple futures are still possible. Think of it as a "choose-your-own ending"—a very adult version of the series I loved as a kid because of the agency afforded the reader. In these books, at a critical point in the story the reader becomes the protagonist, making a choice they reason will lead to their desired ending. We are each protagonists now and we must choose. This is not a storybook, though one may be written about the choices we make now, much as this book reflects on the harmful choices that led to this point.

If we want the ending projected by scientists, we need only participate in politics as usual and business as usual will follow—taking on a green tinge here and there while ultimately eroding the substrate of all life on earth. But if we want to choose a different, better ending, we can't skip to the right page and read the rest of the story, as in the children's series. Rather, we must all act in ways we may not have acted in before, in solidarity with people we have not yet met, in a bold manner powerful enough to finally clear away the muck of the ages. I hope you choose wisely, unafraid and emboldened by the love of life and justice in your heart.

•

I develop the framework presented in this book within the tradition of critical interdisciplinary work that sociologists have undertaken since the discipline's formative period, making clear the connections between capitalist development, social domination, and ecological degradation. From W. E. B. DuBois and Max Weber to Radhakamal Mukerjee and Jane Addams, many sociologists from the beginning were engaged public intellectuals who challenged the social myths and intellectual currents justifying imperialism and class exploitation, as well as the privatization and despoliation of the ecological commons.[36] The discipline took off in the few decades preceding the Dust Bowl, with one of the first distinct sociology departments in the United States forming at the University of Kansas in the 1890s—a Dust Bowl state, as it turns out.[37] The scholars of this era were sophisticated analysts of the developments that eventually made the 1930s disaster possible and conditioned the social response.

To the present day, critical sociologists have been at the forefront in explaining the origins of, and working toward an alternative to, a society built on social division and ecological destruction. I build on their work, in particular the body of scholarship in environmental sociology that continues the critical tradition of analytically linking social and ecological issues, though always in new and innovative ways in response to contemporary crises and social change efforts.

Although I have learned from a broad range of scholars in my field and so many beyond—whose work informs my own and many of whom are referenced in this book—there are key contemporary developments in environmental sociology upon which I draw explicitly for this study and to which I routinely refer. The scholars introduced below are only those directly referenced in this book, with an emphasis on environmental sociology. I introduce them here, especially those I refer to more than once, to avoid repetition and backtracking in later chapters, as well as to situate my work.

Critical to the understanding presented in this book is sociologist Dorceta E. Taylor's theoretical and historical work on the rise of the U.S. environmental movement, segregation within the movement, and the ideological divisions between the mainstream environmental paradigm and the environmental justice paradigm.[38] Taylor's analysis of the impact of race, class, gender, and colonialism in shaping the relationships between people and the land, as well as environmental attitudes, has been invaluable, as has her work on the origins of "business environmentalism."[39]

I also build upon the extensive sociological research into the dynamics distinguishing the "ecological rift" of capitalism from instances in earlier historical periods when human societies despoiled the natural world upon which they depend.[40] This area of research delineates the distinct characteristics of the modern world system that lead to escalating ecological crises today and help explain why it is so difficult to change course so long as these dynamics are in play. Scholars in this area continue the important work of denaturalizing ecological crises. This is crucial in countering narratives in which socio-ecological crises are treated as inherent outcomes of a mythical human nature or the continuation, on a larger scale, of an interminable contest between humans and the rest of nature. Such ahistorical, lazy explanations of our current predicament are promoted too often by those seeking to justify or legitimize the social status quo.

Scholars linking social inequality and ecological decline have shown that the ecological rift of capitalism is "at bottom, the product of a social rift: the domination of human being by human being. The driving force is a society based on class, inequality and acquisition without end. At the global level it is represented by . . . the imperialist division between center and periphery, North and South, rich and poor countries."[41]

Scholars analyzing the ecological rift draw on the ecological insights and political economy of earlier thinkers, especially Karl Marx (considered a classical founder of sociology), as well as contemporary research across a number of fields on the interactions and interdependencies between human society and the rest of nature, described as the social metabolism. John Bellamy Foster, Brett Clark, Rebecca Clausen, Stefano B. Longo, Philip Mancus, David Naguib Pellow, Christina Ergas, Richard York, Camila Alvarez, Julius McGee, and William Wishart are some of the key sociologists contributing to the development and extension of this line of analysis and to whom I refer in this book.[42] In this vein I also incorporate the important research and theoretical work of sociologists Matthew R. Sanderson and R. Scott Frey focused on the Dust Bowl region. Their path-breaking analysis of the ecological and social problems associated with the introduction of industrial agriculture in the plains region under conditions dictated in large part by markets controlled by wealthier financial centers is presented in an article titled "From Desert to Breadbasket . . . to Desert Again? A Metabolic Rift in the High Plains Aquifer," and was an important starting point for my project.[43]

The innovative analyses of sociologist David Naguib Pellow also are of central theoretical importance for this project.[44] His writing expands developments in environmental sociology and links them—including the areas just described (e.g., ecological rift analysis, socio-ecological inequality, environmental and liberation movements, ecological justice)—to other crucial areas of social analysis, including critical race theory and research on intersectionality (building on the work of scholars such as Kimberlé Crenshaw).[45] Pellow's formulations of socio-ecological inequality, the toxicity of race, and total liberation (of all species) have opened new avenues for theoretical and empirical inquiry, as well as activism, and influenced this project from the beginning. His work continues to deepen my understanding of our world and what is possible in research, theorization, and practical action toward social and ecological transformation.

Environmental sociologist Karie Marie Norgaard's explication of the social organization of denial also informs my work. Her book *Living in Denial: Climate Change, Emotions, and Everyday Life* is key to making sense of how and why informed and knowledgeable people with concern for large-scale ecological crises (like climate change) fail to take action commensurate with the problems.[46] The Dust Bowl is difficult to understand without integrating these crucial insights.

In other areas of sociology, scholarship such as that of Evelyn Nakano Glenn—and outside our discipline, going back to Arghiri Emmanuel's classic essay, as well as Patrick Wolfe's body of work—on white settler colonialism as, in Glenn's words, "an ongoing structure rather than a past historical event," is central to this project.[47]

The work of historian Roxanne Dunbar-Ortiz, economist Harry Magdoff, scholar of rhetoric and composition Nancy Welch, and environmental historian Donald Worster are also crucial to my analysis. These scholars' insights into imperialism, colonialism, settler colonialism, indigenous history, neoliberal rhetoric, racism, the environment, economics, capitalism, social movements, and the Dust Bowl run throughout the following chapters.

Also critical for my work and other analyses of the drivers and consequences of the ecological rift are the many contributions of soil scientist Fred Magdoff, especially on the political economy and sustainability of agriculture, from its industrial capitalist forms to traditional and ecological approaches centered on human needs.[48] He collaborates regularly with environmental sociologists. His most recent book with author, activist, and educator Chris Williams, *Creating an Ecological Society: Toward a Revolutionary Transformation*, is an important resource on the subject of capitalism and possibilities for socio-ecological change, and influenced my thinking.[49]

Finally, this book builds on my own previous research, as well as collaborations with some of the authors mentioned above. Herein I continue my work addressing issues of ecological imperialism, unequal ecological exchange, and ecological debt; sociological theory and ecology; the privatization and commodification of science and scholarship; socio-ecological inequality and justice; agriculture and energy policy; race, colonialism, and settler colonialism; environmental politics; and the Dust Bowl, global soil erosion, and the shift in the global water/hydrological cycle.[50]

one

DUST TO DUST: AN AGE BEYOND EXTREMES

> The extraordinary global reach of classical nineteenth- and early-twentieth century European imperialism still casts a considerable shadow over our own times. . . . This pattern of dominions or possessions laid the groundwork for what is in effect now a global world. Electronic communications, the global extent of trade, of availability of resources, of travel, of information about weather patterns and ecological change have joined together even the most distant corners of the world. This set of patterns, I believe, was first established and made possible by the modern empires.
>
> —Edward W. Said, *Culture and Imperialism*, 1993

Historian Eric Hobsbawm deemed the twentieth century—with its cataclysmic wars, economic crises, and abyss between rich and poor—"the Age of Extremes."[1] It is clear, however, that the twenty-first century is poised to surpass the twentieth to become the Epoch of Ecological Extremes. Without a dramatic departure from the status quo, current scientific projections suggest that the ecological instability of global capitalism will routinely, but with increasingly dire and irreversible consequences, bring us to our knees.

In the second decade of the twenty-first century the extraordinary levels of political and economic inequality, associated scale of social misery, and global ecological crisis are bound together as systemic problems. And they are defining features of our epoch, as the 2013 World Social Science Report, *Changing Global Environments*, observes:

> The environmental challenges that confront society are unprecedented and staggering in their magnitude, scope, pace and complexity. They have potentially serious consequences for the wellbeing of people all over the world. The consequences of global environmental change are unfolding now; individuals and communities are already struggling

> to manage often precarious livelihoods; other social, economic and political crises—including persistent poverty, increasing inequalities and social discontent—are intricately linked to and exacerbated by environmental change. Global environmental change changes everything for everyone on this planet—our life support systems, our livelihoods, our ways of life, our actions and interactions with each other.[2]

Nothing better exemplifies the extreme nature of contemporary social and ecological crises than the profound shift taking place in our relationship to land, the climate, and water. The all-encompassing nature of the transformation is clearly reflected in research papers and news stories from around the world that continue to report the development and anticipated intensification of Dust Bowl–like conditions on every continent supporting agriculture.

Today the interconnected issues precipitating the new Dust Bowl era are the culmination of increasingly extreme exploitation—in terms of scale and technique—of the land, of the planet's hydrocarbon repositories, and of freshwater systems. As with the 1930s Dust Bowl, this extreme abuse of the global commons is mirrored in the extreme politics required to make such destruction possible. Also like the 1930s, these developments are associated with high levels of expropriation, social inequality, oppression, and dislocation.

To begin, this chapter introduces salient features of the Epoch of Ecological Extremes contributing to the development of Dust Bowl conditions today. I start with a brief description of transformations under way in the world's soil, energy, and water systems—linking contemporary social, political, economic, and ecological issues.

From Extreme Energy and Agriculture to Extreme Water: The New Dust Bowl Era

The Contemporary Crisis of Soil Erosion and Agriculture

Soil is the earth's incredible and underappreciated living integument. "Wild soils," those free of cultivation, are repositories of much of the earth's remaining biodiversity.[3] And, as biologist Diana Wall explains,

"All above-surface organisms ultimately depend on soil biodiversity for food and habitat. . . . Human health and national economies are largely based on benefits derived from soil."[4] Moreover, humans derive 99.7 percent of our food from cropland; plants, animals, and microbes inhabiting intact soils engage in living processes that regulate many elemental cycles.[5] Healthy, living soils hold and make available nutrients and water needed for plant growth and development, act as natural water filtration systems, and create "a reservoir of organic C [carbon] that greatly exceeds the C [carbon] in the global atmosphere and biosphere."[6]

The formation of soils is ongoing and involves a magnificent interaction between life and the geological substrate of the planet. The process varies geographically based on climate, topography, the local geological material from which soils develop that scientists call parent material, and biological factors. Biological factors include the presence of plants, animals, and microorganisms, and their activities. Plant roots break up rock, animals burrow, and worms, as Darwin observed, dig and till the soil, providing space for water and air.[7] All plants and animals also provide nutrients to the soil. And teams of microorganisms—such as bacteria, fungi, protozoa, nematodes, and arthropods—break down waste, help decompose living matter, and take nitrogen from the atmosphere and transform it into forms that plants can utilize.

All of these interactions and processes take a great deal of time to produce the dynamic, living substance necessary to support life aboveground. In fact, one centimeter of soil can take hundreds to thousands of years to form.[8] For this reason, our remarkable substrate of life is a nonrenewable resource. The Food and Agricultural Organization (FAO) of the United Nations attempted to highlight this fact by making 2015 the International Year of Soils. Associated with this campaign, the FAO published the following statement: "Soil is a finite resource, meaning its loss and degradation is [*sic*] not recoverable within a human lifespan. As a core component of land resources, agricultural development, and ecological sustainability, it is the basis for food, feed, fuel and fibre production and for many critical ecosystem services. It is therefore a highly valuable natural resource, yet it is often overlooked."[9]

Some erosion happens without human interference, "as part of a natural cycle of wearing down and building up that always marked the history of the earth, with the rate of soil formation keeping pace with the rate of soil erosion," explains biologist James B. Nardi.[10] However, today in many parts of the world we are losing soil to erosion much faster than it can replenish itself. Due to accelerating human alterations of the landscape since the nineteenth century, especially through unsustainable agricultural, forestry, and husbandry practices, but also through urbanization and war, "half of the topsoil on the planet has been lost in the last 150 years."[11] According to an FAO report, "the most serious form of soil degradation is from accelerated erosion."[12] It threatens not only food production for people, but the very existence of entire species and ecosystems whose health is dependent on intact soils.

It is fitting that the acronym for the European Union's Standing Committee on Agricultural Research is SCAR.[13] Industrial agriculture has indeed left a scar on the skin of the earth. At the same time it continually expands the wounds. All cultivated soils "are highly modified forms of their wild predecessors."[14] However, contemporary industrial agriculture for private profit, which in many countries is promoted and sustained by an enormous infrastructure of government support—including subsidization, legal and trade protections, university research and extension services—has no historical precedent in terms of the scale of its destructiveness. On the whole, technological advances in modern agriculture have worsened the problem, making it possible to sustain in the short term what ultimately is unsustainable. Plows today cut deep into the earth and quickly expose vast areas of soil to erosion. Synthetic and often dangerous chemicals replace the natural pest-control properties provided by some microorganisms, plants, and animals, and attempt to compensate for nutrients lost by the removal of organic matter. Plant species have been genetically engineered to withstand the dumping of toxic herbicides designed to make weeding unnecessary.

Abuses associated with the modern era's technologically advanced but socially and ecologically regressive farming for profit have contributed to the subjection of 90 percent of global agricultural land to erosion. Eighty percent of the land is affected by erosion classified as moderate to severe.[15] Indeed, "agricultural soil erosion is one of the most destructive human perturbations to soil sustainability."[16]

Anthropogenic erosion happens when the removal of protective vegetation, whether forest or prairie, exposes the soil to wind and rain that can carry it rapidly downriver or across the skies. Tillage is another known cause of erosion.[17] Erosion is linked to other forms of soil degradation affecting agricultural fields including *compaction*—when soil density increases from compression by heavy equipment; *loss of organic matter*—which vitally fuels "the complex soil web of life, helps in formation of soil aggregates, and provides plant growth-stimulating chemicals, as well as reducing plant pest pressures"; and *chemical contamination*.[18] As a result of these widespread problems, from approximately 1975 to 2015 alone, the earth lost a third of arable land to erosion and pollution.[19] Leading agricultural scientist David Pimentel reported in 2006, "30% of the world's arable land has become unproductive and, much of that has been abandoned for agricultural use."[20]

In a *Time* article titled "What If the World's Soil Runs Out?" a scientist was asked: "Why haven't we heard more about this?" He replied: "Probably because soil isn't sexy."[21] Pimentel echoed this sentiment in saying, "The problem, which is growing ever more critical, is being ignored because who gets excited about dirt?"[22] In a 2015 *Guardian* article environmental writer and journalist George Monbiot wrote that "the avoidance of this issue is perhaps the greatest social silence of all," because "war, pestilence, even climate change are trifles by comparison. Destroy the soil and we all starve."[23] Scientists also suggest that soil erosion is as big a threat as global warming.[24] As a result of soil erosion, at the same time international agencies suggest we need to increase food production, some scientists expect a further decline of agricultural productivity of approximately 30 percent in coming decades.[25]

While the public may not be aware of the extent of the problem of soil erosion, governments and policymakers around the world cannot claim ignorance. The fact is that methods of conserving soil have been well understood by national and international agencies concerned with land use for years.[26] In 2015 the FAO and the Intergovernmental Technical Panel on Soils released a report titled *Status of the World's Soil Resources*. The authors write,

> The accelerated loss of topsoil through erosion from agricultural land was recognized as an important threat to the world's soil resource many decades ago. . . . The large difference between erosion rates under conventional agriculture and soil formation rates implies that we are essentially mining the soil and that we should consider the resource as non-renewable. . . . So-called soil loss tolerance levels may help to set objectives for short-term action. However, long-term sustainability requires that soil erosion rates on agricultural land are reduced to near-zero levels.[27]

To this end, the United Nations Convention to Combat Desertification (UNCCD) and the United Nations Environment Programme promote "land degradation neutrality," an official UN Sustainable Development Goal (SDG target 15.3).[28] According to the coordinator of external relations at the UNCCD, Louise Baker, "We should look at realigning the incentive structure that we have away from incentives that degrade the land to those that promote sustainable management."[29] However, the 2015 Economics of Land Degradation report, *The Value of the Land*, suggests that incentives to exploit the land increasingly will override incentives to conserve it "as land scarcity increases and land becomes increasingly seen as a 'commodity.' "[30]

Agro-ecological practices that better preserve soil integrity and sustain healthy, empowered rural communities are widely understood and applied on a small scale in spite of the fact that they garner much less economic and political support than chemical- and energy-intensive monocropping. Yet the removal of natural vegetation, intensive plowing, grazing, and deforestation continue, exposing the topsoil to wind and water, which carry the loosened soil into waterways and the air, polluting both.

Although the public sees little information about the causes and extent of erosion, its consequences are well known, especially by those living near problem areas. Around the world erosion is literally visible in silted rivers, dust storms, and news reports. Media outlets globally report regularly on farm worker unemployment, displacement of people in affected regions, and growing public health problems due to runaway erosion. Increased sediment and pollution in waterways severely damages aquatic ecosystems, threatening communities dependent on them. And dust from blowing topsoil degrades air quality across vast distances. Dust particles lodge in lungs, causing an illness that was known as "dust pneumonia" during the 1930s. Today, however, because of the array of harmful chemicals used in agriculture and other pollutants, eroded soil also carries "arsenic and other heavy metals, agricultural fertilizers and pesticides, as well as a laundry list of bacteria, fungi and viruses."[31] As dust storms worsen in regions around the world, scientists are documenting new health hazards.[32]

We could view the whole problem of soil erosion on the world's limited arable land in a different light if it were the outcome of well-intentioned efforts to feed the hungry. If that were the case and the goal, the problem would be easier to address, especially given the evidence that we could feed as many or even more people by taking different approaches.[33] But one of the most appalling—indeed, tragic—realities of the situation is that despite the extensive social and ecological damage current agricultural practices cause, the world produces more than enough food each year to feed its entire population. However, the system cannot reliably deliver food to the hungry, only to those who can pay. Therefore it fails to adequately nourish the world's people.[34]

In 2015 the World Health Organization reported that 45 percent of the 5.9 million deaths in children under five were related to malnutrition.[35] According to the 2016 Global Nutrition Report, *From Promise to Impact: Ending Malnutrition by 2030*, one in every three people in the world is malnourished.[36] Living in a rich country doesn't guarantee adequate access to nourishing food either.

In the United States, one of the most affluent nations and the country hosting the greatest number of individuals in the top 1 percent of global wealth holders, the Department of Agriculture (USDA) reported in 2015 that 12.3 percent of households, 42.2 million people, were food insecure—rising to 22.5 percent in black households and 18.5 percent in Hispanic households.[37] Food insecurity (representing a 2006 change in nomenclature away from "hunger") is defined as not having enough food for all family members during periods of the year due to "insufficient money or other resources for food."[38]

Perhaps most illustrative of the nature of the agri-food industry and system are the poverty, hunger, and illness among farm workers in the wealthiest of countries. According to the U.S. Bureau of Labor Statistics, the median income for U.S. farm workers in 2015 was $22,542, with 29 percent of farm worker households falling below the poverty line, more than double the national rate.[39] Depending on the region, "reports of food security for farmworker households have found 20% to 80% to be food insecure."[40]

In spite of the great need, farm workers have minimal access to social services, including health care.[41] Therefore, as a group they do not receive adequate care to address sickness and injury due to routinely hazardous work conditions. Pesticide poisoning is a particular threat for farm workers, with those who are children especially vulnerable. In 2017 the UN released a damning report on pesticides, showing that they fatally poison 200,000 people per year worldwide. The report states, "without or with minimal use of toxic chemicals, it is possible to produce healthier, nutrient-rich food, with higher yields in the longer term, without polluting and exhausting environmental resources."[42] Nevertheless, chemical-intensive agriculture remains the norm.

Prolonged exposure to pesticides and other chemicals used in agriculture causes a long list of health problems for farm workers and their children, especially the children who also work the fields to grow our food, tobacco, animal feed, and crops for biofuel production. Farm work is one of the top ten occupations with high fatal injury rates in the U.S. according to the Bureau of Labor Statistics.[43] All of these issues, and the fact that farm labor is just plain hard on the body, contribute to a substantially lower life expectancy for farm workers than for others in the U.S. And this is in one of the richest countries in the world, with a technologically advanced agriculture.

In the second decade of the twenty-first century, the increase in drought conditions in many parts of the world has only worsened the picture for farm workers and the land they work. For example, the western part of the United States is under threat from drought and freshwater scarcity, which will become more severe as climate change progresses. As a result, there is a growing social crisis in farm worker communities in states like California.[44] To illustrate, we may turn to the city of Mendota, cantaloupe capital of the world, which is populated by farm workers with family heritage in El Salvador and Mexico. In good years, unemployment in Mendota is above 20 percent, which would be considered a crisis if it affected mostly white, middle-income Americans. However, by 2014 during the drought, unemployment rose to almost 50 percent. Half of the people there live below the poverty line and two-thirds of the children never graduate high school.[45] Such conditions are not unique to farming communities in California. They exist in agricultural regions across the United States.[46]

The siting of agricultural operations in arid regions that require unsustainable water withdrawals, the methods of cultivation of conventional agriculture that fail to preserve soil moisture, and the promotion of water-intensive crops all put global food production and producers at risk in the New Dust Bowl era. Agriculture is typically estimated by institutions such as the United Nations and World Bank to be responsible for 70 percent of global freshwater withdrawals.[47] However, this only refers to water that is actively taken from a river, lake, or aquifer. The USDA estimates that consumptive water use by crops—that is, water actually consumed over the lifetime of the crop (by retention in the crop as well as evapotranspiration)—is as high as 80 percent in the United States, rising to 90 percent in western states.[48] However, according to what has been called by Sandra Postel, director of the Global Water Policy Project, "the most comprehensive and finest-resolution analysis to date," agriculture's share of global freshwater consumption is closer to 92 percent. This number reflects the additional amount of freshwater required to treat agricultural pollution.[49]

With the jobs of an estimated 42 percent of the world's working population (1.35 billion people) heavily dependent on access to water, and a NASA study indicating that twenty-one of the world's largest aquifers have already passed their sustainability tipping points, the freshwater situation is, according to Jay Famiglietti, senior water scientist at NASA's Jet Propulsion Laboratory, "quite critical."[50] As the planet continues to warm due to unmitigated greenhouse gas emissions, water demand will increase, and the moisture balance in farmed soils in arid regions will decline, leaving them even more prone to erosion—unless we make major changes. The case of Mendota offers a glimpse into the future of communities on the land at the nexus of socially and ecologically extreme agriculture, energy, and water.

Climate Change and the World's Water

A 2012 article in *Science* began with the question, "How bad will global warming get?"[51] The author wrote, "The question has long been cast in terms of how hot the world will get. But perhaps more important to the planet's inhabitants will be how much rising greenhouse gases crank up the water cycle."[52] Findings at the time showed that climate change had intensified the world's water cycle twice as much as global climate models originally predicted. In an editorial for *Environmental Research Letters*, Martin Wild and Beate Liepert wrote, "Variations in the intensity of the global hydrological cycle can have far-reaching effects on living conditions on our planet. While climate change discussions often revolve around possible consequences of future temperature changes, the adaptation to changes in the hydrological cycle may pose a bigger challenge to societies and ecosystems."[53] NASA's Earth Observatory identifies the alteration of the hydrological cycle as one of "the most serious Earth science and environmental policy issues confronting society."[54] This development forms another chamber in the heart of the New Dust Bowl.

The global hydrological, or water, cycle, "describes the pilgrimage of water as water molecules make their way from the Earth's surface to the atmosphere, and then back again. This gigantic system, powered by energy from the sun, is a continuous exchange of moisture between the oceans, the atmosphere, and the land."[55] The shift in the hydrological cycle as a result of anthropogenic climate change is taking place in a period of unprecedented and increasing aquatic ecosystems degradation and overtapping of freshwater resources. Socially, water pollution and local scarcity have led to an increased burden of disease, community displacement, loss of livelihood, and increased mortality, among other effects.[56] These consequences are linked to the havoc facing the rest of nature as a result of pollution and unsustainable water withdrawals.

Already, *National Geographic* notes, "many lakes, rivers, and wetlands around the world are being severely damaged by human activities and are declining at a much faster rate than terrestrial ecosystems."[57] And, "more than 20 percent of the 10,000 known freshwater fish species have become extinct or imperiled in recent decades."[58] The 2016 World Wildlife Fund *Living Planet Report* shows "that on average the abundance of populations monitored in the freshwater system has declined overall by 81 per cent between 1970 and 2012."[59] A world map of the human impact on marine ecosystems published in 2008 showed that "no area is unaffected by human influence and that a large fraction (41%) is strongly affected."[60] Shifts in the hydrological cycle, as well as other effects of unmitigated climate change, exacerbate many existing water issues and make them more difficult to address.

While this is taking place, human demand for water is expected to increase, along with the economic activities driving ecological degradation. According to the UN:

> Global water demand (in terms of water withdrawals) is projected to increase by some 55% by 2050, mainly because of growing demands from manufacturing (400%), thermal electricity generation (140%) and domestic use (130%). As a result, freshwater availability will be increasingly strained over this time period, and more than 40% of the global population is projected to be living in areas of severe water stress through 2050. There is clear evidence that groundwater supplies are diminishing, with an estimated 20% of the world's aquifers being over-exploited, some critically so. Deterioration of wetlands worldwide is reducing the capacity of ecosystems to purify water.[61]

However, only two years after this UN Water report came out, a 2016 study in *Science Advances* indicated that already, of the global population, "about 66% (4.0 billion people) lives under severe water scarcity . . . at least 1 month of the year."[62]

Taken together, these relatively recent developments—the unprecedented demand for water and degradation of aquatic systems, the shift in the global hydrological cycle, and the social drivers and consequences of these changes—indicate a profound shift in the "hydrosocial cycle," or the "historical and geographical" processes "by which water and society make and remake each other over space and time."[63] The shift is a culmination of what some scientists refer to as the "Great Acceleration" of the Anthropocene, and heralds an epochal moment in the historical drama of capitalism's growing ecological rift.[64]

All of this means our current water problems go beyond historical issues. The guiding assumptions of our technological and engineering approaches to water management no longer hold. For example, one foundational concept of water-resource engineering, "stationarity"—"the idea that natural systems fluctuate within an unchanging envelope of variability"—was pronounced dead by a group of scientists in the journal *Science* several years ago.[65] This prospect has ominous implications for communities around the world that rely on knowledge of historical patterns in the water cycle in planning and that lack infrastructure, or rely on infrastructure that was built to accommodate different conditions.

Current projections indicate that difficulties related to water stress will only increase, especially in areas that were struggling even under relatively stable climatic conditions.[66] Scientists have observed that already wet places are getting wetter and dry places drier. As Romm writes in the journal *Nature*, "The impact of anthropogenic global warming [that] will harm the most people in the coming decades . . . is extended or permanent drought over large parts of currently habitable or arable land—a drastic change in climate that will threaten food security and may be irreversible over centuries."[67] The possibility of what one group of scientists termed "perpetual drought" is what first raised again the terrible specter of the Dust Bowl for many commentators.[68]

The world's water and agricultural crises are completely intertwined, and both are made more extreme by the determination of those in power to continue fossil fuel production in spite of the climate crisis, the water-intensity and pollution of energy production, and the implications of these for the future of food and planetary survival. Ongoing developments in the U.S. southern plains region exemplify global trends.

Extreme Energy

Western Oklahoma, which lies at the heart of the region originally identified as the Dust Bowl, is once again literally at the epicenter of extreme ecological havoc. In 2014 Oklahoma surpassed California *three times over* as the most seismic of the contiguous forty-eight states.[69] Then, in November 2015, a spokesman for the Oklahoma Corporation Commission, the body responsible for regulating the state's oil and gas industry, announced that Oklahoma had become unique in the world for the number of earthquakes concentrated in such a small area.[70] To provide a sense of the pace of change, consider that prior to 2009 Oklahoma averaged one to two earthquakes per year of magnitude 3 or larger. By 2015 that number had become *two per day*.[71] Oklahomans have become all too familiar with terminology such as "induced seismicity" and "earthquake swarms." A seismologist at the National Earthquake Information Center reported that between 2013 and 2015 Oklahoma experienced "almost a millennium's worth of earthquakes in two years."[72]

While the change in Oklahoma is shocking, the number of earthquakes throughout the eastern and central United States has also risen dramatically since 2009. All of this is a result especially of the disposal of wastewater associated the sharp increase in U.S. oil and gas production beginning at that time.[73] The year 2009 was the first year of increased oil production in the United States since 1991, and the nation became the world's leading natural gas producer the same year. The boom was facilitated by: 1) legal changes Congress made in 2005, with bipartisan support, exempting oil and gas production from key environmental oversights, and 2) technological developments resulting from the U.S. government's massive, decades-long investment into research and development of new methods for extracting oil and natural gas, like hydraulic fracturing, commonly known as "fracking." These government-supported developments, driven by broader political and economic priorities, made it possible for oil and gas companies to profit from the exploitation of newly accessible hydrocarbon deposits.[74]

Technological development, especially of hydraulic fracturing and directional drilling, has allowed access to geologically "unconventional" or "tight" formations, such as shale and similar rocks, previously considered either inaccessible or unprofitable to exploit because of their relative impermeability.[75] Fracking is a means to extract oil and gas that "typically involves injecting water, sand, and chemicals under high pressure into a bedrock formation via a well. The process is intended to create new fractures in the rock as well as increase the size, extent, and connectivity of existing fractures."[76]

Forcing fractures in bedrock itself leads to increases in induced, or human-caused, seismicity; however, the swarms of earthquakes we see today in Oklahoma mostly are attributed to the injection of saline and chemical-laden wastewater resulting from oil and gas extraction into wells thousands of feet underground.[77] Across the central and eastern United States the dramatic increase in seismicity since 2009 is the result of using such extraordinary means to extract hydrocarbons.[78] And earthquakes are only one concern. Communities around the United States are worried about other ecological impacts that threaten human health and safety, especially given the change in federal laws exempting the oil and gas industry from important environmental regulations.

Congressional Democrats and Republicans worked together to pass the Energy Policy Act of 2005, which exempted fracking from regulation under the federal Safe Drinking Water Act, and oil and gas production and construction sites from regulation under the Clean Water Act. This helped clear the path for industry expansion of multiple forms of unconventional extraction, laid earlier by federal support including tax breaks and subsidies, research and technological development by the U.S. government's Office of Fossil Energy, as well as previous exemptions from environmental laws.

In March 2010, the Obama administration, which oversaw "the largest domestic oil production increase during any presidency in U.S. history," announced that it would expand offshore drilling by opening many areas for the first time.[79] Two months later the "largest spill of oil in the history of marine oil drilling operations" happened in the Gulf of Mexico, which is still attempting to recover.[80] Eight years after the infamous explosion on BP's Deepwater Horizon oil rig, which killed eleven BP workers, massive ecological destruction and economic losses continue to afflict the Gulf region.[81] In the immediate aftermath of the disaster, scholar Michael Klare wrote, "there can be no mistaking the underlying cause: a government-backed corporate drive to exploit oil and natural gas reserves in extreme environments under increasingly hazardous operating conditions."[82]

The company responsible, despite its rebranding as "Beyond Petroleum," has a long history of taking environmental and safety shortcuts to save money and fatten the bottom line—a major factor in the Gulf spill.[83] BP, along with the other major fossil-fuel companies, consistently has used its massive war chest of capital to fight environmental regulations, while promoting through public campaigns a popular green-capitalist mantra—that voluntary, nonbinding efforts under the heading of corporate social responsibility (CSR) are changing the way they do business, obviating, from this perspective, the need for enforceable regulations or broader social change.

BP was so successful in the late 1990s and early 2000s with its rebranding efforts that the United Nations Environment Programme gave BP's CEO (at the time Sir John Browne) an Individual Environmental Leadership Award in 1999. A year later he received the first Award for Responsible Capitalism from *FIRST* magazine.[84] In the years following these decorations BP continued to expand its destructive drilling, including in ecologically sensitive areas, while exposing workers to unsafe conditions. Despite the company's responsibility for worker deaths and unprecedented ecological harm, it continues to promote a green image of itself, while remaining one of the top companies in the world fighting climate policies and other regulations that would protect workers and the planet.[85]

Similarly, many politicians in the model of former president Obama promote their own green image through offering limited support for renewable energy while simultaneously promoting, and failing to oversee effectively through increased regulation and enforcement of existing regulations, ecologically destructive industries. The expansion of fracking and deepwater drilling that occurred under the Obama administration, and the Trump administration's efforts to continue this expansion, are examples of what is really a global transformation.[86] As one *New York Times* headline reads, "New Technologies Redraw the World's Energy Picture."[87]

From Israel to Suriname, governments and industry working in tandem are promoting the expansion of fossil-fuel extraction and production under increasingly extreme conditions and with increasingly dire consequences. The extraction of shale gas, coalbed methane, and tight gas via fracking, along with the exploitation of shale oil, the mining of oil sands, and ultra-deepwater drilling, are some examples of unconventional methods opening vast new stores of hydrocarbons. At the same time, scientists are pleading with the world to leave carbon in the ground for the sake of humanity and the rest of the biosphere.[88]

As in the United States, political leaders around the world are enacting legal changes to support the oil and gas industry and make it difficult or impossible for communities to exercise any democratic control over what's happening to the land, water, and air on which their lives depend. In 2015 an article titled "How Extreme Energy Leads to Extreme Politics" in *Foreign Policy in Focus* documented the legal changes governments have put in motion to promote extreme extraction, protect it from environmental oversight, and prevent both legal recourse for those impacted and community control over whether to allow operations.[89] The article also reported on the increase in protests by communities confronted with upheaval due to the intensification of extraction throughout the Americas to Europe and beyond—and the attempted suppression and repression of such protests. In Asia, too, protests are on the rise as Western companies move in as partners in the exploitation of shale gas deposits.[90]

While all of this state-supported pillaging goes on, some people still expect the same political and economic leaders who have ushered in the era of extreme energy to move us to a new ecological age. However, they are not doing so. In the area of renewable energy and carbon-sequestration technology (such as Carbon Capture and Storage, or CCS), which promoters of the notion that capitalism can "go green" tend to emphasize, a 2015 *New York Times* headline read, "Innovation Sputters in Battle Against Climate Change."[91] The same year, the technologically optimistic International Energy Agency (IEA) reported:

> Indeed, despite positive signs in many areas, for the first time since the IEA started monitoring clean energy progress, not one of the technology fields tracked is meeting its objectives. As a result, our ability to deliver a future in which temperatures rise modestly is at risk of being jeopardised, and the future that we are heading towards will be far more difficult unless we can take action now to radically change the global energy system.[92]

The objectives technology fields are failing to meet are measures required to keep global warming from increasing more than two degrees Celsius—though climate scientists argue that even this is too much to avoid dangerous climate change.[93]

More recently still, under the 2017 headline "Wall Street Sours on $9 Billion Mechanism for Green Projects," *Bloomberg News* reported that "Wall Street investors have gone cold on one of the main mechanisms banks invented to fund the green-energy revolution."[94] Clearly we are not on track via policy or market-driven technological change, in the area of either carbon sequestration (which is only in its infancy and has its own ecological costs) or renewable energy, to avoid even the two-degree mark on climate change.[95]

Furthermore, the emphasis on technology is irrelevant without broader social and economic change. As sociologist Richard York explains in *Nature Climate Change*, the evidence goes against the assumption of many energy analysts and policymakers that the development of renewable energy will displace fossil fuel use. In summarizing research employing cross-national data on energy use from the previous fifty years, York writes that "each unit of total national energy use from non-fossil fuel sources displaced less than a quarter of a unit of fossil-fuel energy use, and focusing specifically on electricity, each unit of electricity generated by non-fossil fuel energy sources displaced less than one-tenth of a unit of fossil-fuel-generated electricity."[96]

In other words, it will take so much more than technology to move us beyond the extreme energy era. Moreover, from the perspective of nature as a whole, including the human species, even technological change is pushing global conditions in the wrong direction. Communities and ecosystems around the world are suffering from earthquakes, violations of indigenous sovereignty and land, oil spills, and other forms of water and land pollution. Most damning is the alteration of the planet's climate system, which is changing everything.[97] These extremes are mirrored in broader social developments.

Life under Fire in the Twenty-First Century

As in the 1930s, severe social and economic dislocation accompanies the widespread ecological degradation defining the New Dust Bowl era. Today it is not hyperbole to say that all life on the planet is under assault. Billionaire investor Warren E. Buffet told a *New York Times* reporter, "There's class warfare, all right . . . but it's my class, the rich class, that's making war, and we're winning."[98] He was referring to the "rich class" manipulating the tax code so that they pay a smaller percentage of their earnings in taxes than the working class, and therefore accumulate an even more disproportionate share of global income. But the consequences of an elite minority wielding so much political power go much further than tax breaks and have enormous impact on the everyday lives of people and the rest of nature.

The modern era has achieved unimaginable levels of social inequality and insecurity.[99] Credit Suisse's *Global Wealth Report 2015* indicated that in 2014 the concentration of global wealth had reached staggering proportions, with the top 1 percent owning half of all wealth while "the richest decile holds 87.7% of assets."[100] By the time the 2016 report was released, the richest 10 percent had increased their share even further. The report stated: "While the bottom half of adults collectively own less than 1% of total wealth, the richest decile (top 10% of adults) owns 89% of global assets, and the top percentile alone accounts for half of total household wealth."[101] As the 2016 report also noted, there is a broader inequity between continents, wherein "North America and Europe together account for 65% of total household wealth, but contain only 18% of the adult population."[102] This illustrates the continuing significance of wealth extraction from the Global South and its concentration in the imperial centers.

By the end of 2017, in the United States, three white men collectively owned more wealth than half of the U.S. population. And the world's richest forty-two people owned as much as the *less wealthy half of the global population altogether*.[103] At the same time, the less-wealthy half contributed a mere tenth of global carbon emissions, while the wealthiest 10 percent were responsible for approximately half.[104] Therefore the expansion of wealth and inequality are linked to another historic milestone, as 2016 topped the previous year as the hottest on earth since record-keeping began in 1880.[105] Coming on the back of the record-smashing year of heat that was 2015, for the first time the hottest three years on record since 1880 are now consecutive.[106]

While the affluent enjoy the benefits of a political-economic system that facilitates the accumulation of wealth and power at the top, and the "accumulation of catastrophe" throughout the biosphere, much of the global human population must worry about having adequate work to procure necessities—if the necessities are even available.[107] Even worse, millions live daily in fear, in the face of routine violence, disease, pollution, and lack of access to essentials such as housing, food, clothing, and even water. This includes people in the world's richest countries.

The UN reported that globally, 2014 was one of the worst years on record for children, who were subject en masse to "war, violence, atrocities, and disease."[108] More people were forcibly displaced in 2014 than at any other time since record-keeping began. The UN

Refugee Agency (UNHCR) reported that "globally, one in every 122 humans is now either a refugee, internally displaced, or seeking asylum. If this were the population of a country, it would be the world's 24th biggest."[109] By 2017 the situation had only worsened, with 65.6 million people forcibly displaced worldwide. "On average," the UNHCR reported, "20 people were driven from their homes every minute" in 2016, "or one every three seconds—less than half the time it takes to read this sentence."[110] Climate change and increasing ecological degradation are exacerbating these trends. As president of the International Rescue Committee and former UK foreign minister David Miliband reported in 2015, "Climate change is going to compound the cocktail that's driving war and displacement."[111] At the same time, António Guterres, then UN high commissioner for refugees and now UN secretary-general, has said that resources are not being directed in any adequate way to provide "the very minimal level of protection and assistance" to those suffering from decisions they did not make and issues for which they are not responsible.[112]

No meaningful democracy or justice is compatible with such conditions. Therefore it should be no surprise that during the 2015 Paris climate negotiations, the political and economic leaders presiding over this suite of developments once again effectively hung the poorest and most vulnerable out to dry (or drown) as the planet's climate system is forced to respond dramatically to the effluence of the affluent. Such decision making is consistent with the politics and economics that allowed us to arrive at this woeful state of affairs.

Beyond the Epoch of Ecological Extremes?

All of this begs the questions of how we got here and what possibilities lie beyond the Epoch of Ecological Extremes. Many have looked back to the concomitant ecological, economic, and social crises of the 1930s as an important analog to the present, seeking lessons for our generation. However, old ways of thinking about the Dust Bowl and ecological crises in general obscure our vision, so that we do not see the direct thread tying the past to the present, the unresolved issues of the period that lead directly to the extreme ecological and social injustices of today. Chapter Two challenges typical interpretations of the Dust Bowl and puts the disaster into a global frame, linking the past to the present. In so doing, the common roots of contemporary and past developments and struggles are revealed. This examination of the political, economic, and social forces that brought us to the brink a century ago and continue to imperil life on our planet helps clarify the drivers and the necessary targets of action if we are to avoid global Dust Bowls, redress injustice, and move toward a new age, beyond capitalist catastrophe.

THE FIRST GLOBAL ENVIRONMENTAL PROBLEM

> The main battle in imperialism is over land, of course, but when it came to who owned the land, who had the right to settle and work on it, who kept it going, who won it back, and who now plans the future—these issues were reflected, contested, and even for a time decided in narrative. As one critic has suggested, nations themselves are narratives. The power to narrate, or to block other narratives from forming and emerging, is very important to culture and imperialism, and constitutes one of the main connections between them.
>
> —Edward W. Said, *Culture and Imperialism*, 1993

The Official Story

Dust Bowl is a term used variously to refer to a historical period, a geographical region, and an ecological disaster. Depending on the perspective, it is presented as a manmade disaster, a natural one, or some balance of the two. A U.S. Department of Agriculture research scientist recounts the official story, in briefest form, as follows:

> The Dust Bowl era was the period of drought from 1931 to 1939 that was coupled with severe wind-driven soil erosion of overgrazed rangeland and soil exposed by the use of farming practices not adapted to the semi-arid Great Plains. The eroding soil from once productive range and crop lands filled the air with billowing clouds of dust that subsequently buried farm equipment, buildings, and even barbed-wire fences; thus, making the living conditions of many Great Plains inhabitants unbearable. On the Great Plains, wind is common and drought recurrent; therefore, farm implements and management methods were developed for producing crops under these conditions. Likewise, farmers have evolved into innovative practitioners of soil and water conservation techniques that rely on residue management practices

> and crop rotations with fallow periods to store precipitation in the soil for later crop use.[1]

The 1936 *Report of the Great Plains Drought Area Committee* is the original basis of the official narrative, asserting that the basic cause of the disaster was the imposition of a system of agriculture suited for humid provinces on a semi-arid region. However, this report also implicates misguided land allotment practices under the Homestead Act of 1862 and unsuitable government policies encouraging settlers to practice "a system of agriculture which could not be both permanent and prosperous."[2] Furthermore, the authors explain that the development of mechanized plowing techniques allowed farmers to plant wheat fields more easily. Fluctuating prices related to speculation, World War I, and shifts in the global market drove them to cultivate as much acreage as they could, thus intensifying and expanding the problem.

As a result of policy and the combined forces of "nature and the market," the 1936 report states:

> One primary source of the disaster has been the destruction of millions of acres of . . . natural cover, an act which in such a series of dry years as that through which we are now passing left the loose soil exposed to the winds. This destruction has been caused partly by over grazing, partly by excessive plowing. It has been an accompaniment of settlement, intensified in operation and effect since the [First] World War.[3]

A cascade of other government publications highlight specific issues related to particular areas of the plains. But this summary captures the general understanding of what became known as the Dust Bowl, after a journalist coined the term in 1935. Geographically, the Dust Bowl tends to refer to the region at the heart of the disaster of soil erosion and drought in the United States, including "considerable portions of Texas, New Mexico, Colorado, Oklahoma, and Kansas."[4]

Most scientists and scholars writing about the Dust Bowl accept, more or less, the general narrative outlined above. They may disagree on many specifics, but this official story is the starting point for nearly all analyses. The main divergence from this view arises from those few defenders of the settlers and boosters for the region who posit the Dust Bowl as a purely natural disaster, overcome by human spirit and ingenuity—we might call them Dust Bowl deniers.

The Dust Bowl Literature

The Scholarly Literature: Geographical Scope and Scale

In the canon of Dust Bowl literature, especially the most cited works—the bulk of which have appeared since the 1970s, when intense droughts and increasingly widespread ecological concern sparked renewed interest in the events of the 1930s across multiple disciplines—scholars consider the Dust Bowl only in national-regional terms, however it is explained or defined in terms of its boundaries. This is in keeping with the official story outlined above and is true of work emanating from the fields of history, soil science, geography, economics, atmospheric science, agronomy, geophysics, and sociology.[5]

Scholars debate the precise boundaries of the Dust Bowl on the plains and the specific cultural, economic, soil, and climatological characteristics shaping the region during the period leading up to and including the 1930s drought.[6] Some refer to character attributes of the local people, specifically the "generally optimistic plainsmen."[7] And now researchers use increasingly sophisticated methodological and technological approaches to explore the crisis in ever finer detail. As a result, much of the literature focuses on proximate causes rather than broader social drivers. In defining the Dust Bowl in very narrow terms, scholars either miss or minimize some of the most important facets of the socio-ecological issues confronting the southern plains in both the past and present. A minority come close to denying the crises altogether.

Recently, historians have used geographic information system (GIS) software that integrates census, soil, and climate data to challenge Worster's thesis that "Jefferson's outward-moving democracy and . . . the shaping of American agriculture by an evolving capitalism" drove the plains to ecological and social despair.[8] Triangulating the results of climate models, demographic data, and GIS analyses to determine just how bad the dust was at the county, and even individual farm, level, some scholars now ask if government intervention was really necessary to save the plains.

Historian Geoff Cunfer writes that "New Deal reformers created the [Dust Bowl] narrative in the 1930s" to justify "their radical efforts to reorganize American agriculture."[9] Cunfer's argument is telling—representing a form of Dust Bowl denial that echoes earlier conservative attacks on the New Deal going back to Herbert Hoover, as well as colonial defenses of settler agriculture—but comes up short. Because dust storms occur regularly on the plains, Cunfer reasons, there was nothing exceptional about the 1930s except the "mass-marketing" of a routine occurrence by an "activist federal government."[10] He writes as if scientists and scholars have ignored earlier dust storms on the plains, which is simply not true. In fact, Worster discusses the fact that plains residents were accustomed to blowing dust. However, the unprecedented problem of soil erosion generated by the expansion of white settlement and cash-crop agriculture in the plains region was recognized, as discussed later in this chapter and even further in Chapter Four, much earlier than the New Deal period by a wide range of observers, scientists, and plains residents—across the political spectrum. The New Deal narrative, in fact, relied on these earlier observations and studies of soil erosion. Moreover, Cunfer's argument that "the Dust Bowl was a temporary disruption in a stable system," which may be reasonably labeled "sustainable" because land-use practices have changed little over a span of decades, has no basis in ecological science and ignores the real ecological issues that persist on the plains as a result of the lack of change. One strand of contemporary environmental politics (antiregulation, defense of the status quo, environmental denialism) is evident in such recent efforts to challenge Worster's interpretation by questioning the severity of the crisis and arguing that the settlers' historical and current agricultural practices are sustainable.[11]

While Worster's famous environmental history, discussed below, is by far the most influential and significant scholarly account of the Dust Bowl, the most cited work written this century is an article published in 2004 by NASA scientists titled "On the Cause of the 1930s Dust Bowl." This study employs a "NASA Seasonal-to-Interannual

Prediction Project (NSIPP) atmospheric general circulation model," building on the work of other studies "using state-of-the-art atmospheric general circulation models (AGCMS)." The researchers find "the drought was caused by anomalous tropical sea surface temperatures during that decade and that interactions between the atmosphere and land surface increased its severity."[12] Despite the title of the article, social factors never enter into the discussion of the "cause" of the Dust Bowl, which the authors refer to simply as a major drought.

Such an interpretation takes us further away from any broader social analysis. Fortunately, there are major exceptions to such narrow perspectives in the Dust Bowl literature. Worster's *Dust Bowl: The Southern Plains in the 1930s* stands out in placing at the center of investigation the systemic problems and extraregional factors that made the Dust Bowl "an extension of, not an exception to, the rest of America" in terms of the maltreatment of the land.[13] Such maltreatment, Worster writes, was the result of the ruling "capitalist ethos," which provided "the cultural impetus that drove Americans into the grassland and determined the way they would use it."[14] In describing this ethos, he adds that "the attitude of capitalism—industrial and preindustrial—toward the earth was imperial and commercial; none of its ruling values taught environmental humility, reverence, or restraint."[15] As a result, "the culture they [settlers] had brought to the Plains—the culture that had brought them there—was ecologically among the most unadaptive ever devised. That was the message written in the darkened skies, shifting dunes of sand, and defeated faces."[16]

Unlike other scholars who focus on the particularity of the region, Worster identifies the larger crisis of agriculture in the United States. Referring to images of other regions published at the time, he remarks: "Those photographs make a convincing argument that the dust storms were neither a trivial matter nor an isolated phenomenon, that everywhere in America the land was in a bankrupt state."[17] Rather than attributing to the plainsmen a peculiar culture, Worster highlights that they, "like American agriculturalists elsewhere . . . increasingly came to view farming and ranching as businesses, the objects of which were not simply to make a living, but to make money."[18] The Dust Bowl came about, then, "because the expansionary energy of the United States had finally encountered a volatile, marginal land, destroying the delicate balance that evolved there."[19]

Going beyond most, Worster refers to social factors, to a systemic push behind the destruction. But his analysis remains expressed in regional and national terms, emphasizing the lives and hardships of white settlers. These issues are related to the fact that the focus of the study is a United States conspicuously extricated from the broader history of colonialism and imperialism marking the era of economic expansion that gave rise to the problem of soil erosion. Worster's discussions of international developments refer to later periods, with problems resulting from the fact that "American agriculture has been powerfully persuasive in the world," especially after the Second World War.[20] This perspective ignores the link between U.S. frontier and Anglo-European colonial policies. Therefore the truly systemic, global patterns present even earlier than the 1900s are obscured, as well as the scale and ongoing unequal ecological and social consequences of these policies in the United States and elsewhere.

A crucial piece of more recent scholarship offers a distinct take on the causes of the "metabolic rift in the High Plains aquifer," referring to the depletion of groundwater as a result of extensive irrigation—one technological "fix" that helps sustain an unsustainable agriculture on the plains. In addressing present-day issues, sociologists Matthew R. Sanderson and R. Scott Frey offer one of the few contemporary sociological analyses of the political economic context that gave rise to the Dust Bowl and the "deeper, socio-structural problems in the human-environment nexus" on the plains.[21] Sanderson and Frey demonstrate a more sophisticated understanding of the relationship between the state and private capital than is presented elsewhere in the literature, showing how they in tandem "incorporated the region as a source of primary raw materials, mainly agricultural products."[22] Their explanation of the "ways in which this region was articulated into broader circuits of capital and exchange" helps make sense, for example, of the persistent barriers to the development of a sustainable relationship to the land and regional water resources on the plains via policy.[23]

Sanderson and Frey explain the inequities of the political economic ties between the plains and wealthier areas of the nation. These areas concentrate capital and political power and shape developments in the plains region to benefit capital accumulation by the affluent centers, at the long-term social and ecological expense of the plains. Their analysis, like Worster's, does not provide a sense of the global problems of the Dust Bowl era. However, perhaps more than any other study to date, the analytical framework of Sanderson and Frey's work makes it possible to link the problems on the plains to global phenomena of unequal exchange and the ecological rift. As a result, their critical insights point an important way forward, especially when articulated with the more global perspective offered here.

The Scholarly Literature: Temporal Delineation

Along with the limited geographical focus in the Dust Bowl literature is the pervasive temporal dimension of all Dust Bowl narratives in which "the plot . . . commences at the moment that Euroamerican settlers began to occupy the grasslands."[24] In an influential article, environmental historian William Cronon, who also focuses on the Dust Bowl as a regional problem, notes that there is "no explicit *backward* extension of the time frame. The precontact history of the Indians is not part of this story."[25]

Indeed, existing scholarship generally ignores the intensive, violent confrontation between settlers, the U.S. government, and private organizations on the one hand, and the indigenous nations on the other. Another oft-cited account of the Dust Bowl illustrates this trend. Environmental scientist William Lockeretz writes:

> Throughout its history of about a century, Plains agriculture has followed a boom-or-bust pattern. Before the arrival of the first settlers—the cattlemen—the undisturbed ecosystem changed in response to variations in weather, but the far-reaching alterations that accompanied each wave of settlement greatly magnified the impact of subsequent weather cycles.[26]

In this account the first arrivals to the plains were white cattlemen, who found an "undisturbed ecosystem." If there were any human costs to settlement of the region, they were to these cattlemen and farmers subject to, among other scourges, bad government policy, speculative capital "from as far away as Europe," market and weather fluctuations, and an undue optimism "founded on a mixture of science, pseudoscience, and hucksterism."[27]

The intensely regional focus and periodization beginning with white arrival to the "undisturbed" plains have had significant consequences for both scholarly and popular understandings of the Dust Bowl. Worster's *Dust Bowl* demonstrates that even when broader, system- or society-level factors are taken into account, including cultural ones, the global drive for white territorial control is left out of the analysis. This means ignoring the role of material-ideological motives such as white supremacy that are linked to, but distinct from, the profit motive, or "capitalist ethos," in shaping the course of events and their outcomes. Removing the experience of the pioneers from the global context hides the colonial nature of the problems on the plains. Focusing on "Jefferson's outward-moving democracy and . . . the shaping of American agriculture by an evolving capitalism," out of context, ignores the reality of racialized social domination inherent in capitalist development but hidden by the rhetoric of expanding democracy.[28]

Further, Worster suggests that emphasizing issues of race and ethnicity, as well as "questions of social justice," is a distraction when trying to understand the ecological impact of capitalist development.[29] In an afterword to the twenty-fifth anniversary edition of *The Dust Bowl* (2004), he writes:

> focusing over much on racial and cultural matters can distract from the larger vision of environmental history. We must never again lose sight of the land itself, of its moral and material significance, its agency and influence; the land must stand at the core of the new history. Nor should we overlook or dismiss the truth claims of the natural sciences, out of misguided deconstructionism or multiculturalism that makes nature whatever any group says it is; for science is our indispensable ally in understanding the past in a fuller and more authoritative light. Nor, in writing the cultural history of ideas about nature, should we obscure the age-old dialogue between ecology and economy. I put that dialogue front and center in this book, for without it there is no new

> perspective on history—there is only an old history of human ideas, perceptions, and values colliding with other ideas.[30]

Just before making this point, Worster mentions that he is aware that different communities were impacted by the Dust Bowl in distinct ways, but even this elides an important point, too often ignored even today, including within mainstream environmentalism, that decimation of the land requires—as a precondition and as an ongoing requirement—the domination of peoples. Addressing issues of racialized social domination does not distract us from understanding the relationship between human economy and ecology, but rather is necessary to understand this relationship. As sociologist David Naguib Pellow puts it, "the domination of the environment is actually reflective of the domination of human beings."[31] The consequences thereof are much deeper and longer-lasting than the unjust distribution of environmental harms once a problem arises.

Toward a Broader View

The following sections point to an alternative framing of the Dust Bowl. First, I show that in contrast to depictions ubiquitous today, and to the canon of contemporary literature, Dust Bowl–era observers situated the crisis on the U.S. southern plains within a broader historical and geographical context. By the 1930s a well-established, international, transimperial body of scholarly literature, government reports, conference proceedings, and periodical articles existed, discussing the growing problem of soil erosion across the colonial world. This literature is written in multiple languages and extends back decades before the Dust Bowl, especially as the early conservation movement was a response to the accelerating ecological degradation associated with Anglo-European and U.S. colonialism and domestic economic activities.[32] So when the dust storms on the plains made headlines around the world, observers interpreted it not as an isolated event, but in light of these historical developments.

Here I draw on examples of commentary published during the Dust Bowl period to summarize international conditions and illustrate how common experiences across colonial contexts allowed writers then (and us now) to understand the dust storms in the United States in broader terms. Doing so makes it possible to resituate the Dust Bowl and make sense of the drivers of socio-ecological changes on the plains and around the world. This was the era of rapid economic expansion via the "new imperialism" of the late 1800s and early 1900s, which violently transformed societies and the land, entrenching the ecological rift of capitalism on a global scale and the related patterns of unequal ecological exchange that persist to this day.

"Dust Bowls of the Empire"

On the front page of the *Springfield Republican* (Massachusetts) on May 25, 1939, a column appeared under the headline "Erosion a World Problem."[33] It reported on the ongoing battle against soil erosion in the United States and around the world. From Canada to Uganda, Ceylon to Australia, erosion had rapidly increased "due to abuse of the soil." The author wrote, "The unskilled farmer has been destroying the soil for many centuries, and Greece, Calabria, Palestine and other regions have been terribly impoverished by this decay."[34] However, the current period marked a break with historical trends. To explain further, the columnist cited a study published earlier the same year in the *Round Table*, Britain's oldest journal of international affairs, titled "Dust Bowls of the Empire."[35]

The *Round Table* article provides an important overview and diagnosis of the expansive anthropogenic destruction of soils throughout the British colonies, in the United States, and around the world by the 1930s. It reminds readers how extensively recognized the problem of erosion had been, years before the "spectacular accounts of the dust storms which enveloped in darkness great areas of the middle and eastern United States during the summers of 1934 and 1935" would move "the popular imagination."[36]

The article traces the dramatic dust storms of the 1930s to the expansion of cash crop agriculture, among other pressures, which changed the relationship of those working the land to the land itself. As a result,

> the men whose conquest of the prairies of the middle west of North America, of the pampas of South America, of the wheat-belt of Australia, let loose that flood of wheat and other food which enabled the population of the world to take its unprecedented upward leap in the nineteenth century, were rarely farmers in any real sense of the word. They were simply miners of whatever fertility had accumulated through the ages in the virgin soils.[37]

The author explains that within the colonial context, while "erosion takes various forms in the different African colonies . . . it is to be noticed that much of the pressure upon the land has arisen through the introduction of crops for sale."[38] Also, "Ceylon and the island colonies nearly all report serious cases of erosion . . . of the same character," arising "from shifting cultivation, deforestation and overgrazing."[39]

These activities left scars on the land across continents to feed a growing global market for food and other resources, servicing those who could pay. However, for locals, "the increase of such money crops, even maize" resulted "in the neglect of the food crops for the family and in a deterioration in the native dietary."[40] It was clear, wrote the author, that "the erosion menace" was "threatening certain tribes."[41] Indeed, the article cited all too common features of the new imperialism of the late nineteenth and early twentieth centuries, which involved a massive colonial land and resource grab and the restructuring of global food systems along capitalist lines.

Moreover, the social and ecological problems arising from colonial expansion, including the causes and consequences of soil erosion associated with cash-crop agriculture, were well understood—even as conditions worsened. The unnamed "Dustbowls of the Empire" author writes that "some years before these events," numerous reports presented evidence that "all showed how rapid was becoming the decline in the productive capacity of much of the land in Africa," and that these reports drew the attention of governments across the continent.[42] Indeed, our author writes,

> specialists had often reported on particular cases, but their warnings carried little weight with Governments, who are occupied more with the political aspects of agriculture than with the fate of the land. At last, however, Governments have been forced to realize that matters cannot be allowed to drift, even though the measures that must be adopted in order to preserve the land as a means of production involve actions of a kind to which all Governments are most averse, namely, interference with traditional methods of farming and the right of man to do what he likes with his own land.[43]

By 1914, "there was a select committee on erosion" in South Africa.[44] The spread of experience and information meant that "from one source or another there sprang up a general consciousness of the gravity of the problems presented by soil erosion in almost every country where recent settlement or the growth of the population had led to an intensification of agriculture."[45]

Another example of the many early warnings came from India in 1915, when British superintendent Albert Howard lamented a lost opportunity to conserve the soil. In the context of describing a wider problem, he wrote, "It is in the planting areas of the East . . . that the most striking examples of soil denudation are to be seen. In the hill tracts in the centre of Ceylon, an area which is now covered with tea estates, the original forest canopy was removed to make room for coffee which later gave place to tea. Little or no provision was made at the time to retain *in situ* the fine soil of the original forest and, in consequence, the loss of soil has been enormous and is still going on."[46]

Despite such warnings, the stripping of the soil continued.

Many 1930s publications lament the ignored warnings and document the nature of the crisis internationally. Writing in the *China Press* in 1937, Dr. Chatley, engineer-in-chief of the Whangpoo Conservancy Board, noted, "This state of things [soil erosion] occurs noticeably in Northern China and also in the 'Dust Bowl' in the upper part of the Mississippi basin."[47] The authors of a 1944 article in the *Empire Forestry Journal* write that in the British colonies alone, soil erosion had transformed eastern Africa, South Africa, and the West Indies.[48] It was also a serious issue in what the colonial administration then called the Northern Territories of the Gold Coast in western

Africa, as well as in Palestine, Cyprus, Ceylon, Malaya, Hong Kong, Trinidad and Tobago, and the Falkland Islands.[49] In 1938 the *Journal of the Royal African Society* published a supplemental volume providing a transcript of a high-level discussion hosted by the society on the subject of global soil erosion. Agricultural scientist Sir Daniel Hall is quoted as saying,

> What I want just to impress upon you is that this soil erosion question is not one of Africa alone. It is one that affects the whole world, and in particular the British Empire. I had occasion to point out how one form of erosion, wind erosion, is playing havoc in Western Canada. Again South Africa suffers from it. Of Australia we read now many accounts of how the grazing grounds are becoming open to wind erosion and the whole of the somewhat exiguous vegetation that they once carried is now disappearing. We get erosion from rain creating difficulties in an old country like India. In Ceylon the tea crop has suffered from soil erosion. Jamaica, too. It is a problem that is world-wide.[50]

The same year, underlining that the problem of soil erosion was neither local nor confined to arid regions, Gorrie R. Maclagan published an article titled "The Problem of Soil Erosion in the British Empire with Special Reference to India" in the *Journal of the Royal Society of Arts*, explaining that colonials in various global regions understood that "their problems are merely local phases of the same widespread phenomenon."[51] Elspeth Huxley, writing in the *Japan Times* in 1937, highlighted the altered purpose of agriculture in Africa—how it had been redirected with great success by colonial governments toward exports—at the expense of local food production, social systems, and soil health:

> For the past century in Africa vegetative cover has been slowly but steadily stripped from the land, and the process continues today at an accelerated rate. This has been done in three ways: by deforestation, by extension of cultivation, and by overgrazing. All these methods have been greatly stimulated by European rule . . . [T]he drives which nearly all Colonial Governments have undertaken in recent years to increase production of native-grown crops for export have been extremely successful; so successful that very much larger areas are now under cultivation than (so far as is known) ever before.[52]

Of everything written during the Dust Bowl era, Graham Vernon Jacks and Robert Orr Whyte's *The Rape of the Earth: A World Survey of Soil Erosion* is one of the most thorough. It covers every continent, tracing the expansion of soil erosion along with the "rapid development of the New World" and explicitly linking it to ecological imperialism and conditions of what we now call unequal ecological exchange.[53] The authors write that "the main economic cause of recent accelerated erosion has been the transfer of capital across regional or political boundaries and its repayment with soil fertility" in the form of food and other agricultural commodities imported to wealthier regions.[54] They refer to erosion as "a disease to which any civilization founded on the European model seems liable when it attempts to grow outside Europe" and "a warning that Nature is in full revolt against the sudden incursion of an exotic civilization into her ordered domains."[55]

In placing the U.S. case within this overarching framework, they explain:

> The history of erosion in the United States is bound up with the pioneer phase in the nation's development, through the stages of deforestation for agricultural land, timber, fuel, and potash in the east, the development of the monoculture system of agriculture for maize in the Corn Belt and cotton to the south, overstocking and ploughing of the natural grassland areas of the Great Plains, gross overstocking and maltreatment of the range country, overgrazing and over-cultivation on the Pacific coast, and deforestation in the Pacific north-west.[56]

The dust storms on the plains, then, "were not freaks of Nature"[57] but the result of bringing land to an "almost desert state by over-cultivation of the original semi-arid grasslands, much of which should not have been ploughed in the first place."[58] In so summarizing the U.S. condition, these writers recognize what seems to have escaped many contemporary writers on the Dust Bowl, namely, that "in the Great Plains States, depression and drought have only accentuated a situation which has long been developing."[59]

Moreover, *The Rape of the Earth* contains an extensive comparative overview providing suggestions regarding how, moving forward, the colonial powers might address the linked problems of the "native," the poor white, the ongoing drive for economic expansion and territorial acquisition, and soil erosion. This is because one major preoccupation at the time, the late 1930s, was addressing soil erosion in order to retain white territorial control.[60] Jacks and Whyte suggest "jettisoning the promising experiment of Indirect Rule," though "everywhere it would mean denying the natives some of the liberty and opportunity for material advancement to which their labours should entitle them."[61] However, it would "enable the people who have been the prime cause of erosion and who have the means and ability to control it to assume responsibility for the soil."[62]

"At present," Jacks and Whyte write,

> humanitarian considerations for the natives prevent Europeans from winning the attainable position of dominance over the soil. Humanity may perhaps be the higher ideal, but the soil demands a dominant, and if white men will not and black men cannot assume the position, the vegetation will do so, by the process of erosion finally squeezing out the whites. . . . It is kind to the natives to allow them their due rights in a civilized community but hard on the soil, and soon in Africa the soil will be more insistent on its right to have a ruler than the natives are on theirs. Either the white man or the wild vegetation is destined to become dominant on the soils which the former now administers but does not rule.[63]

For this reason, they conclude, "the white man's burden in the future will be to come to terms with the soil and plant world, and for many reasons it promises to be a heavier burden than coming to terms with the natives."[64] This sentiment was echoed in the *Springfield Republican*, which commented in reporting on soil erosion worldwide that the "white man's burden grows heavier year by year."[65]

Similarly, District Commissioner of Nyeri, Kenya, A. M. Champion wrote, "so grave is the present position [of soil erosion] . . . that legislators and others interested, at home and abroad, should be made to realize that the condition of some of our African Possessions is such that we have reached the position in which it is kinder to be cruel, for by doing so we shall save the negro from worse to come."[66]

Prof. E. P. Stebbing, a British forester and entomologist in India, wrote in the *Journal of the Royal African Society* to report on his joint expedition with the French to assess the erosion problem in Nigeria. He held out little hope that, despite the best-intentioned efforts of white colonists to help them, Africans could save the soil or themselves: "It has been said in some quarters that the education, now being so liberally given to the African, will result in his becoming soil-conscious, and that he will become aware of the present wasteful methods of soil utilization which have come down to him from his ancestors." However, he continued, "to await the dawn of some problematic future when the educated African will take the necessary action himself is to risk either the migration (if possible) or starvation of no inconsiderable percentage of the population. Or, as a least of the dangers, a decrease in their well-being and a lessening in the amount of food production in regions which are under our administration."[67]

In 1940 Isaiah Bowman, U.S. geographer and president of Johns Hopkins University, cited in *Scientific Monthly* a 1929 edition of the *Empire Cotton Growing Review*, which stated that "nearly all countries which have been opened up for any kind of 'planting' afford striking object lessons in what ought *not* to be done." Bowman concluded that "the exploiting white man has been unable to make his economic scheme take account of the science that has given him power over the native and his land. . . . We have assured profits for the time being to commercial enterprises in the far-flung acreages that now lie devastated and barren. We have equally assured the destruction of the soil. All our other scientific achievements in tropical exploitation will fall if the base is destroyed, and that base is not profits but the land upon which tropical peoples dwell."[68]

Despite increased knowledge and appreciation of soil erosion in all quarters of the British Empire, and better coordination between colonial offices and government departments to address it, the authors of the *Empire Forestry Journal* article nevertheless conclude that by 1944 it remained "one of the chief agricultural problems with which the Colonial Empire is faced."[69]

These examples make clear that the Dust Bowl was one spectacular instance of a global problem of soil erosion associated with capitalist colonial expansion. While the official interpretation suggests that agriculture suited for a humid region was imported to an arid region, precipitating the crisis, these contemporaneous accounts illustrate how much larger the crisis was, tied up with specific social and economic developments that imposed new socio-ecological relations upon peoples of the world and upon the land irrespective of local climatic conditions. The common denominators across the world, from North to South America, Australia to Africa, and Southeast to East Asia, were not climate and geography, but capitalism and colonialism.

Ultimately, therefore, we can only answer the question of what caused the Dust Bowl by understanding the social and economic developments driving the changing relations of humans to one another and to the land globally in the period immediately preceding it. This is the subject of Chapter Three.

IMPERIALISM, WHITE SETTLER COLONIALISM, AND THE ECOLOGICAL RIFT

> The colony of a civilized nation which takes possession, either of waste country, or of one so thinly inhabited that the natives easily give place to the new settlers, advances more rapidly to wealth and greatness than any other human society.
>
> —Adam Smith, *An Inquiry into the Nature and Causes of the Wealth of Nations*, 1776

> The national idea . . . [that] regarded the frontiers of the state as being determined by the natural boundaries of the nation, is now transformed into the notion of elevating one's own nation above all others. The ideal now is to secure for one's own nation the domination of the world, an aspiration which is as unbounded as the capitalist lust for profit from which it springs. . . . These efforts become an economic necessity, because every failure to advance reduces the profit and the competitiveness of finance capital, and may finally turn the smaller economic territory into a mere tributary of a larger one. . . . Since the subjugation of foreign nations takes place by force—that is, in a perfectly natural way—it appears to the ruling nation that this domination is due to some special natural qualities, in short to its racial characteristics. Thus there emerges a racist ideology, cloaked in the garb of natural science, a justification for finance capital's lust for power, which is thus shown to have the specificity and necessity of a natural phenomenon.
>
> —Rudolph Hilferding, *Finance Capital: A Study of the Latest Phase of Capitalist Development*, 1910

German sociologist Max Weber turned down a meeting with President Theodore Roosevelt in order to visit the U.S. southern plains in 1904, not long after the government opened the region more fully, by force, for white settlement. Based on his observations of what was then still nominally Indian Territory, Weber wrote that "with almost lightning speed everything that stands in the way of capitalistic culture is being crushed."[1] He was referring both to the rapid devastation of the regional environment and to the violent dispossession of indigenous nations, especially through the federal policies of expropriation, privatization, and allotment of communal land.[2]

Weber made these observations at a time when much of the world in addition to the southern plains was subject to "lightning speed" transformation brought about by capitalist development via the new imperialism. These political, economic, and social developments imposed on the world a racialized division of humanity and the rest of nature on a global scale that persists to this day.[3] At the heart of this transformation, sociologist and activist W. E. B. DuBois observes in "The Souls of White Folk" (1920), was the capitalist powers' "vast quest of the dark world's wealth and toil," which destroyed communities and transformed the land.[4] "With the dog-in-the-manger theory of trade, with the determination to reap inordinate profits and to exploit the weakest to the utmost there came a new imperialism."[5]

A distinguishing feature of the new imperialism, which took off in the wake of the U.S. Civil War and abolition of slavery, was the marked increase in the rate of territorial acquisition by Europe, the United States, and Britain to three times the rate of the previous period.[6] Japan also extended its imperial reach in this era. As economist Harry Magdoff explains, by 1914, "as a consequence of this new expansion and conquest on top of that of preceding centuries, the colonial powers, their colonies, and their former colonies extended over approximately 85 percent of the earth's surface."[7] Control of the circuits of finance and trade, in addition to direct colonial rule, meant that "economic and political control by leading powers reached across almost the entire globe."[8]

As historian Roxanne Dunbar-Ortiz has researched extensively, the "essential ideology of colonial projects," white supremacy, was part of the "culture of conquest" energizing Anglo-European and U.S. expansion and justifying the murderous treatment of peoples.[9] DuBois, who experienced and addressed these developments as they unfolded, recounts that "as to the darkest and weakest peoples there was but one unanimity in Europe—that which Herr Dernberg of the German Colonial Office called the agreement with England to maintain white 'prestige' in Africa—the doctrine of the divine right of white people to steal."[10] The gospel of imperial expansion, identified by DuBois as the "new religion of whiteness," proclaimed that "whiteness is the ownership of the earth forever and ever, Amen!"[11]

U.S. imperialism, including wars against the plains tribes and colonial expansion west of the Mississippi, was encouraged at the turn of the century and lauded as contributing to white control of the world's peoples and resources. During this time the United States seized Hawai'i, Alaska, Puerto Rico, Guam, American Samoa, the Marshall Islands, and the Northern Mariana Islands.[12]

As imperialists put boots on the ground across the globe, communities and nations forcefully resisted subjugation. As Edward W. Said wrote, "it was the case nearly everywhere in the non-European world that the coming of the white man brought forth some sort of resistance."[13] In the face of a growing anti-imperialism—expressed in mutinies, plantation rebellions, and anticolonial revolts, as well as in the writings and activism of Americans like Mark Twain and sociologists DuBois and Jane Addams—the United States took up the "white man's burden" on an ever-increasing scale.[14] As England's Nobel Prize–winning poet Rudyard Kipling had urged and glorified in his 1899 poem "The White Man's Burden: The United States and the Philippine Islands," the United States waged a brutal colonial war against the Philippines to prevent its independence.

On the Fourth of July in 1901—while the United States celebrated the 125th anniversary of the adoption by the Second Continental Congress of the Declaration of Independence—President William McKinley appointed William Howard Taft as the colonial governor-general of the Philippines during a war of atrocity waged against the recently declared Philippine Republic. More than 200,000 Filipinos were killed in the onslaught, most of them civilians and children.[15] On the same day in 1901, McKinley proclaimed the remaining lands of the Kiowa-Comanche, Apache, and Wichita—in what would become the Dust Bowl region—open for settlement. The U.S. government faced fierce resistance to this land theft and a legal challenge to allotment led by Kiowa chief Lone Wolf that went all the way to the Supreme Court. The court reinforced U.S. colonial policy, ruling that Congress had jurisdiction over the tribes, for whom there was no recognized legal recourse in such cases.[16]

The racially justified expropriation of the land and people enriched and increased the capacities of Global North nations and their economic elites—who financed, carried out, and benefited from this expropriation—to reinforce their rule. As David Naguib Pellow writes, "natural resources are used and abused to support racial hegemony and domination and have been at the core of this process for a half-millennium."[17] Thus, expropriation, exploitation, and domination paved the way directly to the Dust Bowl and the global crisis of soil erosion by the 1930s.

The following pages explain the immense changes that took place in the decades preceding the Dust Bowl and made its development possible.

The New Imperialism and the Political Economy of Conquest

Well before the U.S. Civil War broke out in 1861, the inherent instability of slavery, marked by constant revolt and rebellion, and the growing global abolition movement, greatly concerned merchants and manufacturers worldwide. Whether individual capitalists and statesmen supported slavery's expansion or abhorred the institution, the wealth of nations hinged on it. Indeed, the incredible growth and global integration of Anglo-European capitalism was completely dependent on the accumulation of capital made possible by the brutal extraction of slave labor and resources, alongside a vast theft of land and the exploitation of wage workers that often began when children were very young and led many to an early grave. Slavery, land theft, cruel colonial warfare, and the sadistic treatment of people were part and parcel of what historian Sven Beckert redesignates "war capitalism," a term that describes the activities of capitalist nations during this period more accurately than "mercantile capitalism."[18]

Describing processes to which social scientists refer as original or primary accumulation—mostly building on Marx—Beckert's concept of war capitalism represents not so much a distinct period as the barbaric side of capitalist development that persisted in the industrial period.[19] This barbarism was common knowledge among both its perpetrators and, of course, its victims and resisters. As Beckert notes, "Marx's argument that 'bourgeois civilization' and 'barbarity' were joined at the hip . . . was simply common sense in elite circles."[20] As Marx himself put it, "The colonial system ripened trade and navigation as in a hot-house. . . . The colonies provided a market for the budding manufactures, and a vast increase in accumulation which was guaranteed by the mother country's monopoly of the market. The treasures captured outside Europe by undisguised looting, enslavement, and murder, flowed back to the mother-country and were turned into capital there."[21]

Because of slavery's centrality in the global economy, its uneven abolition was viewed by many capitalists and statesmen as a crisis in the first half of the nineteenth century, and led by the second half to a push to identify new sources of cheap labor and land, alongside the ongoing search for new repositories of natural resources and markets for industrial goods. Among other concerns, the prospect of diminishing, unpredictable, or more costly supplies (such as food and inputs for manufacturers) in a postslavery context sent capitalist states scouring the globe for new territory to bring under direct colonial control and cultivation in the mid-nineteenth century. This search became frantic as civil war in the United States, one of the most important suppliers of slave-produced cotton and other crops to the industrial centers of the world, appeared inevitable.

In the aftermath of the abolition of slavery in the United States, this expansionary thrust became even more frenzied as the second industrial revolution gave birth to the new imperialism, widely recognized as lasting from 1870 to at least the First World War, alongside the rise of monopoly capital—a new phase of capitalist development.[22] During this period capital headquartered in the leading capitalist nations consolidated, including through the fusion of finance and industrial capital—becoming larger, more concentrated, and more powerful, with the largest business firms (corporations) dominating the economy.

Thus, the second industrial revolution involved the centralization of production, concentration of capital, ascendancy of finance, and technological development that gave capitalists the means and the might to reorient the economies of entire regions and nations toward production for an emerging global market. This revolution required increasing, and increasingly stable, sources of raw materials and crops. As Beckert notes, "heavy advances in industrial production, a novelty in human history, demanded a constant supply of land, labor, and money."[23] New developments in technology and finance made capital available for overseas ventures on a greater scale and made feasible the transport of bulk materials and food over long distances, while enhancing the military capabilities of the colonial powers to hold territory.

Capitalists also wanted new investment outlets and manufacturers desired new, continually expanding markets for their increased industrial output, as well as an end to competition from indigenous industries. Through economically and legally coercive means, as well as "a staggering degree of violence," communities around the globe were compelled to abandon their traditional occupations and cultivate crops for export to global markets.[24] Swelling urban populations, often the result of social dislocation in the countryside, brought a growing demand for cheap food and other agricultural products, such as cotton.[25] As a result, explains Magdoff, "the pressures and opportunities of the later decades of the nineteenth century" meant that "more and more of the world was drawn upon as primary producers for the industrialized nations."[26] During this era of gunboat globalization, "self-contained economic regions dissolved into a world economy, involving an international division of labor whereby the leading industrial nations made and sold manufactured products and the rest of the world supplied them with raw materials and food."[27]

Within thirty short years, Africa, for example, went from being nearly free of colonial occupation, except along the coasts, to being almost entirely claimed by competing European nations. The British statesmen James Bryce gives a breathtakingly brazen account of the changing colonial perception regarding the African continent in this period. In his *Impressions of South Africa* (1897), he writes:

> It is apt to be forgotten that the Cape was not occupied with a view to the establishment of a European colony, in our present sense of the word. The Dutch took it that they might plant a cabbage-garden; the English took it that they might have a naval station and half-way house to India. Not till our own time did people begin to think of it as capable of supporting a great civilized community and furnishing a new market for British goods; not till 1869 was it known as a region whence great wealth might be drawn. . . . The tide of English opinion began to turn about 1870, and since then it has run with increasing force in the direction of what is called imperialism. The strides of advance made in 1884–85 and 1890 have been as bold and large as those of earlier days were timid and halting . . . until the advent on the scene of other European powers, whom it was thought prudent to keep at a distance from her own settled territories, impelled her to join that general scramble for Africa which has been so strange a feature of the last two decades.[28]

With the rise of new challenges to British economic, political, and military hegemony, a fierce rivalry ensued among the major capitalist powers to gain control of these new markets for industrial goods, new opportunities for the export of accumulated capital in the form of foreign investment, and new sources of raw materials and labor. Nevertheless, the English economist John Hobson believed that imperialism was a bad policy for Britain. In 1898 he laid out from the standpoint of a fictional interlocutor what he considered to be the hegemonic but sorry defense of the indefensible expansion of British imperialism:

> However costly, however perilous, this process of imperial expansion may be, it is necessary to the continued existence and progress of our nation; if we abandoned it we must be content to leave the development of the world to other nations, who will everywhere cut into our trade, and even impair our means of securing the food and raw

> materials we require to support our population. Imperialism is thus seen to be, not a choice, but a necessity.[29]

Hobson argued that all of these justifications for imperialism were wrong. Moreover, imperialism was morally and socially unjustifiable, and not a panacea for domestic economic troubles resulting from the lopsided nature of the British economy suffering from the concentration of wealth at the top.

Despite all the arguments and protests against colonialism, capitalist states were locked into advancing the economic interests of their most powerful industries and investors against competition from other Great Powers and defending white "prestige" (see DuBois quote above) and territorial control.

Globalizing the Ecological Rift of Capitalism

Further motivating the search for new sources of agricultural land and inputs (such as fertilizer) was the degradation of soil in Europe, England, and the eastern United States, as a result of the capitalist transformation of agriculture before the 1870s. By the mid-nineteenth century, as noted by environmental sociologists John Bellamy Foster, Brett Clark, and Richard York, European scientists were sounding the alarm with respect to "the loss of soil nutrients—such as nitrogen, phosphorus, and potassium—through the transfer of food and fiber to the cities."[30] Soil erosion was also a major problem in this period, which furthered the loss of nutrients.

In place of the soil nutrient cycling associated with traditional farming, the commodification of agriculture meant that, increasingly, "essential nutrients were shipped hundreds, even thousands, of miles and ended up as waste polluting cities."[31] Leading soil scientists in the nineteenth-century, such as Justus von Liebig, viewed this disruption of the soil nutrient cycle as a system of robbery. The reduction of complex ecosystems, as well as more ecologically integrated farms, to monocropping for sale on the market resulted in the disconnection and disruption of natural processes. Foster writes that "with the development of the capitalist division of nature, the elements of nature are reduced to one common denominator (or bottom line): exchange value. In this respect it does not matter whether one's product is coffee, furs, petroleum, or parrot feathers, as long as there is a market."[32] Karl Marx saw this transformation of the land and agriculture as an original source of the modern rift in the metabolism between human society and the rest of nature, or what environmental sociologists and others now refer to as the ecological rift of capitalism.

The ecological rift became global as the colonial powers sought to compensate for the environmental overdraft of the metropole, and feed the growing urban market, by combing the earth for the necessary nutrients to replenish degraded and depleted soils and bring under production new agricultural land. In one of the first "resource wars" of capitalism, the violent and ecologically destructive guano trade was one result of this push, as were the undertaking of phosphate mining in the United States, the expansion of tropical plantation agriculture, and the development of export-oriented agriculture in the expanding white settler colonies and states. As a result, "the transfer of nutrients was tied to the accumulation process and increasingly took place on national and international levels."[33] Marx observes that globalized capitalist agriculture benefits the "main industrial countries, and it converts one part of the globe into a chiefly agricultural field of production for supplying the other part, which remains a pre-eminently industrial field."[34]

White Territorial Control and the Development of Global Agriculture

The transformation of one part of the globe into a "chiefly agricultural field of production" was predicated on the worldwide trend toward "renewed seizures of indigenous peoples' lands."[35] In the post-abolition era this meant that governments and private capital encouraged the expansion of white settlement and the development of new forms of coercive labor—such as sharecropping in the United States—still divided along racial lines, throughout the colonial world.

These were the conditions of capitalist expansion and reorganization of global agriculture and labor, constituting what environmental historian Edward Melillo refers to as the "first green revolution" and the industrial division of nature and labor on a planetary scale.[36] Through these processes the first global food regime came into existence.[37] Sociologist Phillip McMichael describes the first global food regime, which sociologists date from 1870–1930, as combining

> tropical imports to Europe with basic grains and livestock imports from settler colonies, provisioning emerging European industrial classes, and underwriting the British "workshop of the world." Complementing mono-cultural agricultures imposed in colonies of occupation (compromising their food systems and ecological resources), nineteenth-century Britain outsourced its staple food production to colonies of settlement (over-exploiting virgin soil frontiers in the New World). Here, the establishment of national agricultural sectors within the emerging settler states (notably USA, Canada, and Australia), *modeled* twentieth-century "development" as an articulated dynamic between national agricultural and industrial sectors.[38]

From this context the global problem of soil erosion emerged by the turn of the century, associated with the vigorous seizure of native lands and displacement of peoples, the imposition of racist land tenure policies, the spread of cash crops, and continuation of plantation-style agriculture.[39]

The introduction of colonial agriculture required the destruction of regional ways of life and, as Beckert notes, "rested ideologically on the naturalizing of certain historically specific ways of organizing production, and was thus enabled by economic, social, cultural, and even racial hierarchies it had helped produce."[40] This means the colonists treated local and indigenous knowledge and ways of provisioning, including cultivating crops, as backward or irrational, even in places where they survived or profited only by adopting local methods.[41] Colonial occupiers often appropriated local knowledge to serve their ends even as they demeaned it to justify the expropriation of its bearers.

Polish-German social scientist and activist Rosa Luxemburg described how capitalism needed to completely overturn all preexisting social relations in order to spread, in contrast to previous societal changes:

> The European conquerors are the first who are not merely after subjugation and economic exploitation, but the means of production itself, by ripping the land from underneath the native population. In this way, capitalism deprives the primitive social order of its foundation. What emerges is something worse than all oppression and exploitation, total anarchy and a specifically European phenomenon, the uncertainty of social existence.[42]

Previous conquerors had robbed, stolen, and plundered; had distorted and assimilated the cultures that they absorbed into their empires. However, none had aimed for the complete eradication of previous social relations and implantation of something completely alien: a commoditized economy and society. Luxemburg's evocative and disturbing phrase "the uncertainty of social existence" still resonates today.

Glorifying these horrid developments throughout the era of the new imperialism, England, the United States, and Europe hosted international exhibitions that extolled white supremacy and capitalism as the unified goal and pinnacle of historical social and economic development. The exhibitions were "designed to celebrate progress, technology, and colonialism."[43] For these purposes they kidnapped, confined, and put on display indigenous peoples from U.S., British, and European colonies and occupied territories around the globe. To give one example among many, explorer, anthropologist, and missionary Samuel Phillips was hired to deliver African, Inuit, Native American, and Filipino people to the St. Louis World's Fair in 1904 (where Max Weber gave a lecture before visiting Indian Territory) for an anthropology exhibit, wherein indigenous people from North America and colonies around the world were displayed in supposed replicas of traditional villages.[44] Historian Nancy Egan estimates that "25,000 indigenous people were brought to fairs around the world between 1880 and 1930," in what were essentially "human zoos."[45] Such exhibitions of indigenous peoples went on as late as 1958.[46]

Literally setting up a human zoo and illustrating the deep connections between colonialism, racism, and environmentalism in this period, William Temple Hornaday—a major figure in the U.S. conservation movement, friend of Teddy Roosevelt, and first director of the Bronx Zoo—infamously put Congolese man Ota Benga on display in the zoo's monkey house in 1906. Benga had previously appeared in St. Louis. Reacting to the outcry from the Colored Baptist Ministers' Conference, among others, Hornaday was unrepentant. In a letter to Madison Grant, secretary of the New York Zoological Society (a Columbia-educated eugenicist, conservationist, and author of the racist tract *The Passing of the Great Race*, one of Hitler's favorite books), Hornaday said it was "imperative that the society should not even seem to be dictated to" by black ministers.[47]

While scholars rightly emphasize the "ruling capitalist ethos," this cannot be disentangled from the white supremacist logic driving and legitimizing the domination of indigenous peoples, as well as the expropriation and exploitation of their land. The combined result was an unprecedented expansion of the global economy, white territorial control, social dislocation, and ecological degradation. Putting events on the U.S. southern plains in this context helps explain both the timing of the Dust Bowl and the rapidity of soil erosion on a global scale by the end of the nineteenth and beginning of the twentieth centuries.

Dunbar-Ortiz notes that "US policies and actions related to Indigenous peoples, though often termed 'racist' or 'discriminatory,' are rarely depicted as what they are: classic cases of imperialism and a particular form of colonialism—settler colonialism."[48] Because depictions of the Dust Bowl focus on the experience of white settlers, typically without referring to them as such, the whole story is taken out of the context of the broader history of U.S. and Anglo-European colonial expansion. What follows is a summary of the policies and practices on the U.S. plains that gave rise to the Dust Bowl and link that region to global developments.

The New Imperialism on the Southern Plains: Prologue to the Dust Bowl

By the 1860s northern industrialists, among others, were agitating increasingly for national agricultural development and access to other resources by expanding the territory of the United States. This, they argued, required that the state extend infrastructure, especially the railroad and irrigation, remove native peoples, privatize the land, and introduce a working settler class to the West.[49] While supporters of slavery saw westward expansion as an opportunity to expand the institution, many northern manufacturers were confident that the nation would prosper by expanding both its territory and the regime of wage labor into the western countryside, a regime that could effectively mobilize and discipline large numbers of workers, as they had shown in their factories.[50] President Abraham Lincoln obliged.

Lincoln, in his presidential campaign, promised free acreage in the West, including the plains region, to settlers. This moment marked an escalation of U.S. government imperialist policies and practices. Following his victory in the election of 1860, President Lincoln signed the Homestead Act in 1862, which required the military removal of the peoples living in the plains and elsewhere in order to allot land to settlers. Even before his election, the U.S. Army had six of its seven departments "stationed west of the Mississippi, a colonial army fighting the Indigenous occupants of the land."[51]

When the Civil War broke out, the new president recalled federal troops to fight in the East. In their stead volunteers assembled from the western states and territories carried on "military campaigns against Indigenous nations," constituting "foreign wars fought during the US Civil War, but the end of the Civil War did not end them."[52] After the Civil War, "the US Army hardly missed a beat before the war 'to win the West' began in full force. As a far more advanced killing machine and with seasoned troops, the Army began the slaughter of people, buffalo, and the land itself."[53]

The connection between destroying ecosystems and societies was encapsulated by the U.S. military's indirect and direct actions to annihilate the buffalo in order to deprive Native Americans of both sustenance and culture. In charge of the Department of Missouri from 1869 to 1870, Lt. Gen. John M. Schofield wrote succinctly of his aims: "I wanted no other occupation in life than to ward off the savage and kill off his food until there should no longer be an Indian frontier in our beautiful country."[54] The settler-occupiers carried on, as Dunbar-Ortiz writes, "destroying the natural tall grasses of the Plains and planting short grasses for cattle, eventually leading to the loss of topsoil four decades later."[55]

In 1871 the U.S. government passed legislation further attacking tribal sovereignty, stating that "hereafter no Indian nation or tribe within the territory of the United States shall be acknowledged or recognized as an independent nation, tribe, or power with whom the United States may contract by treaty," although this did not legally invalidate U.S. legal obligations under previous treaties.[56] During this same period William Tecumseh Sherman, who replaced Ulysses S. Grant as the commanding general of the U.S. Army, "sent an army commission to England to study English colonial campaigns worldwide, looking to employ successful English tactics for the US wars against the Indigenous peoples."[57] By the 1890s, although military attacks still took place, as did armed acts of resistance, "most of the surviving Indigenous refugees were confined to reservations, their children transported to distant boarding schools."[58] However, political and economic elites supporting westward expansion in what would become the Dust Bowl region and beyond did not consider these actions against the indigenous nations adequate.

Massachusetts senator Henry Dawes, who represented some of the most powerful manufacturers in the Northeast and who had his own financial interests at stake, argued that the reservation system and all holdings of communal land were too socialist. He insisted, as colonial administrators around the world did during this time, using various rationales, that privatization and allotment of land to individual tribal members were necessary—leaving the remainder for U.S. citizens to settle, and paving the way for a massive land grab by the railroads and private capital more broadly. Dawes reported on his trip to Indian Territory and the Cherokee Nation to the Board of Indian Commissioners:

> The head chief told us that there was not a family in the whole nation that had not a home of its own. There is not a pauper in that nation, and the nation does not owe a dollar. It built its own capitol, in which we had this examination, and built its schools and hospitals. Yet the

> defect of the system was apparent. They have got as far as they can go, because they hold their land in common. It is [Socialist writer] Henry George's system, and under that there is no enterprise to make your home any better than that of your neighbors. There is no selfishness, which is at the bottom of civilization. Till these people will consent to give up their lands, and divide them among their citizens so that each can own the land he cultivates, they will not make much progress.[59]

Property ownership, for Dawes, was necessary to instill "selfishness, which is at the bottom of civilization." And, importantly for Dawes's economic and political position, it satisfied the interests of private capital, especially the railroads, manufacturers seeking cheap raw materials, extractive industries, bankers, and land speculators.

The Five Civilized Tribes removed from the South by Andrew Jackson's army via the Trail of Tears in the 1830s initially were exempt from the Dawes Severalty [Allotment] Act (1887), along with a few other indigenous nations and areas, because their territories were still sovereign by law.[60] In the end, however, the federal government overcame a fierce resistance to allotment and violently imposed a division of much of the remaining tribal lands held in common to form what eventually became the contiguous United States.[61] In Oklahoma, the "unassigned lands" left after allotment were opened for settlement, setting the stage for developments that helped to bring about the Dust Bowl within a very short time. Three-fourths of the "Indigenous land base that still existed after decades of army attacks and wanton land grabs" was taken and redistributed to non-Native peoples in this period.[62] At the same time, part of the vast capital accumulated under the "war capitalism" of Britain, the United States, and Europe "poured into the West" as investment in infrastructure such as railroads, new extractive industries such as logging, and agricultural expansion.[63]

Just after the Dawes Act was passed, South Africa passed the Glen Grey Act under the administration of Cecil Rhodes to accomplish the same task with its own local flavor.[64] New Zealand took a similar approach, as did other settler colonies. The installment of new private property regimes favoring the colonial powers thus required the destruction of communities and local land rights. British, Japanese, and European overlords often sought to coerce rural cultivators to labor on the very lands just expropriated from them, land that had previously provided their industry, subsistence, and other necessities of social reproduction. The colonial powers promoted a new wave of settlement and colonial occupation to help manage this coercion.

On the U.S. southern plains the settlers, reliant upon government support—including military backing, land subsidies, agricultural assistance, and the development of infrastructure, including water supplies—became the greedy bankers, landowners, and poor whites later portrayed in scholarly and popular literature about the Dust Bowl.

Many of the settlers in the plains region were themselves capital's dispossessed and dislocated from Europe, the former slave states in the South, or the Northeast.[65] However, many settlers were also aware that they were part of a broader colonial project, glorified in racial terms at the time by politicians, academics, school textbooks, and popular and "high" culture. When the United States invaded Cuba in 1898, "a third of Teddy Roosevelt's Rough Riders . . . were recruited from Oklahoma Territory."[66]

White supremacy and racial division under capitalism have long been crucial tools of ruling-class elites for "neutralizing the class antagonisms of the landless against the landed."[67] As civil rights lawyer and law professor Michelle Alexander argues in *The New Jim Crow* (2010), seizing native land for settlers served, among other purposes, as a political safety-release valve for Europe, the United States, and England, all teeming with new masses of the economically dispossessed.[68] Abolitionist and author Frederick Douglass explained in 1882, "The hostility between the whites and blacks of the South is easily explained. It has its root and sap in the relation of slavery, and was incited on both sides by the cunning of the slave masters. Those masters secured their ascendency over both the poor whites and the blacks by putting enmity between them. They divided both to conquer each."[69]

Arriving on the U.S. southern plains, settlers became caught up in relations of unequal exchange with the wealthier industrial and financial centers and, as the first systematic federal report on the Dust Bowl stated, "a system of agriculture which could not be both permanent and prosperous."[70] The plains became integrated into the global economy as a cash crop–producing region, a condition made possible and encouraged by the U.S. government and private capital.[71] It served at least three objectives for the elites, as professor of sociology and geography Harriet Friedmann notes: "Wheat was the substance that gave railways income from freight, expanding states a way to hold territory against the dispossessed, and diasporic Europeans a way to make an income."[72]

Cash-crop agriculture is very different in its social and ecological consequences from subsistence agriculture, or even farming by locals to supply local markets. It is volatile, subject to global market fluctuations. And there is an insatiable quality to it, as long as there is money to make or, because of the role of finance in agriculture and taxes, debts to pay. As a consequence, fields are planted when they should rest, herds are expanded when they should be reduced, and so on, leading to the rapid degradation of the land. This happened on the plains despite many advance warnings that the region couldn't handle this kind of agricultural development and that the problem of soil erosion was becoming intractable.

The same pressures and outcomes were apparent around the world due to the global commodification of nature and creation of a world market in agricultural commodities, at a then-unprecedented rate. Whether the region was tropical or arid, every place capital put boots on the ground was subject to social and ecological dislocation and violence. The global problem of soil erosion was one result.

The Necessity of Deeper Conceptions of Environmental History, Justice, and Solidarity

In *Environment and History: The Taming of Nature in the USA and South Africa*, historians William Beinart and Peter Coates write:

> Much American frontier history has suffered from an exaggerated sense of exceptionalism, yet beneath the euphemistic veneer of

> "settlement," the American frontier struggle against indigenous people and natural world was essentially no different from the white imperialist in southern Africa. The European conquests of our regions were but two aspects of the global expansion of capitalism whose tentacles fingered the globe's farthest recesses in the wake of Columbus and de Gama.[73]

The Dust Bowl, and the way it is almost universally depicted in mainstream environmental discourse, including the academic literature, against the backdrop of frontier history, illustrates the persistence of American exceptionalism. Moreover, memories of westward expansion, including the Dust Bowl, like memories of the Boers' trek in South Africa, are "whitened" so that the links between the ongoing social legacies of colonialism and ecological degradation are mostly obscured.[74]

All of this is related to problems in U.S. environmentalism and the academic environmental literature with the conceptualization of environmental crises and environmental justice. Environmental injustice often is viewed as the unequal distribution of outcomes of environmental harm. Colonized peoples are homogenized and described as one group of "stakeholders" in environmental conflicts.[75] Mainstream environmental organizations, those on the privileged side of the segregated environmental movement globally and more linked to power, are encouraged to diversify their staff and memberships and pay attention to issues of "justice."[76] However, the deeper aspects of social domination required to maintain the economic, social, and environmental status quo frequently are denied, minimized, or simply ignored.

Wider recognition of what Evelyn Nakano Glenn refers to as the "ongoing structure" of settler colonialism and imperialism would be a great advance in the mainstream environmental movement, the environmental social sciences, and also in Dust Bowl and frontier historiography.[77] It would keep alive the recognition of the original and ongoing injustices imposed, as well as their continuing effects.

Addressing these issues among environmentalists (both activists and academics) requires moving beyond superficial approaches to historical changes associated with imperialism and capitalist development.

Superficial treatments of this history too often allow activists and scholars "to safely put aside present responsibility for continued harm done by that past and questions of reparations, restitution, and reordering society" when discussing current, interrelated environmental and social problems and environmental justice.[78]

Shallow approaches to addressing racism, white supremacy, oppression of indigenous peoples, and other forms of social domination preclude the possibility of building a deeper solidarity across historical social divisions. This is critical as the future of environmentalism—whether it can play a part in creating a genuinely green and just world—will hinge on whether anti-imperialist struggles for such solidarity are continuously fought and won, and whether we can move past ahistorical conceptions of ecological disaster that conceal the reality: massive ecological change is impossible without massive social change.

The following chapter drives home this point by making absolutely clear that ecological crises are not resolved by increased scientific understanding, commonly held knowledge, sophisticated technological development, advance warnings, or a slew of proconservation elites attempting to tackle the problems. Rather, the historical record shows that there are mechanisms built into the capitalist system that prevent the incorporation of society's knowledge into efforts that might truly address the pace and scale of ecological crises. These mechanisms clearly are still at work today. Without addressing the social drivers of crises directly—by taking on the system that produces crises and building solidarities that challenge permanently the social status quo—all the scientific knowledge and technological development in the world couldn't prevent the global crisis of soil erosion that developed by the 1930s, any more than it has prevented its acceleration and expansion in subsequent decades. Our solutions to soil erosion and ecological crises in general must thus lie elsewhere.

Chapter Four shows how extensive our social knowledge of soil erosion has been, and the devastating limitations of efforts to address it within the parameters of the social and economic status quo.

four

THE WHITE MAN'S BURDEN, SOIL EROSION, AND THE ORIGINS OF GREEN CAPITALISM

> Where land-utilization practices are firmly established and have become the basis of the country's economy, the adoption of a new land-utilization programme conforming to the limits imposed by the natural environment, may well involve a social and political revolution. Therein lies the supreme difficulty of applying effective erosion control. We now know fairly precisely what agricultural, pastoral, forest and engineering principles must be adopted to stop the earth from rotting away beneath our feet, but we cannot, or dare not, apply them forthwith on a scale commensurate with the gravity of the situation.
>
> —Jacks and Whyte, *The Rape of the Earth*, 1939

The colossal contradiction between the great possibilities of science and the grim reality of the political economy has plagued capitalism since its inception. This quotation from British soil scientists Graham Vernon Jacks and Robert Orr Whyte captures the irrationality of a society with an increasingly sophisticated scientific understanding of ecological problems and, relative to the scale of their development, a decreasing ability to solve those problems in spite of the efforts of individuals, communities, governments, and businesses.[1] Imperialism, white supremacy, and racism are central to this contradiction. They lie at the heart of understanding the historical impotence of environmental politics that take the current political economic order for granted or defend it outright in the face of large-scale ecological crises.

Rather than advocating decolonization, the redress of injustice, and a radically democratic, egalitarian alternative, such politics assume the possibility, desirability, and in some cases inevitability of a more ecologically friendly, sustainable, or green capitalism. The term *green capitalism* refers here to the broad swathe of environmental politics that take the political economic system of capitalism and its dominant institutions for granted and posit that the negative ecological impacts of exploitative economic activities can be addressed adequately by better state policies and regulation enforcement, adjustments to market and industry operations, improvements in science and the use of technology, increased knowledge and education, the work of environmental NGOs, and/or the voluntary actions of businesses and individuals. This is in spite of the fact that all historical evidence of capitalist development points in the opposite direction. The growing problem of soil erosion is an important case in point, which makes the dynamics of the system that prevent substantive change clear and concrete.

This chapter presents evidence that knowledge of both the dangers presented by soil erosion, and the means to successfully address it, exist deep in the memory and experience of agricultural societies and were understood by the white settlers who colonized North America. Yet, even as knowledge of the problem and efforts to contain it in the United States and around the world grew, so did the erosion crisis. It is my contention that this socio-ecological contradiction is the inevitable outcome of an expansionary society where the people in power promote, enshrine in law, and treat as sacrosanct certain ideological assumptions in order to justify their practices, social position, and the economic order over which they preside, including: white ethno-racial supremacy; the right of individuals to claim parcels of the earth as private property and to do what they want with them; and, above all else, the right to make a profit. These are central ideological tenets of the dominant capitalist societies that serve to naturalize the subordination of social and ecological priorities to those of capital accumulation by those at the top. They undergird the culture of conquest, help to legitimize land degradation, and facilitate the denial of responsibility for ecological and social harms by those making decisions about land use—from policymakers and investors to individual farmers and property owners. In 1908 President Theodore Roosevelt summarized one manifestation of this ideological triumvirate in a succinct description of the white settler attitude toward the land: "When he exhausted the soil of his farm, he felt that his son could go West and take up another."[2]

As the erosion crisis developed in colonial societies, addressing its root causes was out of the question for those in charge because doing so, as Jacks and Whyte observed in the 1930s, "may well require a social and political revolution." These authors provide insight into a clear instance of what we now call "ecological denial."[3] "Literal denial," following sociologist Stanley Cohen's terminology, refers to the outright denial of a crisis in spite of the available information. "Interpretive denial" does not deny the facts, but gives them a different meaning, creating "an opaque moat between rhetoric and reality" that misassigns responsibility, downplays harms, and denies accountability.[4] The Jacks and Whyte quote reflects a third form, known as "implicatory denial."[5] This is denial of the "psychological, political, or moral implications that conventionally follow" recognition of large-scale crises or atrocity.[6] Implicatory denial, in Cohen's terms, involves recognizing the facts of disaster and atrocity, but rejecting the responsibility and necessity of commensurate social action.[7]

Colonial officials and colonists could not consider the radical social change needed to address the root cause of extreme socio-ecological crises because such change would threaten the racialized colonial social order. Jacks and Whyte recognized this denial as the primary obstacle to addressing erosion. However, these colonial scientists themselves fell in line with the dominant ways of thinking. In their *The Rape of the Earth*, they identify colonial expansion as the root cause of the global crisis, but advocate further colonial control to solve the problem—preserving the position of the white settler and colonial regimes, regardless of the costs to the "native." Put another way, they describe a form of what sociologist John Bellamy Foster refers to as "the third stage of denial"—in which the social system is implicated as the cause of the crisis, but then, in a twist of logic, is said also to offer its resolution.[8] This is the denial represented by green capitalist and colonial approaches to ecological problems, which dominated early conservationists' attempts, and dominate contemporary efforts, to address soil erosion.

With respect to preventing and overcoming ecological crises, sociologist Kari Marie Norgaard, in *Living in Denial: Climate Change, Emotions, and Everyday Life*, writes: "we need a mode of social organization that promotes organized responsibility rather than organized irresponsibility and denial."[9] Given that the early twentieth-century scientists and policymakers understood the disastrous social and ecological consequences of such crises and how they could be prevented, it is my contention that the Dust Bowl was only possible as a result of the socially "organized irresponsibility and denial" made possible by the deeply entrenched racism and colonial outlook with respect to the earth and its inhabitants that has always accompanied the imperial expansion of capitalism.

A Foreseen Crisis

Students of the history of agriculture know that since the advent of agriculture, soil erosion and exhaustion have accompanied human farming, and efforts to prevent and address them extend far back in time.[10] Long before modern agronomy and soil science developed, generations of farmers passed down their knowledge of the causes and consequences of soil erosion, as well as the methods they devised to avoid it. Ancient Chinese and Vedic texts address soils and erosion, and evidence of agricultural practices to reduce erosion is found throughout Africa, the Middle East, South America, East and Southeast Asia, North America, and beyond, testifying to the existence of extensive historical knowledge.[11] Roman agriculturalists cited the ancient Greeks, like Plato, who detailed the effects of erosion in the Attic peninsula. By the first century B.C.E., Varro, the Roman writer and student of soils, had declared farming a science and described methods of planting to avoid erosion. A hundred years later, Columella elaborated on practices to prevent erosion. Roman law even included provisions making farmers responsible for the consequences to their neighbors of soil erosion on their land.[12] The annals of agricultural societies record an astounding diversity and sophistication of analyses and practices addressing the devastating social and ecological toll of erosion.

English-language writers were aware of the ancient lineage of such knowledge. For example, in an address to England's Royal Society in 1675, writer and diarist John Evelyn described the writings of ancient Roman agriculturalists.[13] In 1862 the U.S. Department of Agriculture's first commissioner, Isaac Newton, submitted a report to President Abraham Lincoln that referred at length to such classical texts and asked whether the United States would learn the lessons of history to avoid Roman-style self-destruction.[14] Long before the 1930s dust storms grabbed headlines and the international imagination, historical records show that no one concerned with agriculture, least of all the literate political, economic, and land-owning elites, could claim ignorance of the causes or consequences of soil erosion.

By the late nineteenth century, modern scientific understandings of erosion and conservation, and the means to disseminate this information internationally, had grown significantly.[15] At the same time, destruction of the soil was accelerating on an ever-widening scale. Greater scientific understanding did not prevent increased soil degradation any more than greater knowledge of climate science in more recent decades has prevented the quickening of climate change. Which is not to say that efforts to address erosion, such as changes to government policies and programs, have not made a difference, but that *despite* these improvements, the problem has expanded and worsened overall. Indeed, in many cases ill-considered efforts to address erosion introduced new and even more destructive ecological and social crises, as I will discuss in Chapter Five.

Dust Bowl scholars often cite the repeated warnings in the decades leading up to the Dust Bowl of the dangers of removing the plains grasses protecting the soil through unsustainable agriculture and ranching—warnings that went unheeded. They frequently refer to documents such as the *Report on the Lands of the Arid Region of the United States*, published in 1878 by John Wesley Powell, who was in charge of the U.S. Geographical and Geological Survey of the Rocky Mountain Region.[16] Powell's report is still considered "a pioneering work recognizing the West's unique environmental character, advocating irrigation and conservation efforts in it, and calling for the distribution of Western lands to settlers on a democratic and environmentally realistic basis."[17] However, there also existed an extensive body of literature on soil erosion that ensured policymakers and the reading public, including farmers with access to agricultural periodicals, were well versed in specifics of the problem.

This literature shows, as the Dust-Bowl era writers discussed in Chapter Two noted, that soil erosion was a well-understood problem long before the 1930s and was not limited to arid lands but also, it is important to understand, heavily impacted tropical and temperate regions. Most accounts of the Dust Bowl repeat the official explanation that agriculture suited for humid regions was inappropriately introduced to the plains. But the reality is that cash-crop agriculture leading up to and during this period of rapid colonial expansion and economic growth was not ecologically suitable or sustainable under any conditions.

Colonialism and Soil Erosion

The relationship between the spread of colonial agriculture and soil erosion (from wind and water) was understood centuries before the Dust Bowl occurred, as historian Richard H. Grove documents in his classic work *Green Imperialism.* In early colonial contexts planters attempted to implement soil conservation measures, but they could never keep pace with the increase in land degradation and soil loss. While soil degradation, including erosion, also accompanied the expansion of cash-crop agriculture in Europe and Britain, the rapacious destruction of colonial lands proved unprecedented in its social and ecological violence. By the mid-seventeenth century, Grove asserts, "the hard reality of the destructive impact of metropolitan capitalism on the tropical island at the European periphery served to demonstrate the contradictions between capitalist development and the preservation of the paradisal vision. It was in the context of this contradiction and of the realization of it that colonial conservationism began to develop."[18]

Cultivation always causes soil erosion to some degree, and agriculturalists throughout history and across continents have developed a variety of means to address it. This helps explain why, as environmental historians J. R. McNeill and Verena Winiwarter have established, in all of human history there have been only three waves of significant growth in soil erosion. We are now living through the third great wave of erosion, which since 1945 has brought "human-induced soil erosion and the destruction of soil ecosystems to unprecedented levels."[19] The first wave was associated with the "expansion of early river-basin civilizations, mainly in the second millennium B.C.E."[20] For another three thousand years "farmers in Eurasia, Africa, and the Americas gradually converted a modest proportion of the world's forests into farmland or pasture and thereby increased rates of soil erosion, but the fertile soils of the world's grasslands were little affected."[21]

That changed in the era of capitalist expansion via colonialism. Beginning in the sixteenth century and accelerating sharply in the nineteenth, the second great wave of soil erosion spread across the land as "stronger and sharper plowshares helped break the sod of the Eurasian steppe, the North American prairies, and the South American pampas. The exodus of Europeans to the Americas, Australia, New Zealand, Siberia, South Africa, Algeria, and elsewhere brought new lands under the plow."[22]

It wasn't simply that new lands came under the plow but that political economic imperatives dictated the form of agriculture. As historian Vimbai C. Kwashirai explains, colonial states "sought to orient farmers towards the production of export crops . . . [and] the perennial cultivation of the same crop on the same field."[23] Depending on the region, growers replaced diverse local crops with cotton, tobacco, sugar, tea, coffee, corn, and wheat, of varieties demanded in industrial centers. Once they were linked to the global market, farmers experienced mounting economic pressures to increase production of export crops in the short term, regardless of whether the crops or the techniques employed to raise them were suited to local conditions.

By the mid-eighteenth century, colonies and frontier regions that had transformed to produce crops and raw materials for export to the growing urban market were experiencing persistent environmental crises, which prompted international environmental concern among policymakers and agricultural experts. The growing problem of soil erosion became central to an emerging "global environmentalism."[24] At the same time, concerned with expanding production and territorial control, colonial authorities facilitated official and informal knowledge-sharing networks among imperial states and capitalists worldwide.[25] Newspapers in metropolitan centers and colonies reported regularly on global events, including the growing crisis of soil erosion predating the 1930s Dust Bowl. By the nineteenth century, conservation and agricultural literature warning of the harms of erosion circulated widely.[26] Government-issued reports and bulletins took stock of the problem and made recommendations.

The following sections draw on literature on soil erosion, conservation, and colonialism from the mid-1700s up to the Dust Bowl period, with an emphasis on the United States and the British Empire and Commonwealth. References from this period illustrate the ways in which writers at the time understood soil erosion—as a problem confronting nations and farmers around the world, linked in particular to imperial economic expansion and other ecological issues, and as part of the larger "white man's burden" of conservation.

Land Murder and Settlement

As noted earlier in this chapter, before Anglo-European colonization of North America, English and European writers expressed concern for soil erosion. Settler colonists carried knowledge of this problem to the "new world." Early on, settler writers recognized an emerging pattern of land abuse, which degraded the land and created Dust Bowl–like conditions of soil erosion, encouraging a continual westward movement to cultivate new lands. The colonies adopted laws to try to check erosion associated with cropping and grazing. In the 1730s, for example, Massachusetts implemented rules to regulate grazing because, during dry periods, the exposure of sandy soils led to wind erosion, threatening coastal regions with sandstorms and drift. Connecticut farmer, minister, and doctor Jared Elliot wrote the first book on American agriculture in the 1740s, in which he noted the persistent westward movement of settlement caused by land degradation.[27] Colonists elsewhere described dramatic sandstorms that prefigured the Dust Bowl. In Maryland and Delaware, one observer wrote in 1807, "it is not uncommon, in great droughts, when high winds arise, to see the sand raised from the fields . . . thirty or forty feet high, and carried a considerable distance. If corn fields be situated near the dwellings of planters, the drifting sand, in dry weather, and in high winds, enters every door and crevice, in like manner as drifting snow."[28]

Post-independence, the United States' first leaders and elites saw the related problems, for them, of how to capture indigenous land and address land-use issues as principal concerns. Patrick Henry reportedly said that after fighting the Revolution, the greatest sign of patriotism was preventing gullies, which are an ugly outcome of severe water erosion.[29] George Washington warned against monocropping and laid great stress on erosion control.[30] Thomas Jefferson expressed his view that nothing was more beautiful than land properly contoured.[31] However, according to famed U.S. soil scientist Hugh Hammond Bennett, Jefferson also argued that "it was less expensive . . . to clear a new piece of ground than to fertilize an old field."[32] Thus, early in the republic's history, economic priorities trumped the prevention of environmental damage, though not for want of knowledge of the consequences.

As the decades went on, writers decried the crimes against nature and humanity at the heart of the U.S. agricultural economy. The abuse, degradation, and exploitation of people and the land were seen as going hand in hand. In 1856 an article on "southern land-murder" for the *Friends' Review* asked of slave-owning farmers, "What possible apology can these vandals offer to posterity for the destruction?"[33] Writers in the United States compared the condition of the land in North America with other eroded places in the world as far away as Palestine.[34] International commentators wrote of North America's wasteful exploitation of the land and compared it to similarly problematic practices in Europe, Britain, their colonies, and elsewhere.[35]

Westward expansion of the erosion problem in North America was made possible by government policy, financing from the imperial urban centers, technological change, and military conquest. In 1862, President Lincoln helped set the stage for the conquest of western lands and eventually the Dust Bowl when he signed four acts: the Homestead Act, the Morrill Land Grant College Act, the act establishing the U.S. Department of Agriculture, and the act granting federal lands and funds for construction of the Union Pacific–Central Pacific railroad to connect the coasts and inland agricultural markets.[36] The purpose of the Department of Agriculture and the land-grant colleges was to increase the productivity of agriculture and the wealth of the nation. As the USDA's first director, Isaac Newton, wrote: "The surplus of agriculture not only allows the farmer to pay his debts and accumulate wealth, but also does the same for the nation. To increase the surplus, therefore, to develop and bring out the vast resources of our soil, and thus create a new additional capital, should be the great object of the Department of Agriculture and of legislation."[37] Citing an unnamed political economist approvingly, Newton quoted the comment that "every acre of our fertile soil . . . is a mine which only awaits the contact of labor to yield its treasures, and every acre is opened to that fruitful contact by the homestead act."[38] The federal government's imperialist agricultural policies in the 1860s gave short-term accumulation of capital another fateful edge over the long-term preservation of the land. The consequences of policymakers advocating and celebrating the "mining of the soil" were well understood even then.

In 1864, American diplomat and philologist George Perkins Marsh published what would become a conservation classic, *Man and Nature*. After witnessing land degradation in his home state of Vermont, as well as in Europe and Northern Africa, Marsh wrote that clearing land for cultivation left the soil "bared of its covering of leaves, broken and loosened by the plough, deprived of the fibrous rootlets which held it together, dried and pulverized by sun and wind, and at last exhausted by new combinations."[39] As a result, "the face of the earth is no longer a sponge, but a dust heap" subject to erosion.[40] Within the first decade of its publication, *Man and Nature* was already "a classic of international repute."[41] In the United States, "Marsh's profoundly important book on the devastation that humanity had already inflicted on the planet had deeply impressed itself upon the American imagination."[42] But whatever impact Marsh may have had on readers, his warnings fell on the deaf ears of landowners and policymakers. The next few decades would prove that humans mired in the operational logic of capital were capable of environmental destruction on a global scale.

As discussed in previous chapters, the decade following the Civil War initiated an accelerated and brutal period of capitalist expansion known as the new imperialism. The Europeans, British, Americans, and Japanese engaged in a global land grab, seeking new sources of raw materials, markets, labor, and agricultural land. The United States, while pushing westward and conducting ongoing wars against North American indigenous nations, also expanded its imperial presence beyond the continent. Conservation, white supremacy, and colonialism fit hand in glove in this era.

Blood and Soil

Often celebrated for his role in the conservation movement, Theodore Roosevelt published his multiple-volume opus *The Winning of the West* in 1889. In it he writes:

> The most ultimately righteous of all wars is a war with savages, though it is apt to be also the most terrible and inhuman. The rude, fierce settler who drove the savage from the land lays all civilized mankind under a debt to him. American and Indian, Boers and Zulu, Cossack and Tartar, New Zealander and Maori—in each case the victor, horrible though many of his deeds are, has laid deep foundations for the future greatness of a mighty people . . . . it is of incalculable importance that America, Australia, and Siberia should pass out of the hands of their red, black, and yellow aboriginal owners, and become the heritage of the dominant world races.[43]

At the time, President William McKinley, who began the conservation work Roosevelt continued and made famous, promoted conservation at home and colonial expansion and exploitation abroad in the name of humanitarianism, "an unselfish duty conscientiously accepted."[44]

By the late 1800s many elites saw caring for nature as another white man's burden; the civilized had a duty to the land as part of their broader noblesse oblige.[45] Attention to soil erosion increased along with the colonial conquest of portions of every continent where cotton, tobacco, sugarcane, or food crops could grow. Concern for erosion in the United States accelerated as people realized that in North America there would be no more "virgin soils" (a term evoking colonial conceptions of *terra nullius* that ignored indigenous land use before white settlement and helped justify land theft and genocide). In the plains region recently open to white settlement, according to Hugh Bennett, "wind erosion affected many localities when soil conditions favored blowing shortly after cultivation was introduced. Drifting of the soil was reported in parts of Oklahoma four years after the sod was broken and in North Dakota six years after settlement (1888). . . . Wind erosion became such a menace that in some areas, whole communities were mobilized to fight it. . . . The life of the community was threatened."[46]

In 1894 the U.S. Department of Agriculture published a farmer's bulletin titled *Washed Soils: How to Prevent and Reclaim Them.*[47] In 1896, Harvard geologist Nathaniel Southgate Shaler wrote in *National Geographic:*

> The old view that the earth was firm set and that on it we could build "for aye" has gone the way of many ancient opinions. In every region which geologists have investigated they have had occasion to note many and profound alterations in the form of the surface which have taken place since man has occupied the earth. They have come to recognize the fact that man himself is, through his arts, particularly those of agriculture, one of the great agents of change, and that through these interferences with the course of nature the operation of many forces has been greatly increased in energy.[48]

Shaler's article "The Economic Aspects of Soil Erosion" highlights the risks of erosion associated with tilled land left bare. "A brief comparison of the effect of a heavy rainfall on a newly tilled surface bare of vegetation and on a like area which is protected by the natural covering of living and dead plants," Shaler writes, "will show the peculiar influence of the vegetable shield on the history of soils."[49] This covering acts as a "natural roof," the maintenance of which prevents erosion in the woods and grasslands.[50] Even on meadows, where rainfall "may, indeed, pass to the permanent streams quite as rapidly as from the plowed ground . . . it is kept from contact with the soil by the closely set and entangled stems through which it cannot break, even when gathered into considerable streams."[51] During this same period, soil conservation articles appeared in newspapers across the United States. For example, on May 10, 1898, the *Topeka Weekly Capital* in Kansas published Fry's Farm Letter on "how to prevent washing away of soil."[52]

The study of soils and dissemination of information was thus well established by the late nineteenth century. Focused on the future Dust Bowl region itself, in 1908 the U.S. Department of Agriculture published a bulletin titled "Blowing Soils." Hugh Bennett later cites it to show that the government was well aware at the time that "the problem of wind erosion became serious in western Kansas; northwestern Texas; western Oklahoma; eastern Colorado; and parts of the Dakotas, Nebraska and other Western States."[53] In other words, contrary to scholarly accounts and popular perception, decades before disaster struck and any serious action was taken, officials had identified the problem that would become the "Dust Bowl."

By the early twentieth century, if any U.S. policymaker, politician, or reader of the country's major newspapers managed to remain oblivious to the risks of soil erosion, the Conference of Governors on the Conservation of Natural Resources in 1908, and the widely disseminated reports of it, made ongoing ignorance impossible. In May of that year, the extent of the degradation of nature engaged the attention of conservationists around the world, including President Theodore Roosevelt, who hosted this national conference focused on the "conservation of natural resources." In his opening address, one of the key topics was soil erosion. "We began with soils of unexampled fertility," Roosevelt told his audience, "and we have so impoverished them by injudicious use and by failing to check erosion that their crop-producing power is diminishing instead of increasing."[54]

The president asked his listeners to consider seriously "what will happen when our forests are gone, when the coal, the iron, the oil and the gas are exhausted, when the soils shall have been still further impoverished and washing into the streams, polluting the rivers, denuding the fields, and obstructing navigation."[55] He noted that the attitude of the American settler was always that "when he exhausted the soil of his farm, he felt that his son could go West and take up another. . . . When the soil-wash from the farmer's field choked the neighboring river, the only thought was to use the railway rather than the boats to move produce and supplies. That was so up to the generation that preceded ours."[56]

Many speakers proceeded to address the problem of soil erosion associated with cultivation, from the governor of Texas to railroad industrialist James J. Hill. In the end, as the governors summarized their common commitments in a final declaration, they agreed, among other items, "that the land should so be used that erosion and soil-wash shall cease."[57]

Despite pointing the finger at settlers for their cavalier attitude toward land degradation, the president was a great defender and champion of these pioneers, and colonial spirits were high during the conference. Hawaii's colonial governor, Walter F. Frear, reminded attendees that "obviously one of the most effective methods of conserving the natural resources of the United States is by taking advantage . . . of the vast natural resources of other countries and especially those of China, which are perhaps, next to those of the United States, the richest in the world and as yet practically untouched."[58]

This conference raised the profile of conservation efforts and linked them to broader U.S. strategic interests and plans for the new century. An article in the journal *Science* declared it a "notable occasion." It was "the consensus of opinion that the condition and probable duration of our leading resources were summarized more completely than ever before."[59] The conference, wrote the author, marked a new era of cooperation: "So far as the relations among the states and between these and the national government, are concerned, the general opinion expressed in public addresses and personal conversation was that the conference marked a new era, comparable only with that opened by the Philadelphia Conference in 1787, at which the constitution was framed."[60] The governors' joint declaration, unanimously adopted by all present, was "regarded as the chief tangible result of the conference."[61] Major newspapers covered the conference. The *Philadelphia Inquirer* reported: "Startling was the warning sounded today at the conference of Governors at the White House, of the danger the nation confronts in soil waste and forest depletion."[62]

The attitude toward conservation illustrated by this high-profile conference might seem remarkable from today's perspective, when a litmus test of U.S. politicians seems to be whether they adequately shun any acknowledgment or expression of concern for environmental issues. But in the early 1900s, conservation was a high priority for elites around the globe. As the decades wore on, awareness of and attention to the problem of soil erosion became a matter of course.

In the region that would soon be ground to dust, the Oklahoma State Board of Agriculture announced in 1908 plans to hold farmers' institutes that included lectures "on soils and erosion."[63] In 1910 the USDA released a bulletin offering advice on "the control of blowing soils." The bulletin contained a prefigurative photograph taken during a twelve-hour dust storm in the Great Plains that resulted in the loss of at least an inch of topsoil.[64] The topic of soil erosion also remained newsworthy in the popular press. In a huge spread on February 26, 1911, the *New York Times* ran an article on politician and forester Gifford Pinchot titled "We Are the Richest, But Most Wasteful People."[65] In it, Pinchot warned that "erosion is the death knell of fertility" and that "we have already lost in this country thousands of millions of dollars in actual value by permitting the unrestricted erosion of our soils . . . and with them the productive power which all the centuries of nature's efforts had put into them." He went on to say,

> The greatest losses have taken place in the Southeast, among the steeper lands of the Piedmont and mountain region, from Maryland to Alabama, but vast losses have occurred elsewhere. The National Conservation Commission estimated that the annual loss to farmers throughout the United States from erosion, a calamity which can be prevented by good management of forests, amounts to about half a billion dollars annually. This is all due to unintelligent forestation and to ancient and unscientific methods of cultivation.[66]

With respect to other parts of the world, Pinchot told the reporter, "there are sections in Asia which have become uninhabitable through similar mismanagement, and are now desert wastes. Once they were fertile and productive. That we should permit similar conditions to begin in this, the newest of the continents, seems quite incredible, but it is quite true."[67]

In 1913, William Temple Hornaday, a friend of Roosevelt's and a leader in the conservation movement, suggested an alternative to unsustainable farming practices. He and Roosevelt had worked together to found one of the early conservation societies in America.[68] As discussed in Chapter Three, Hornaday was and is infamous for holding a kidnapped Congolese man, Ota Benga, in the monkey display house at the Bronx Zoo, where he was director.[69] He viewed conservation work as the next stage, after securing territory through conquest, of tending nature for future (clearly only white) generations.

Hornaday wrote in 1913 that the United States was finally accepting "its share of the white man's burden" at home and in its new colonies.[70] He praised "the brave and hardy men who are making for the British people a grand empire in Africa" for their game-preservation work and wrote that they were probably "greater men than far-distant people realize":

> To them, the white man's burden of game preservation is accepted as all in the day's work. A mere handful of British civil officers, strongly aided by the Society for the Preservation of the Fauna of the British Empire, have carved out and set aside a great chain of game preserves reaching all the way from Swaziland and the Transvaal to Khartoum. Taken either collectively or separately, it represents grand work, characteristic of the greatest colonizers on earth. Those preserves are worthy stones

> in the foundation of what one day will be a great British empire in Africa. The names of the men who proposed them and wrought them out should, in some way, be imperishably connected with them as their founders, as the least reward that Posterity can bestow.[71]

It was in this context of concern for wildlife preservation that Hornaday entered into the discussion of U.S. agriculture and the soil. He saw the problems with agriculture as the result of farming unsuitable land in the first place. He considered success in "dry farming" semi-arid lands very unlikely. As an alternative to continuing the practice, he suggested that one third of the United States comprised of marginal lands for agriculture, including the eroded area that would become the Dust Bowl, be used instead as game reserves.

Although I focus here on English-language publications, with an emphasis on the United States, during this era a great deal of literature on soil erosion and conservation was published and circulated in multiple languages throughout the world. By the 1920s, the problem of soil erosion was understood as an international crisis linked to broader ecological changes. While some radical and farsighted thinkers and activists had noted these tendencies decades earlier and posited social alternatives, by the late nineteenth and earlier twentieth centuries, mainstream commentators and bureaucrats regularly acknowledged the destructiveness of imperial expansion.[72]

The sophistication of the science of the era was reflected in the work of writers like Robert Lionel Sherlock, senior geologist of the British Geological Survey, who further developed the line of thinking introduced by George Perkins Marsh and others writing in the nineteenth century. Reflecting the acceleration of crises since Marsh famously wrote that "the art of man" was capable of "Geographical Revolutions," Sherlock, closer to the understanding of our time, wrote *Man as a Geological Agent* in 1922.[73] The author places soil erosion within a broader context of advanced environmental degradation, including climate change, associated with the modern period.

Sherlock marks environmental change using a periodization we are familiar with today and prefigures contemporary debates regarding the Anthropocene. Discussing the transformation of Britain, for example, he recognizes that there was a historical break associated first with "the general enclosure of the land" and second with "the growth of the towns and of industries during the last hundred years, with the necessary accessories of paved roads, railways, canals, reservoirs, etc."[74] While Sherlock believed man had always altered the environment and denuded the earth, "we have found . . . that by far the greater part of Man's work was done during the last century, and it follows that at the present time, in a densely peopled country like England, Man is many times more powerful, as an agent of denudation, than all the atmospheric denuding forces combined."[75] He notes that "from the earliest times a certain amount of excavating must have been done by Man, but with the increase of civilization and population and the growth of industry the quantity has increased by leaps and bounds, so that the amount of denudation before the eighteenth century is very small as compared with that effected since."[76] He goes on to say we should also consider man's role in "accumulation," by which he means something like ecological restoration: "Man is a rock-maker as well as a rock-destroyer. Nevertheless, accumulation is small compared to denudation."[77]

With respect to soil erosion, Sherlock describes the ways in which clearing forests and draining lands for cultivation increase the vulnerability of the soil to erosion, impact rivers, and add to the total "amount of carbon dioxide in the atmosphere as the result of the burning of fuel, and the probable effect on climate of such an increase," which he predicts would likely "be in some degree inimical to the higher animals" and "raise the average temperature of the earth."[78] He draws on contemporary and historical examples from around the world—Russia, China, France, Idria, Dalmatia, Herzegovina, Montenegro, Carniola, Croatia, Italy, Greece, Syria, Persia—to illustrate the effects of soil erosion. Using the example of northwest China, in the Hoang-Ho [*sic*] (Yellow) River Basin, Sherlock writes: "Originally the country was doubtless a plain, under rich vegetation. When the land began to be cultivated the soil was bared, and ravine formation began and has continued four thousand years. Now the Hoang-Ho is the richest in mud of all the great rivers."[79]

Similar effects could be seen in the Rhine, Po, and Oxus river basins, among other places where the rivers must traverse "deforested country and a great spread of cultivated land."[80] "Even in England," he writes, "indications of ravine formation, due to cultivation of the land, have been observed."[81]

Foreshadowing scenes that would generate world headlines in the following decade, Sherlock writes,

> the destruction of forests has also led to the formation of moving sand-dunes. In Russia, during the last thirty or forty years, many moving sands have originated which threaten to destroy the neighboring cultivated lands. During storms in dry seasons, the soil and subsoil is lifted by the wind and deposited against hedges, hollows in the ground, or in fact wherever wind is more feeble. . . . On a small scale the same effect is observable in England.[82]

But erosion was "considerable in a great part of the Russian plain."[83] He notes, citing Russian geographer Alexander Ivanovich Woeikof, that "ravines [from erosion] do not form either in forests or on prairies, vegetation acting as a preventative. Man assists destructive agencies by cultivating the soil, for cultivated plants are not as a rule so deeply rooted as wild ones, and, moreover, there is an absence of mosses, lichens, and dried leaves to hold the rain as in a sponge."[84]

Another significant expression of international concern for, and understanding of, erosion on a different continent is the 1923 South African Drought Investigation Commission Report, which officials disseminated throughout the United States and beyond (my copy included a hand-written note from the South African drought investigation commissioner, Heinrich du Toit, to the dean of Oregon State University's agricultural school). It concludes:

> Your commissioners are convinced by the evidence submitted that, as a result of conditions created by the white civilization in South Africa, the power of the surface of the land, as a whole, to hold up and absorb water has been diminished, that the canals by which the water reaches the sea have been multiplied and enlarged, with the result that the rain falling on the sub-continent to-day has a lower economic value than in days past. Herein lies the secret of our "drought losses."[85]

The report emphasizes that scientific and governmental understanding of soil erosion went back at least a half century, though this knowledge was ignored. The text discusses "sand drifts" in various regions, blames the "natives" and "poor whites," and presents a blend of eugenicist and environmental views, which were regular bedfellows in the early conservation movement.[86]

With a shared global community of soil scientists and government officials working on agricultural issues, as well as the development of the fledgling science of ecology in the early twentieth century, reports from particular countries were widely shared, with the understanding that administrators and landowners everywhere faced similar challenges.[87]

Colonial Environmental Management

It was directly out of this "colonial crucible" that the cadre of American conservation professionals formed, many of whom would become the first responders to the Dust Bowl crisis.[88] Historian Paul S. Sutter writes, "Scholars of American conservation have begun to paint a picture of that movement that is both transnational and trans-imperial, one that challenges exceptionalist invocations of America as 'nature's nation.' "[89] He points out the imperial nature of the federal government's growing concern with the environments of its newly acquired territories, and notes the colonial backgrounds of key figures in the history of U.S. environmentalism:

> One of the most striking lessons of the rise of the American environmental management state is just how much it was influenced by international and imperial examples. The founding figure in American conservation, George Perkins Marsh, was a diplomat and thorough internationalist who learned conservation by observing Old World examples of environmental degradation. Gifford Pinchot, the founder of professional forestry in America, trained in continental forestry methods with European foresters who had cut their teeth in imperial settings. Elwood Meade, a pioneering irrigationist, worked across the Pacific transferring water management expertise between Australia and the western United States. And Hugh Hammond Bennett brought

to his tenure as the head of the Soil Conservation Service substantial experience in Latin America.[90]

Indeed, Bennett, often called the "father of soil conservation" and cited as the architect of the U.S. government response to the Dust Bowl, served as a consultant for colonial administrators and elite planters from Cuba to South Africa.[91] In his coauthored book *The Soils of Cuba*, he wrote that "one can not but express admiration for the native skill frequently shown by some of the early pioneers both in Cuba and the United States in their selection of those areas upon which colonization was first effected."[92] He viewed his work as building on the earlier efforts of white settlers by introducing a more scientific understanding of soils and conservation.

The significance for global environmental politics today of the colonial roots of conservation cannot be overstated. Sociologist and historian of environmentalism Dorceta E. Taylor writes, "From the outset, conservationism and preservationism were divorced from the inequities prevalent in society."[93] The forbears of modern environmentalism "did not challenge social injustices such as slavery, the appropriation of land from indigenous people, the expulsion of Native Americans from their traditional territories, the creation of the reservation system, widespread poverty, and rising inequalities."[94] Rather, some of the major figures in the history of environmentalism were white supremacists and eugenicists, as well as agents and cheerleaders of imperialism. This is reflected in the comments of Theodore Roosevelt and other conservationists cited above, and is well documented in the historical literature on colonial environmentalism and in the writings and work of the figures who shaped what became mainstream environmentalism by the end of the nineteenth and beginning of the twentieth centuries.[95] Taylor explains, "The adherence of early activists to the social dogmas of their time is reflected in the nature of the conservation and preservation organizations they established. . . . The legacy of race and class discrimination and the practice of separating environmental issues from those of social inequality are challenges that the conservation movement has had a difficult time overcoming. Discussions and conflicts about these issues still occur regularly even today."[96]

The hegemonic environmentalism that came about in the decades preceding the Dust Bowl as an outgrowth of colonial developments reflected the concerns of the power elite, and as such retained a commitment to the racialized status quo that continues to have a pernicious effect on today's mainstream environmentalism, strengthening allegiances to green capitalism over alliances with communities upon whose backs capitalism is built.[97] This "white man's burden" version of environmentalism informed the policy response to the growing crisis of erosion and the Dust Bowl, precluding the possibility of change of the kind and on the scale necessary to avoid the disaster, as discussed in Chapter Five.

Thus, in spite of sophisticated knowledge and international networks of information exchange, capitalist development resulted in a seeming paradox: a growing understanding of ecological crises on the one hand, and deepening entrenchment of those crises on the other due to a lack of sufficient social action. The Dust Bowl was one devastating consequence of this contradiction; our problem today with land degradation, freshwater scarcity, and climate change is another.

five

ECOLOGICAL RIFTS AND SHIFTS: THE ACCUMULATION OF CATASTROPHE

> It [the Dust Bowl] was an ironic and tragic situation; and the great drive toward a sounder basic culture in our country began full force, it is strange to recall, only after the most spectacular mass sacrifice to strictly commercial *mores* in the history of mankind.
>
> —Russell Lord, "Progress of Soil Conservation in the United States," 1945

The only universal, transhistorical reality of the human condition, as Karl Marx succinctly puts it, is that "man must *live* from nature, i.e., nature is his *body*, and he must maintain a continuing dialogue with it if he is not to die."[1] Central to this dialogue is the labor process, which is "first of all, a process between man and nature, a process by which man, through his own actions, mediates, regulates and controls the metabolism between himself and nature."[2] Through our labor as humans we transform nature and therefore ourselves. Altogether this represents "the universal condition for the metabolic interaction [*Stoffwechsel*] between man and nature, the everlasting nature-imposed condition of human existence."[3]

Every society develops its own social metabolic order, its own way of interacting with the rest of nature. How it manages this interaction determines the character of the relationship, whether in ecological and social terms it is sustainable, healthy, and just. In nonegalitarian societies, social inequality plays a defining role in determining this relationship. David Naguib Pellow explains:

> At its most basic level, inequality means that if you are "on top" of, or higher on the social ladder than someone else, then you possess or have access to greater resources, wealth, and social privileges. But more importantly—and from the standpoint of ecological politics—

> your elevation above others also means that your *life* is of greater value than others living within that social system. You likely own or control and affect more of the planet and its constituent ecosystems than others, you likely own or control and affect more living beings (and therefore likely produce more death) than others, and you likely control and benefit from the ideational systems that give meaning and legitimacy to such dynamics. Inequality is a means of ordering the human and nonhuman worlds for the relative benefit of some and to the detriment of others.[4]

Inequality in a capitalist society—a class-based socio-economic system with its social metabolic order based on accumulation and the privatized, racialized, and gendered control of the vast majority of the land and productive infrastructure—results in an elite minority having more power to determine how production is organized, under what socio-ecological conditions we labor, and to what ends. The most powerful segment of that elite minority still resides primarily, though not exclusively, in the original colonial centers of the Global North—Europe, Britain, and the United States—and to this day remains overwhelmingly white and male.

Since the earliest days of capitalist development, colonized, dispossessed, dehumanized, and exploited working people have waged heroic struggles to push back against capitalism's tendency to concentrate and privatize its benefits at the top while socializing its costs—war, poverty, ecological harm—and concentrating social immiseration at the bottom. Without these struggles today's world would be much crueler, less just, and in even greater ecological chaos. Yet it remains true that a tiny minority of the global population is "on top" of the social ladder, as Pellow puts it. Their accumulation of wealth and power depends on their exploitation of other people and the planet. This dynamic is the key to understanding why, despite our sophisticated understanding of social and ecological problems, we keep failing to resolve them.

From the perspective of capitalists, so long as it is profitable, the point always is to continue the basic activities of "business as usual," however much individual entrepreneurs adopt the language of disruption, change, and even revolution. Capital must grow or die. Businesses must work to increase profits and market share or risk losing investors and going under. To compete for investment, capitalists are compelled under normal circumstances to extract as much labor power as possible from workers and to minimize costs by keeping wages low, avoiding taxes, and otherwise externalizing costs of production, including environmental degradation. National governments of every political stripe, even if they support conservation work or environmental regulation to some extent, facilitate these activities to maintain "competitiveness" and a "favorable climate for investment."[5] This is in part because the typical capitalist state, whether rich or poor, is run by politicians heavily influenced by and dependent on the financial backing of industry and wealthy donors, and who are either wealthy themselves or are afraid of the economic, political, and even violent repercussions if they fail to play according to the rules.

Because of our material circumstances, formal and informal education, and socialization in a culture steeped in capitalist-friendly ideology and procorporate propaganda, most of us living in such societies, most of the time, actively or passively support the aims of capitalist development—even if we would prefer to adopt a different economic model or to change the status quo and reduce inequality (as polls show many people in the world do).[6] Often unable to believe in the possibility of wider social change, we worry about our jobs, our ability to pay rent. Our very existence, as we are repeatedly told, depends on a "healthy economy," which our society defines in terms of the profitability of business and returns on investment—in short, successful capital accumulation.

Small-time businessmen and farmers work under the same pressures as everyone else. They are blown about by the same winds, but do not have the same power as more highly capitalized operations to shape their broader economic circumstances. The large firms that dominate the economy and government policy, along with the routine functioning of the "free market," dictate conditions that make it extremely difficult for small operators to "do the right thing" in ecological and social terms. Those exceptional small operations that succeed under a different model tend to require extensive community support and loyalty, including political activism, to survive. And anytime they are "too" successful, they face extraordinary efforts on the part of large firms to move in, take over the niche, and put them out of business, either by acquiring them or imitating their model to lure away supporters and customers to capture market share. While examples abound across sectors, a 2015 *Washington Post* article examined the fate of bought-out small organic producers under the headline: "Your Favorite Organic Brand Is Actually Owned by a Multinational Food Company."[7]

This is not to say that supporters of the system are not trying to address ecological crises, through "conscious capitalism," or some other means.[8] However, the deeper social changes necessary to reverse the overall trend of ecological decline and redress injustice are impossible to achieve without challenging the status quo and business as usual. Such a challenge is not yet on the agenda of mainstream actors in environmental politics. Therefore, current efforts by world leaders, the United Nations, international conferences, corporations, and environmental NGOs to address capitalist environmental crises have proven inadequate in scale at best, or, at worst, have created new crises or shifted problems from one ecological system to another, one community to another, or down the line so that future generations are burdened with the same problem or the consequences of false solutions.

Social scientists have documented the historical tendency of capitalist societies to shift ecological problems technologically, ecologically, geographically, temporally, or socially in order to continue business as usual. Brett Clark and Richard York write that "rather than acknowledging metabolic rifts, natural limits, and/or ecological contradictions, capital seeks to play a shell game with the environmental problems it generates, moving them around rather than addressing the root causes."[9] Technological and market mechanisms, or other means of shifting ecological rifts, such as moving dirty industries into poorer regions and more disenfranchised communities, are the norm. Mainstream environmentalism has facilitated such shifts by winning environmental gains in one area but not challenging business as usual, which simply continues elsewhere. These approaches seem to resolve issues in the short run, or at least give the appearance of doing so in a particular time and place, but serve to deepen crises in the longer term. Nowhere is this clearer than in the history of capitalist agriculture.

Capitalist agriculturalists addressed the early European soil crisis, caused by the expansion of agricultural production for profit, by seeking to replace the lost nutrients in the soil with fertilizers, rather than rebuilding the soil for its long-term health and fertility. Nations went to war over access to natural sources of nitrates and phosphates, the primary ingredients in commercial fertilizers. The War of the Pacific (1879–83) saw Peru and Bolivia at war with Chile to secure access to nitrogen- and phosphorus-rich guano, a war encouraged and supported by the British government and investors.[10] U.S. president Millard Fillmore made guano an important topic of his 1850 State of the Union speech, noting that "Peruvian guano has become so desirable an article to the agricultural interest of the United States that it is the duty of the Government to employ all the means properly in its power for the purpose of causing that article to be imported into the country at a reasonable price. Nothing will be omitted on my part toward accomplishing this desirable end."[11]

In response to the dire need for nitrogen fertilizer to overcome soil exhaustion, particularly in the slave South, the United States passed the Guano Islands Act in 1856 (legislation that remains on the books today) and laid claim to dozens of guano-strewn rocks and islands across the Caribbean and Pacific over the next two decades. This land grab continued to be important to the ambitions of the leading imperial powers into the twentieth century. Historian Gregory T. Cushman writes:

> U.S. claims under the 1856 Guano Islands Act represent an important landmark not only in the history of U.S. imperialism but also for the place of remote islands in global geopolitical history. Not to be outdone the United Kingdom claimed Kirimati (Christmas) and Malden Islands in the Central Pacific and belatedly annexed Namibian guano

> islands. Claiming a guano island became a favored way for a country to assert itself as a colonizing power: France, the Kingdom of Hawaii, Japan, Mexico, Germany, and Australia, among others, all joined the scramble in the Pacific. Ecuador and Chile colonized remote islands with other resources. In later years these islands took on new geopolitical importance as coaling stations, relay points for telegraph cables and eventually air bases.[12]

The fact that so many countries across the globe were desperate to secure supplies of nitrate for their fields underlines the magnitude and widespread nature of the soil fertility crisis of the 1800s.

Over the decades cultivated soils have become more exhausted and eroded. Agricultural science often has been applied to mask the effects of this degradation rather than to restore natural soil fertility. Moreover, the increased use of insecticides and herbicides in lieu of more ecological approaches to controlling weeds and insects, and synthetic fertilizers to replace lost soil nutrients, has led to further problems. These chemicals pollute the land and waterways, poison farm workers, and have led to an evolutionary-chemical arms race, as plant and animal species adapt by selecting for resistance to pesticides and herbicides. Scientists involved with the "planetary boundaries" project explain, "At the planetary scale, the additional amounts of nitrogen and phosphorus activated by humans are now so large that they significantly perturb the global cycles of these two important elements."[13] Scientists identify nine critical boundaries as representing "the safe operating space for humanity with respect to the Earth system." These are thresholds "associated with the planet's biophysical subsystems or processes."[14] To date, we have transgressed the safe boundaries defined for biogeochemical cycles (phosphorus and nitrogen), as well as for climate change, loss of biosphere integrity (includes extreme rate of biodiversity and genetic diversity loss), and land-system change. Two of these—climate change and biosphere integrity—are "core boundaries" whose significant alteration could "drive the Earth System into a new state."[15] Each of these boundaries is significantly impacted by commercial agriculture, and their transgression will alter agriculture around the world.

Marx was an early articulator of the paradox now routinely observed, that as our technological capability and scientific understanding of ecological crises expand, so do the crises themselves. In relation to the emerging agricultural science of the nineteenth century and the development of agricultural technology, he wrote,

> all progress in capitalist agriculture is a progress in the art, not only of robbing the worker, but of robbing the soil; all progress in increasing the fertility of the soil for a given time is a progress towards ruining the more long-lasting sources of that fertility. The more a country proceeds from large-scale industry as the background of its development, as in the case of the United States, the more rapid is this process of destruction. Capitalist production, therefore, only develops the techniques and the degree of combination of social process of production by simultaneously undermining the original sources of all wealth—the soil and the worker.[16]

More recently, historian William H. McNeill proposed the "law of the conservation of catastrophe" to explain this contradiction of human social development, wherein society's greater ability to understand and manipulate nature results in the potential for catastrophe on an ever-greater scale such that "the conservation of catastrophe may indeed be a law of nature, like the law of conservation of energy."[17]

"Catastrophes," McNeill writes, "recur perpetually on an ever-increasing scale as our skills and knowledge grow" and are "a price we pay for being able to alter natural balances and to transform the face of the earth through collective effort and the use of tools."[18] John Bellamy Foster develops this concept into one with more concrete historical content:

> Indeed, what distinguishes our time from earlier centuries is not so much the *conservation of catastrophe*, which has long been recognized, but rather the accelerated pace at which such destruction is now manifesting itself, i.e., what I am calling the *accumulation of catastrophe*. The desertification arising in pre-capitalist times, partly through human action, manifested itself over centuries, even millennia. Today changes in the land, the atmosphere, the oceans, indeed the entire life-support system of the earth, are the product of mere decades.[19]

This acceleration is crucial to understanding the disaster of soil erosion and degradation that engulfed the U.S. southern plains by the 1930s. The Dust Bowl is a perfect example of the accumulation of catastrophe, the result of decision makers shifting ecological problems down the line and denying the nature of the changes required to develop sustainable farming on the plains. As a result, the plains and the people living there in the 1930s suffered what Russell Lord, who worked for the Soil Conservation Service, called "the most spectacular mass sacrifice to strictly commercial *mores* in the history of mankind."[20]

Dust Bowl's Eve

The online textbook company Cengage Learning describes itself as "a leading publisher of research and reference resources for libraries, schools, and businesses" and provides material for in-class use by schoolteachers. Its curriculum includes *Historic Events for Students*. The Dust Bowl entry Cengage provides contains a section describing the onset of the dust storms entitled "The Unforeseen Arrives."[21] However, as I make clear in Chapter Four, the problem of soil erosion on the U.S. southern plains was not unforeseen, but well understood in advance of the 1930s. In 1910 the USDA even provided photographs of dust storms in the Great Plains region, and multiple publications, going back years earlier than the 1910 bulletin, described methods for "the control of blowing soils."[22]

Into the 1920s, reports and calls to action on soil erosion only increased. Instead, economic conditions in the 1920s induced more intense exploitation of the soil. After the agricultural boom years of the First World War, farmers in the United States and around the world were hit hard by the postwar decline in demand for key agricultural commodities. As Russell Lord explained to an international audience in 1945, "when that boom had ended, our soil lay wounded, and even that soil, still hard driven, was piling up what we called 'surpluses' of food and fiber—surpluses only in that needy consumers in our own and other countries did not have the money or credit to pay for them."[23] Because hungry people could not afford to buy the stockpiled grain, prices fell and plains farmers suffered. Lower market prices led them to intensify production in order to make up for lost income.[24] New technologies and crop varieties made expanded cultivation possible in less time and with less labor. Farmers needed to further expand cultivation to pay for more expensive equipment and inputs, which they often purchased on credit, thus increasing their indebtedness and leading to a vicious cycle of agricultural intensification to avoid destitution and eviction—which induces still more production, destitution, eviction, or abandonment.

Because cash-crop agriculture means specialization rather than diversification and self-sufficiency, farmers were increasingly vulnerable to fluctuations in commodity prices that determined their income, as well as fluctuations in the costs of farm and other family necessities. Moreover, because a substantial number of farmers in the Dust Bowl region were hired workers or tenants, they had neither the means nor the long-term connection to the land required to implement methods of soil conservation. Absentee owners were happy to take what they could from the land and the tenants, whom they often encouraged to move along after an annual contract was fulfilled.[25] But farms occupied and worked by their owners suffered, too. Thomas Jefferson's idealized, privately owned and operated family farm offered no panacea.[26]

Ironically, and with clear parallels to today's climate catastrophe, the crisis on the land was deepening at the same time a sophisticated global soil science was developing. In 1927 the first World Congress of Soil Science convened in Washington, DC. This congress was based on the success of a series of international soil conferences that had begun in 1909 in Budapest. More than a thousand people attended the 1927 meetings, including representatives from every European country and Australia, as well as colonial representatives from many countries in South and Central America, Africa, and Asia. Soil scientists, government officials, agronomists, industrialists, and the like attended. Papers were presented and collated in dozens of languages. The proceedings from this conference offer impressive documentation of the role of science in the colonial project and the state of the land during this period, including the problem of soil erosion. In one notable presentation, USDA land-use expert O. E. Baker laments the problem on the U.S. plains. He refers to settlement and changes in land use spreading "like an advancing army" and states that the new soils "should have never been plowed."[27] He attributes the fact that farmers overplowed to their prioritizing peace and protection "from the natives" over soil fertility.

A year later, in 1928, the USDA published Circular 33, whose title says it all: *Soil Erosion a National Menace*. The report refers to soil erosion as the "greatest enemy to the most valuable asset of mankind (the agricultural lands)" and states that "to visualize the full enormity of land impairment and devastation brought about by this ruthless agent is beyond the possibility of the mind."[28]

When the global economy began to crawl, before crashing as the decade ended, the bottom fell out of agricultural commodity prices, prompting even more planting among desperate farmers, and thus more soil erosion. An article in the *Daily Oklahoman* in July 1930 gives a sense of the scale of the problem on the southern plains. It reports the results of a survey of state agricultural lands by Oklahoma A & M College, which found that at the beginning of the decade, only twenty-three years after the territory became a state, erosion affected thirteen of sixteen million acres under cultivation. As a result, "81 percent of soil [had been] damaged" in state farmlands.[29]

Elected in 1928, President Herbert Hoover was, like his Republican predecessors, an avid supporter of conservation. He provided more federal funding for agencies like the Forest Service than any previous president. However, he was also a proponent of voluntary approaches to ecological and economic problems, which proved no match for the unrelenting forces of capital. Hoover had faith that self-interest or altruism would lead landholders and business owners to voluntarily make short-term sacrifices in order to reap the long-term benefits of conservation. This trust was a precursor to today's misguided and historically unfounded belief that business can and will treat each component of the so-called triple bottom line (social, ecological, and economic/financial) with equal concern, or even put social and ecological priorities ahead of profit—and it was then, as now, as historian Kendrick A. Clements writes, "quite simply, too optimistic."[30] Even Hoover came to recognize, as he once said to a friend, that "the only trouble with capitalism is capitalists; they're just too damned greedy."[31]

In 1931 a bumper crop contributed to a further drop in agricultural prices, and in the spring of the following year a period of drought set in alongside the global economic collapse.[32]

1930s Dust Bowl and Depression

The historical record makes it clear that the Great Depression and severe droughts of the 1930s only exacerbated an existing problem of land degradation and soil erosion. By the time the droughts hit the southern plains, with heat scorching the bared earth till it dried up and blew away, darkening the sky and choking the lungs of all living creatures, soil scientists and policymakers understood what they were dealing with. They knew the situation was dire. No one, however, could forecast how long the economic and ecological troubles would last, nor how much the calamity would cost socially, economically, and ecologically. From the vantage point of the late 1970s, Worster wrote, "in no other instance was there greater or more sustained damage to the American land, and there have been few times when so much tragedy was visited on its inhabitants. Not even the Depression was more devastating, economically. And in ecological terms we have nothing in the nation's past, nothing even in the polluted present, that compares."[33]

The private and initial public response to the unfolding disaster could not check its ugly progress. It was too little, too late. The Hoover administration was confronted with competing diagnoses of the concomitant economic, humanitarian, and environmental disasters and competing priorities, given the increasingly global market collapse and the millions of Americans who had lost their jobs by 1930. In addition, the government was aligned with powerful interests that represented a legacy of opposition to government relief, especially for the poor in the plains region, and it was therefore reluctant to step in.[34]

Drought expert Donald A. Wilhite explains that on the Great Plains "the drought relief of the 1850–1900 period proceeded in an 'anti-relief' environment."[35] Land speculators, railroad men, local politicians, and newspaper owners in the recently settled plains states long worried that honest news regarding conditions there would decrease immigration and opportunities for profit. They didn't want any negative attention. Aside from their active promotion of white settlement in the region, U.S. presidents before Hoover nearly always took a hands-off approach to the wretched conditions of plains settlers, as they did in general where the nation's poor were concerned. In the United States the poor, then as now, more often encounter police or the national guard in response to their demands for reprieve from hunger, destitution, and oppression, or their expressions of despair such as stealing food, than the benevolent hand of government. Therefore, drought-relief organizations that relied on voluntary contributions had been the primary means for addressing crises on the plains since as far back as the 1860 Territorial Relief Committee. Hoover expected this tradition to continue.

The president's ideological and political commitments led him to denounce Congress's efforts to send emergency relief to the plains and elsewhere as "a raid on the public treasury."[36] Expressly concerned with preserving the ethos of capitalism and individualism, Hoover responded to proposals for emergency relief to hungry farmers by invoking Grover Cleveland's 1887 claim "that though the people support the Government, the Government should not support the people."[37] Hoover believed the Department of Agriculture and extension services could give advice on what to grow and the Department of Commerce could provide advice on how and where to sell, but the federal government should not be required to provide anything or intervene to ease the people's suffering. As an adamant proponent of volunteerism, he saw this as the work of state and local private efforts and a matter for the Red Cross. Even so, in 1930 Hoover granted approval for one of the first federal initiatives meant to save the plains "from utter ruin"—"a $45 million seed-and-feed loan fund."[38] And in 1931 he supported a national conference on land utilization.

The administration also authorized further federal intervention, a fact left out of most accounts of Hoover's response to the agricultural depression and ecological calamity. To address white unemployment,

> in the late 1920s and early 1930s, under the president's watch, a wave of illegal and unconstitutional raids and deportations would alter the lives of as many as 1.8 million men, women and children—a threat that would seem to loom just as large in 2017 as it did back in 1929. . . . What became colloquially known as the "Mexican repatriation" efforts of 1929 to 1936 are a shameful and profoundly illustrative chapter in American history, yet they remain largely unknown—despite their broad and devastating impact.[39]

Some of these deportations took place in the Dust Bowl region, especially Texas. The Republican's race-based job-creation strategies continued under the Democrats and Roosevelt. This entailed the federal deportation and exodus of Mexican and Filipino nationals, among others, as well as Latino U.S. citizens—including in California to make way for local whites and "Okies" seeking jobs. Many of these refugees from white supremacy left because they were subject to threats, state and local deportation efforts, anti-immigrant and racist campaigns, and the refusal of white owners to hire them.[40]

For their part, state officials often indulged their wealthy, and overwhelmingly white, landowners in many ways. These landowners welcomed the social-control efforts of the federal government, but they often wanted neither government-imposed conservation nor relief for their tenants or sharecroppers. Therefore, at the start of the Dust Bowl years the wealthy and their representatives at the state, as at the federal, level promoted self-sufficiency and local, private assistance. Some landowners wanted to keep their workers near starvation so they could be induced to continue laboring under the inhumane conditions endemic to U.S. farm labor. One Red Cross chapter in a drought-stricken part of the Arkansas delta reported, "We do not believe we should give enough food to be comfortable for this would destroy the incentive of our negroes to work and might even ruin our labor force for years."[41]

The brutal consequences of such social views—as well as Hoover's conviction that the market should sort itself out and that private initiative could solve economic and ecological crises—led to his downfall, when Franklin Delano Roosevelt's victory in the 1932 election signaled the ascendancy of the New Deal coalition. Initially Roosevelt also ignored the particular plight of the southern plains. However, initiatives started during the first hundred days of his administration, such as the Agricultural Adjustment Administration, the Federal Emergency Relief Administration, and the Farm Credit Administration, would prove critical to the recovery, however unstable, of southern plains agriculture.[42]

The crises of the Depression and Dust Bowl made room for many innovative programs and new ideas in spite of the enormous conservative opposition to New Deal programs (an opposition that survives to this day). Roosevelt knew there had to be change in order to keep the overall system intact. His administration faced pressure from the popularity of movement organizations such as the Communist Party and Southern Tenant Farmers' Union, whose radical activism was growing in appeal, as well as from older civil rights organizations like the NAACP. As a result, Roosevelt's government was compelled to become more responsive to the voices of African-Americans than any previous administration (which is, truly, not saying much). It also faced pressure from the campaigns of other popular politicians, some of whom were not progressive in other ways, but had run and won elections based on platforms focused on wealth distribution and a social safety net. The 1930s was a tumultuous period, with, on the one hand, exciting, innovative, and in some cases multiracial movements promoting a more just, democratic, and ecological vision for the future, and, on the other hand, the threat of fascism. Political and economic elites were particularly concerned with suppressing the popularity of socialism, communism, and other revolutionary perspectives. Upending the social status quo lay at the heart of many political movements. But, as it turned out, it was decidedly not on the agenda of the Roosevelt administration.

Where social protections for the poorest and issues of land ownership and land use were concerned, FDR's government reinforced the position of the white and propertied. Like colonial regimes throughout the world facing similar crises at this time, the minority "at the top" dominated policy. The administration's goal became to return to business as usual in the countryside, though with new, limited government support. As journalist and author Ta-Nehisi Coates observes,

> The New Deal is today remembered as a model for what progressive government should do—cast a broad social safety net that protects the poor and the afflicted while building the middle class. When progressives wish to express their disappointment with Barack Obama, they point to the accomplishments of Franklin Roosevelt. But these progressives rarely note that Roosevelt's New Deal, much like the democracy that produced it, rested on the foundation of Jim Crow. . . . The omnibus programs passed under the Social Security Act in 1935 were crafted in such a way as to protect the Southern segregationist way of life. Old-age insurance (Social Security proper) and unemployment insurance excluded farmworkers and domestics—jobs heavily occupied by blacks. When President Roosevelt signed Social Security into law in 1935, 65 percent of African Americans nationally and between 70 and 80 percent in the South were ineligible. The NAACP protested, calling the new American safety net "a sieve with holes just big enough for the majority of Negroes to fall through."[43]

This should not surprise anyone today, given that, as geographers Anne Bonds and Joshua Inwood write, "white supremacy is not only a rationalization for race; it is the foundational logic of the modern capitalist system . . ."[44] This is why Malcolm X said in an interview, "It's impossible for a white person to believe in capitalism and not believe in racism. You can't have capitalism without racism. And if you find one and you happen to get that person into a conversation and they have a philosophy that makes you sure they don't have this racism in their outlook, usually they're socialists or their political philosophy is socialism."[45] In other words, a confrontation with white supremacy entails a confrontation with the entirety of capitalist development, and this was not FDR's agenda.

Despite conservatives' claims to the contrary, Roosevelt was no socialist, even if he believed in and supported efforts to ameliorate the worst conditions of the poor, including, in a way, of communities of color. Rather, his administration's commitment to defending the racialized system of private profit, its appeasement and in some cases reinforcement of white supremacy, strictly limited the rural agenda.

A New Deal for the Land?

Soil scientists Fred Magdoff and Harold van Es explain in *Building Soils for Better Crops* (2009), a widely used handbook today, that there are two general approaches to effective erosion control: building structures and changing agronomic practices.[46] Examples of structures include terraces and diversion ditches. Terracing reduces the erosion of hillsides by altering their slope. Ditches divert water to a desired area to help prevent soil wash from fields. Agronomic practices include cover cropping, reducing tillage, increasing the amount of crop residue and other organic material left on land, perennial-crop rotation, and planting vegetation to hold the soil in place and slow erosion from wind or water.

These recommendations are standard today, but they reflect long-understood principles of erosion control and were central conservation measures promoted by the Soil Erosion Service, which became the Soil Conservation Service (SCS).[47] In 1944, when Russell Lord, then working for the Tennessee Valley Authority (TVA), drafted an article describing the wonderful results of new agricultural methods promoted by New Deal soil scientists in the foothills of the Great Smokies, a leader in the TVA and scientist at the University of Georgia, S. G. Chandler, told him he only had to change one word of what he had written.[48] Chandler said to take out the word "new" when describing soil conservation methods, because "it isn't that we didn't know."

Recalling the exchange a year later, Russell agreed. "That was true. When you come to examine the essentials, we have invented nothing new in detail in our entire New Deal agricultural program. We have simply gone back to neglected or forgotten wisdom and applied it in a new working pattern or combination that suits our land and climate."[49] Although the wisdom was old, the Soil Conservation Service was newly established as a permanent agency in the U.S. Department of Agriculture in 1935, headed by Hugh Hammond Bennett. This move was part of the larger New Deal program that included a series of legal reforms, new government agencies, and overhauls of existing federal agencies, policies, and programs to facilitate government intervention in U.S. agriculture's ecology and political economy.

Historians often describe the New Deal as having two parts. The first is associated with Roosevelt's first two years in office (1933–34) and "consisted of *ad hoc* salvage or bailout measures, principally aimed at helping business, coupled with work relief programs"—with the "lion's share of New Deal expenditures at the outset . . . devoted to salvage operations."[50] The second began in 1935 in response to pressure for more comprehensive reforms and was much bolder than the first phase, reflecting the administration's decisive turn to the left. This shift was "made possible by the great 'revolt from below' of organized labor in the 1930s."[51] As journalist David Greenberg writes, "Elected overwhelmingly in 1932 on the strength of the public discontent, FDR found himself jarred into action by recurring waves of dissent."[52] Revolt also helped clear the path for an attempt on the part of some in the administration to implement what sociologist and historian Jess Gilbert identifies as a third New Deal, which would have delivered even greater structural reform had it succeeded.

As part of the First New Deal, Congress passed public works legislation providing employment and projects for the social good while stimulating the deflated economy. Soil conservation was identified as one of the goals of the Civilian Conservation Corps, founded in 1933. By 1934, government-supported surveys revealed that across the nation 200 million acres of cropland were "seriously eroded, leached, or depleted by overcropping without proper replenishment or care. To put it in still another way, about half our present cropland of 400 million acres showed signs of having been abused by careless or faulty culture when we started this national campaign of repair and restitution in 1934."[53] In the same year, as NASA scientists confirmed in a 2014 study, farmers suffered "the worst North American drought year of the last millennium."[54] Dust storms lifted the exposed, dry soils of the plains and spread them "across most of the United States east of the Central Plains."[55] Sixty-five percent of the Great Plains had been further damaged by wind erosion by the end of the year. Aside from the dust, water shortages meant that "conditions for pasture, corn, and tame hay (hay cut from cultivated grasses) were considered extremely poor over most of western North America (WNA), from Texas and New Mexico and up through Montana and the Dakotas."[56]

In 1934, in the face of extreme levels of devastation, Roosevelt finally requested a massive drought-relief package, which took steps to help farmers and ranchers, such as providing feed and buying starving cattle to give meat to the hungry.[57] Other provisions included jobs to poor farmers, cash supports, government acquisition of marginal lands with relocation of rural residents, loan and shelterbelt programs, and more.[58] As conditions worsened, businessmen and landowners changed their tune and became some of the biggest cheerleaders of government aid.[59]

The situation in the Dust Bowl region was dire. Between 1930 and 1935 the counties in the heart of this region lost a third of their population. One in every four houses was abandoned, and some counties saw rates of abandonment around 40 percent. By 1938 an estimated 275,000 people, 28 percent of the farm population of Oklahoma, had moved to a new farm in the previous year.[60] Remember that even before the Dust Bowl, living conditions on the southern plains had been challenging. In the 1930s most residents were not landowners and were not wealthy. Most farms had no electricity, no indoor plumbing, and no telephone. Transience was part of the social landscape.[61]

When the Dust Bowl descended, Native American communities in the region were already reeling from the loss of 90 percent of their landholdings between 1890 and 1933 and from some of the worst poverty rates in the country.[62] The government-commissioned 1928 Meriam Report, *The Problem of Indian Administration*, noted that among a much longer list of social deprivation and economic ills, "an overwhelming majority of Indians are poor, even extremely poor, and they are not adjusted to the economic and social system of the dominant white civilization . . . the general death rate and infant mortality rate are high. Tuberculosis is extremely prevalent. . . . The prevailing living conditions among the great majority of the Indians are conducive to the development and spread of disease. With comparatively few exceptions the diet is bad."[63] The report discussed that the state of Oklahoma had "evidenced a great desire to get control or possession of Indian property" and "little tendency to protect the Indians or provide requisite developmental work."[64] With respect to the land, "frequently the better sections . . . originally set apart for the Indians have fallen into the hands of the whites"; therefore, "many . . . are living on lands from which a trained and experienced white man could scarcely wrest a living." Nevertheless, the report still blamed Native Americans for their condition because "from the standpoint of the white man the typical Indian is not industrious, nor is he an effective worker when he does work."[65] Such racism bled into the New Deal treatment of the indigenous nations, despite attempts to reform U.S. policy toward indigenous peoples and again recognize a limited tribal sovereignty.

These conditions and treatment meant that during the Dust Bowl Native American farmers had it especially hard. State and local relief efforts were often denied them, under the justification that they were wards of the federal government and not a local responsibility. Native American farmers wrote to the federal government requesting a small portion of the funds held "in trust" for the tribes to be released as relief; the requests were denied.[66]

In 1934 Congress passed the Indian Reorganization Act (also known as the Wheeler-Howard Act), which was meant to end allotment, legally (according to white law) reinstate tribal governments, and improve tribal economic conditions, including increasing landholdings. This legislation formed the centerpiece of what was known as the Indian New Deal. In Oklahoma, Native American communities faced further attack in the wake of this act. Because of the vigorous opposition of its white businessmen, landowners, and politicians, the state's tribal nations were initially excluded from the 1934 Reorganization Act and further disenfranchised. Although they were included two years later, times remained hard.

The plight of the poor whites, communities of color, and Native American communities in the Dust Bowl region in the first two decades of the century—before the drought—had been so grim that it gave rise to radical, and in some cases multiracial, organizing. It also led to "the most vigorous, ambitious, and fascinating socialist movement of all," strongest in Oklahoma, but extending throughout the southeast and southwest.[67] Socialists and other radical groups were immediately subjected to massive, violent repression from the state and private white militias, including eventually the Ku Klux Klan, especially during and just after the First World War. But these early efforts inspired the formation of imperfect and unstable, but nevertheless significant, multiracial alliances of workers and the unemployed during the 1930s. They pressed for better conditions on farms and in factories, as well as for better support for the unemployed and elderly.[68]

Partly due to their efforts, and others like them throughout the United States (and around the world), Roosevelt expressly saw social reform as part of the effort to save the capitalist system. As he put it to businessmen in 1936 to gain support for reform efforts, change was necessary "because we cherished our system of private property and free enterprise and were determined to preserve it as the foundation of our traditional American system."[69]

As previously mentioned, beginning in 1935 the Second New Deal "produced some of the most lasting and impactful policies of the New Deal."[70] Thanks to the persistent activism of organizations like the Southern Tenant Farmers' Union, the Second New Deal included measures to help tenants and sharecroppers, providing land ownership and resettlement programs, new jobs, better terms with landlords, and direct relief. However, because of the racist manner in which the new programs were implemented, white tenants and sharecroppers benefited far more than black, Latino, or Native American farmers. For example, the Agricultural Adjustment Administration (AAA) paid (mostly white) landowners to keep land out of cultivation in order to reduce supply, raise the price of agricultural commodities, and conserve the soil. But when racist landowners kept money that was intended to relieve their farm workers, or kicked tenants and sharecroppers off the land because they no longer needed their labor, the federal government looked the other way.[71]

Another manifestation of naked racism was the exclusion of agricultural and domestic workers from key social legislation, as noted earlier in this chapter. Sociologist and National Urban League member Ira De A. Reid, writing in the 1930s, stated that "so far as the Negroes in the South are concerned the AAA . . . might just as well be administered by the Ku Klux Klan."[72] And historian Harvard Sitkoff observes that "no other department was controlled by white supremacists both in the bureaucracy and in Congress as was the Department of Agriculture."[73] The New Deal did benefit black communities, enough to maintain their electoral support for the Democratic Party over the Republicans, but many New Deal provisions intentionally excluded black farmers and communities in order to appease racist white landowners, businessmen, and politicians.

Maintaining the racial hierarchy and social status quo in agriculture put limits on the ecological, as well as social, agenda. However, during this period, the federal government took important steps to address soil erosion. Two key initiatives were the establishment of the Soil Conservation Service as a permanent agency of the USDA with expanded duties, and federal encouragement of state and county authorities to implement "democratically organized soil conservation districts to lead the conservation planning effort at the local level."[74] Taking further action, Roosevelt convened the Great Plains Drought Area Committee, which published an influential report in 1936 containing recommendations to address more fundamental and long-term problems with plains agriculture. Coming right after the worst impacts of the Dust Bowl, this was the first major government report analyzing the systemic causes of the crisis and providing direction for ongoing government intervention in the region.[75]

One crucial outcome of the federal response to the Dust Bowl was the spread of soil conservation through the nationwide expansion of demonstration projects. The Soil Conservation Service (SCS) and the Civilian Conservation Corps (CCC)—a program designed to give out-of-work men a job on projects that would benefit communities—together created demonstration projects on private land to educate farmers in new techniques. Historian Neil M. Maher writes that "Although the Soil Conservation Service supplied the technical know-how by assigning agronomists to demonstration areas, the CCC supplied the muscle needed to physically alter farmers' fields in ways that halted soil and water erosion."[76] This muscle, underwritten by the federal government, had a big impact. Illustrating what can be done when planning, labor, and resources are directed in a socially useful way, "by January 1938, Corps projects on the nation's 175 soil demonstration areas affected approximately 11.5 million acres of farmland in 48 states. Corps enrollees helped farmers contour till nearly 2 million acres, strip crop more than 770,000 acres, plant cover crops on more than 250,000 acres, and terrace 1,136,553 acres of farmland throughout the United States."[77]

Still, these efforts proved inadequate. In the words of Roosevelt, "Demonstration work has been undertaken but much remains to be done. The conduct of isolated demonstration projects cannot control erosion adequately. Such work can only point the way."[78] The federal government could not address erosion on private land, but the states could. So the USDA and SCS urged Roosevelt to argue for state-led, rather than federally mandated, soil conservation districts. In a 1937 letter to state governors, the president encouraged legislation to implement the districts. He warned,

> I need not emphasize to you the seriousness of the problem and the desirability of our taking effective action, as a Nation and in the several States, to conserve the soil as our basic asset. The Nation that destroys its soil destroys itself. . . . The problem is further complicated by the fact that the failure to control erosion on some lands, particularly if such eroding lands are situated strategically at the heads of valleys or watersheds, can cause a washing and blowing of soil onto other lands, and make the control of erosion anywhere in the valley or

> watershed all the more difficult. We are confronted with the fact that, for the problem to be adequately dealt with, the erodible land in every watershed must be brought under some form of control.[79]

Most states adopted the legislation, which brought together farmers and government officials who made decisions and worked together to legally regulate farming practices and implement conservation works.

In terms of rural policy, Jess Gilbert explains that a short-lived third New Deal attempted to institutionalize democratic land-use planning and, some hoped, restructure the economy from the bottom up. In the late 1930s, the plethora of New Deal agencies and programs represented a disjointed, sometimes contradictory tangle. In an effort to coordinate action across agencies and programs, and democratize the work of these agencies, Secretary of Agriculture Henry Wallace reorganized the entire USDA in 1938–39, aiming "to advance the new initiative, cooperative land-use planning, which constituted the nation's first attempt to link local citizens with the administration of public policy at all levels of government."[80] The initiative was implemented at the county level, where planning committees headed by farmers and including representatives of federal and regional extension agencies decided what their counties needed and then coordinated among the various programs to implement a range of social improvements. The goal was to integrate the efforts of farmers, experts, educators, and policymakers, cocreating policy informed by discussions of broader social issues, with an educational component. These planning committees achieved wonderful results. They coordinated everything from conservation efforts to cooperative medical and hot food programs, along with youth and adult education on subjects ranging from the philosophy of democracy and ecology to nutrition and home canning, thus improving the health of the land and people.

At the center of the third New Deal, this new form of "cooperative land-use planning . . . combin[ed] new types of continuing education and participatory research with unprecedented citizen planning."[81] Within the government the project was promoted by a group of what Gilbert calls (drawing on Gramsci) "organic intellectuals" who "invented a tradition of democratizing agrarian reform."[82] Gilbert sees these efforts as representative of "low modernism"—"meaning decentralized programs that involved local citizens in substantive, meaningful ways," combining top-down and bottom-up approaches to policy—in contrast to the more elitist "high modernism" theorized by political scientist and anthropologist James C. Scott, which attempts to engineer society from the top down, justified in scientific terms.[83]

In spite of its accomplishments and its potential to facilitate agricultural development for a broader swath of the American population in the postwar period, the third New Deal had powerful opponents and was soon extinguished. The program suffered a decisive defeat (even if aspects of cooperative planning continued) when Congress defunded it at the urging of the conservative American Farm Bureau Federation, which represented influential white landowners and corporate agriculture, and part of the "growing anti-New Deal coalition that would soon destroy other progressive agencies, including the FSA [Farm Security Administration]."[84] To seal the deal, Gilbert explains, eventually "conservative politicians and administrators suppressed institutional economics and reformist rural sociology in the land-grant colleges as well as in USDA, banishing ideas and programs. . . . A rabid anti-New Dealism, eventuating in the postwar Red Scare, purged these economic planners and agricultural professors from the ranks."[85] The consequences were that "the intellectual head of the planning program thereby got lopped off, and the nation forfeited an informed, wide-ranging debate on the future of American agriculture."[86]

Even in the plains region, which struggled to recover, Worster writes, "whenever the New Deal really tried to become new and innovative, plainsmen turned hostile. The fate of the plains lay in the hands of Providence, and Providence, not Washington, would see them come out all right."[87] This attitude prevailed in spite of the fact that the plains region in the end received "more federal dollars than any other, along with reassurance, solicitation, and encouragement."[88]

With the coming of the Second World War, priorities and the political environment shifted. While conservation work continued, the spirit of social reform wouldn't be so strong again in the United

States until the movements of the 1960s brought social and ecological change back onto the mainstream political and policy agenda. "After World War II," Gilbert concludes, "national policies set the United States on a rapid course of unrestrained capitalist development with little regard to its cost or its victims, ecological as well as human."[89]

Prior to the war, Hugh Hammond Bennett—student of the global history of soil conservation, father of soil conservation in the United States, first head of the Soil Conservation Service, and proponent of business-oriented conservation until his death—would become a kind of international celebrity, influencing conservation and development policy around the world. Colonial administrators outside the United States, confronting their own ecological crises, found themselves mesmerized first by dramatic images of the plains dust storms they saw in the international press and then by the work of Bennett's SCS to tackle the problem.[90]

Bennett may have been popular among colonial officials because he represented just their kind of man, and his version of environmentalism soothed their anxieties at a time when the soil erosion crisis called into question white territorial control. However, in historian David Anderson's view, Bennett and his U.S. cohorts did not deserve the acclaim they received. Though the know-how was available to do so, they did not avert the catastrophe. They only responded to it under duress. He writes,

> The Dust Bowl, at its height in 1935, and its cost spectacularly measured in pounds of soil lost per person and square feet of topsoil blown hundreds of miles across country, had made conservation of the environment an international issue. This impact did much to push the [British] Colonial Office to tackle the issue on an equally grand scale. Administrators from the colonies and bureaucrats from Whitehall traveled to America to see the devastation at first hand and, more importantly, to view the anti-erosion measures being applied by the United States Soil Conservation Service. But the Americans, for all their efforts to deal with the problem, were barely worth their acknowledged status of 'experts' on soil conservation. Having created one of

> the most serious single environmental disasters known to man they simply had to set about trying to solve it. In a sense, there were no 'experts'; only those who were doing something. More of necessity was being done in North America than elsewhere, and so it was primarily from this pool of experience that the Colonial Office drew its ideas.[91]

In the long run, by failing to challenge the social status quo, the environmentalism of Hugh H. Bennett and the other probusiness environmentalists that dominated policy did not prevent or resolve any ecological problems. This truth is evident in today's global, ongoing, and intensifying problems with climate change, soil erosion, desertification, and general land degradation. As Worster concludes:

> Agricultural conservation at the New Deal era was, on balance, a failure in the Great Plains. Neither the federal land-use planners nor the ecologists made a lasting impact on the region. The agronomists and soil technicians, although they were more successful in getting their version of conservation translated into action, were ultimately ineffectual, too. Give them credit for this: the region would not have come back so spectacularly without their assistance. Farmers did learn from these advisors a few tips that stayed with them, making them more of an "expert profession," as Hugh Bennett had hoped. But all the same, the agronomists' success in reforming the plains was, to put it in the best light, partial, and, to put in the most critical light, self-defeating. Nothing [leading soil erosion expert H. H.] Finnell and his fellow conservationists said in the thirties could have encouraged plainsmen to think of the land as something more than a commodity—a "resource"—for their enrichment. They offered farmers a technological panacea for ecological destructiveness, when the root issue is motivation and values—a deeply entrenched economic ethos. The return of dust-bowl conditions in the 1950s demonstrated, or should have demonstrated, the inability of a technical assistance program by itself to reform the old ethos. And that program was, in the end, by far the major legacy of New Deal conservation.[92]

Indeed, in the United States, the "filthy fifties" brought "dirty thirties" Dust Bowl–like conditions back to the plains.

One western Kansan had forewarned in 1949, "We aren't [*sic*] kidding ourselves that it won't come again. There isn't a thing being done to prepare for it. If it starts again, within two or three years . . .

it will catch us as ill-prepared or almost so as it did in the middle thirties. Only this time it will be much more widespread with so much more land broken up out there in Colorado."[93] But the drought in the 1950s occurred in the middle of a decade of economic expansion, in stark contrast to the 1930s. Although it sparked a revival of interest in conservation, it was not until the environmental and social movements of the 1960s and 1970s that popular pressure would again significantly change the course of federal policy. The response to the crisis in the 1950s mostly repeated the solutions of the 1930s: rather than creating a truly drought-resilient agriculture that conserves soil and water, farmers relied on technical solutions, artificial fertilizers, and a shift from one problem to another. Today, the major issue in the plains region is the mining of groundwater, which is itself now facing rapid depletion, resulting in what sociologists Matthew R. Sanderson and R. Scott Frey have called the "metabolic rift on the High Plains aquifer."[94]

All of this may sound like a harsh judgment. However, in late 2016, University of Chicago and NASA scientists published in *Nature Plants* the results of a study on the potential for drought-induced agricultural losses under climate change. The authors of the article, titled "Simulating US Agriculture in a Modern Dust Bowl Drought," warn that another period of drought like that in the 1930s, anticipated to be more frequent under climate change, would result in "unprecedented consequences," in spite of our greater scientific knowledge and understanding of ecological issues, technological advances, and innovations in agricultural practice that have increased productivity.[95]

In an interview, research scientist and coauthor of the article Joshua Elliott said, "We expected to find the system much more resilient because 30 percent of production is now irrigated in the United States, and because we've abandoned corn production in more severely drought-stricken places such as Oklahoma and west Texas. . . . But we found the opposite: The system was just as sensitive to drought and heat as it was in the 1930s."[96]

This chapter's account of the avoidable crisis of the Dust Bowl, the New Deal's response, and its ultimate failure to resolve the long-term problem of soil degradation and unsustainable agriculture makes it clear that it is time to reexamine the limitations of mainstream 1930s environmentalism. This is all the more important because "the Progressive era conservation policies of the New Deal . . . stand at the root of modern environmentalism."[97] And because for many environmentalists the "Green New Deal" has become a rallying cry. Such a reevaluation is the subject of Chapter Six.

six

"WE'RE NOT STAKEHOLDERS": BEYOND THE *LANGUE DE COTON* OF CAPITALIST ENVIRONMENTAL MANAGEMENT

> The future of our earth may depend upon the ability of all women to identify and develop new definitions of power and new patterns of relating across difference. The old definitions have not served us, nor the earth that supports us. The old patterns, no matter how cleverly rearranged to imitate progress, still condemn us to cosmetically altered repetitions of the same old exchanges, the same old guilt, hatred, recrimination, lamentation, and suspicion.
>
> —Audre Lorde, "Age, Race, Class, and Sex: Women Redefining Difference," 1980

> The proper treatment of environmental problems requires an end to the 'totalitarianism of economics' and work toward the practical and theoretical reconstruction of the unity of politics and economics. Conventional thought has not gone down this road and conventional political forces have not taken any action in this direction. The debate surrounding the environment remains, under these conditions, the powerless expression of wishful thinking.
>
> —Samir Amin, "Can Environmental Problems Be Subject to Economic Calculations?" 1993

At a 2001 conference titled "Breaking the Links Between Land Degradation, Food Insecurity, and Water Scarcity," a representative of the U.S. government explained its decision to become a party to the UN Convention to Combat Desertification (CCD):

> One important reason the United States is committed to combating desertification is that we have been there. Farmers moving onto the

> fragile plains persisted in using agriculture methods that were inappropriate for that environment. As a result, when a series of droughts hit, their land literally dried up and blew away. Conditions were so terrible that, it is claimed, farmers could actually hear the ground cracking as it dried. So, one reason I am here today is that the United States created one of the most famous examples of desertification ever. But the other side of that is the fact that the United States eventually managed to recover from this disaster. The US response to this crisis was a successful community-based soil and water conservation program that is still fighting the ever-present threat of desertification in the American West. Through research on soil conservation measures, technology transfer to farmers, and education and training of farmers, ranchers, and local communities—this should sound familiar to all of you knowledgeable about the CCD—the Dust Bowl was eventually mitigated and the affected lands returned to productivity.[1]

From this simplistic perspective, the problems on the plains in the 1930s, like the problems today with land degradation, were caused by insufficient money, inappropriate technology, and a lack of scientific knowledge. Therefore, they could be resolved through financing and educating the ignorant or misinformed local population, while updating well-intentioned, if misguided, policy.

This assessment positions wealthy countries (for example, in the CCD context) as benevolent overseers of positive ecological change carried out through seemingly objective science and technology-based solutions. Within countries, such a view situates those attempting to make a living on marginal and degraded lands, or using traditional farming methods, as poor and ignorant people in need of proper shepherding and financing down the path of ecological righteousness and modern sustainable development.

Inherent in this government official's remarks is the environmental version of what anthropologist James Ferguson calls the "modernist master narrative of progressive phases."[2] In the social sciences, this narrative is best represented in the work of scholars advocating varieties of green capitalism. Examples include the ecological modernization school of thought, which assumes an ecologically "reflexive" or "green modernity," and draws on classical modernization theory as well as the work of writers like sociologist Ulrich Beck.[3] Another prominent example is the "natural capitalism" perspective building on the work of authors Paul Hawken, Amory Lovins, and Hunter Lovins.[4] From such perspectives, disasters represent opportunities to learn from our mistakes, make corrections, and continue the cumulative process, however uneven, of greening capitalism, primarily through technological change.

As Hawken, Lovins, and Lovins explain, it's perfectly possible to redirect capitalism toward ecological sustainability and make it not only greener or more "natural," but simultaneously more profitable. To these ends they propose

> a new approach not only for protecting the biosphere but also for improving profits and competitiveness. Some very simple changes to the way we run our businesses, built on advanced techniques for making resources more productive, can yield startling benefits both for today's shareholders and for future generations. This approach is called natural capitalism because it's what capitalism might become if its largest category of capital—the "natural capital" of ecosystem services—were properly valued.[5]

For ecological modernizationists this means promoting, in the words of proponents Arthur P. J. Mol (sociology) and Martin Jänicke (political science), "the possibility, actuality and desirability of a green Capitalism."[6]

There is a consensual undertone to the advocacy of proponents of green capitalism, the sense that we are all in this together: the capitalists make more money, the people have more and better jobs, and the environment is protected; the whole earth is well tended. Everybody wins or loses together. As Beck claims, "climate change may yet prove to be the most powerful of forces summoning a civilizational community of fate into existence."[7]

Ecological modernizationists inside and outside the academy reserve their strongest criticism for environmental activists who focus on issues such as social justice or more substantive democratization of the economy, rather than on the environment (or an aspect of the environment) as a separate issue. They deride activism that alienates environmentalism from institutions of power that, in their eyes, "make a difference."[8] In other words, they consider environmentalism at its best when it aligns with the agenda of powerful private and public actors (such as industry and government). For advocates of ecological modernization, questions of substantive social change explicitly don't enter the picture.

Regrettably, mainstream environmentalism has moved closer toward this line of thinking over the last forty years, though challenges to the trend persist.[9] Incomplete and misleading stories about the New Deal and Dust Bowl conservation serve to reinforce the notion that with the right set of techniques, policies, and/or voluntary adjustments by individuals and industry, capitalism is well suited to solving our ecological crises. Many see the New Deal of the 1930s as evidence that the system can be reformed and the state geared toward social and environmental improvement, even in the heart of the empire of capital. This has led to repeated calls over the years for a Green New Deal.

A Green New Deal?

After decades in which austerity and the rollback of environmental gains have led to escalating ecological degradation and social insecurity, many around the world look back longingly at the 1930s New Deal. For some, this was capitalism's finest hour, proof of the potential for reflexivity even in a leading capitalist nation.[10] In recent years calls for a Green New Deal have reverberated from the halls of the United Nations to the pages of *Forbes* magazine, and in electoral campaigns across a number of countries.[11] Contemporary proponents suggest that the original New Deal serves as a model for how we might address linked social and ecological challenges; all we need is the political will.

In the wake of the 2007–2008 Great Financial Crisis, the New Economics Foundation and the United Nations Environment Programme (UNEP) called on member countries, especially the G20, to implement policy and investment strategies consistent with a Global

Green New Deal.[12] Economist Edward Barbier, the author of an important report informing the proposal, explained in the journal *Nature*, "UNEP started its policy initiative in December 2008, when the world faced multiple crises—fuel, food and financial. Overcoming these required a package of policy measures similar to the New Deal of former US President Franklin D. Roosevelt in the 1930s, but on the global scale and embracing a wider and greener vision."[13]

As countries developed stimulus packages to address economic recovery, UNEP recommended investment in five key areas: energy efficiency in buildings, renewable energy, sustainable transportation technology, the earth's "ecological infrastructure, including fresh waters, forests, soils and coral reefs," and sustainable agriculture.[14] In sum the proposal recommended that 1 percent of global gross domestic product (GDP) be spent on green development, with G20 countries shouldering most of the burden. It also "showed that the need for improved agriculture, freshwater management and sanitation in developing countries provides key green business opportunities."[15] These measures were meant to accompany policy changes that removed perverse subsidies supporting ecologically damaging economic activities, such as unsustainable agriculture and fossil-fuel extraction.

China's green stimulus investments were held up as a model of the "everybody wins" payoff—you can clean up the environment, stimulate economic growth, and provide jobs, pleasing nearly every sector of society. UNEP's 2009 report, *Rethinking the Economic Recovery: A Global Green New Deal*, highlighted efforts in Mexico, Germany, France, the United States, and South Africa. South Korea's Green New Deal plan allocated 95 percent of its fiscal stimulus in response to the crisis, or 3 percent of its GDP, to green initiatives. In contrast, in the United States the Obama administration apportioned only 12 percent of the funds allocated for the American Recovery and Reinvestment Act to green initiatives, or 0.7 percent of GDP.[16] In its update to the report intended to inform the G20 meeting in Pittsburgh of progress toward a Green New Deal, UNEP said that "much more needs to be done" and that "in many cases, there remain large gaps between government declarations and practice" when the goal is to address the urgency of social needs and the pace of ecological degradation.[17] The G20 overall fell far short of its original commitments to so-called green investment and poverty reduction.

An assessment a year after the Pittsburgh meetings—where G20 leaders had pledged implementation of the Global Green New Deal—showed that "to date, the G20 has failed to deliver on these promises."[18] This is in spite of the fact that the Global Green New Deal was explicitly nonthreatening to the social status quo, representing industry-friendly environmentalism. As political scientist Timothy W. Luke writes, "while a backlash against neoliberalism reverberates in these plans for a green new deal, neoliberal articles of faith remain. Indeed, the superstructure of the green new deal rests upon many foundations, and one of the deepest is 'natural capitalism.' "[19]

That a Green New Deal still couldn't get sufficient traction to meet its goals is evidence that contemporary calls for an ecological replica on a world scale of Roosevelt's New Deal were taking place in a vastly different political and economic climate than the original. For example, in the depths of the 1930s global economic depression, revolutionary parties and radical ideas about democratizing the economy, land reform, and abolishing the credit system were gaining ground, and the Russian Revolution was held in high regard by members of the working class, anticolonial, civil rights, and national liberation movements around the world. Reform, Roosevelt himself explained, was necessary to save capitalism. The 1930s New Deal, like UNEP's Global Green New Deal, was not meant to upend the social status quo, only to ameliorate some of the worst symptoms of the social order and get the economy back on track, with ample support for, and collaboration with, industry.[20] However, as explicitly unthreatening as UNEP's version of the Green New Deal was, global political elites (with a few countries excepted) did not feel sufficient pressure to change, in spite of the wave of global protests linked to agricultural, ecological, and economic crises, the Occupy movement in the United States, and support for the Green New Deal by major environmental organizations.[21]

A decade after the 2007–08 crisis began, UNEP's proposal for a Global Green New Deal has fizzled out of the news. However, the concept of a Green New Deal lives on around the world, reflecting the power of this interwar period in the United States in the global contemporary progressive and green imagination.[22]

In the 2016 U.S. presidential elections, climate change and the environment barely gained a mention in the official presidential debates between Republican Donald Trump and Democrat Hillary Clinton. However, the Green Party of the United States, with Jill Stein as its presidential candidate, made the Green New Deal central to its platform. The Green Party's version included an economic bill of rights, a green transition involving green jobs and the green economy, financial reform, and a promise of increased democracy and transparency in government and the economy.[23] After the election of Donald Trump, Naomi Klein reported in the *New York Times*, "The good news is that the sectors that have made common cause with Mr. Trump represent less than a quarter of all unionized workers. And many other unions see the enormous potential in a green New Deal."[24]

Monica Frassoni, cochair of the European Green Party, wrote in March 2017, "I believe there are two fields, in particular, that could determine whether we will triumph against or succumb to the rising wave of populism and authoritarianism: the 'Green New Deal' and the quality of our democracy."[25] This statement echoed the sentiments of French economist Thomas Piketty, who called in 2016 in the *New York Review of Books* for a New Deal for Europe (though his emphasis was not ecological). He wrote, "Only a genuine social and democratic refounding of the eurozone, designed to encourage growth and employment, arrayed around a small core of countries willing to lead by example and develop their own new political institutions, will be sufficient to counter the hateful nationalistic impulses that now threaten all Europe."[26]

Northern Ireland's Green Party is calling for a Green New Deal to create a "world-class renewable energy industry." The party says income from business taxes, such as a corporation tax, could fund a "Green New Deal, an energy efficiency retrofit programme that would sustain up to 15,000 jobs as well as reduce fuel poverty and lower carbon emissions."[27] The Green New Deal was on the agendas of parties in 2016–2017 elections in the Netherlands and Austria as well, among others across Europe.[28] Rwandan author and scholar Oscar Kimanuka writes, "Africa needs some form of Green New Deal with development partners not just to rescue them from crisis but to ensure that their long-awaited rise is as smooth as it can possibly be and that their countries do not become the last bastion for business-as-usual, but the premier frontier for the green economy."[29]

In the United Kingdom, a Green New Deal group that has met since early 2007 includes a wide range of participants, from the economics editor of the *Guardian* and Green Party representatives to academics and leaders or former leaders of environmental organizations like Greenpeace and Friends of the Earth.[30] The Green New Deal is an important part of the identity of the U.K.'s Green Party as it works to distinguish itself from the increasingly popular Labour Party led by Jeremy Corbyn.[31] As a final example, confronted in the fall of 2017 with one of the most violent Atlantic hurricane seasons on record, the *New York Times* published another appeal: "In Hurricane Harvey's Wake, We Need a Green 'New Deal' " (August 31, 2017).

All of this illustrates the astounding amount of hope placed in a Green New Deal, which takes its cue from a ninety-year-old government program mythologized as a panacea for a range of social and ecological ills. In this idyllic vision, a Green New Deal will not only make capitalism more sustainable; it will facilitate the regrowth of democracy and lessen nationalistic and xenophobic political currents by creating millions of green jobs.

There are compelling reasons to look back to an idealized, or in some cases mythical, 1930s New Deal. Looking soberly at the ecological degradation engendered by today's dominant politics is utterly chilling. In 2016, a United Nations report attributed an estimated 12.6 million human deaths per year to environmental degradation—a quarter of all deaths worldwide.[32] UNEP projects an increase in annual fatalities as climate change continues. To put the numbers of dying in perspective, consider the fact that during the six years of the Second World War there were an estimated 15 million battle deaths and 45 million civilian deaths. Sixty million died over six years, or approximately 10 million per year, during the bloodiest conflict in world history.[33] This means that environmental degradation and unhealthy environments are causing millions more deaths each year than violent conflicts in the present as well as the past.

And not just humans are dying. The same year this UN report was released, the World Wildlife Fund published the 2016 version of their *Living Planet Report*, stating that between 1970 and 2012 the earth's vertebrate populations overall declined by 58 percent, while freshwater populations declined by an estimated 81 percent. "If the trend continues," the report projects, "then by 2020 the world will have lost two-thirds of its vertebrate biodiversity," including mammals, birds, fish, and other vertebrates. And there are no indications that this rate of loss of life will decrease. The proximate cause is habitat destruction resulting from "logging, agriculture and the disruption of freshwater systems such as rivers."[34]

In the face of such an enormous assault on life—and current levels of inequality rivaling those of the 1920s, with political power increasingly concentrated at the top—we find value and comfort in looking to past hard times and how they were handled.[35] The Green New Deal is also attractive to environmentalists who feel bullied by the "jobs versus the environment" trope used by industries to pit their workers against environmentalists, even when they are from the same community and care about the same problems. However, in the face of our current calamity, is reaching back to the New Deal really the best we can do? What are the consequences of drawing on it as a referent? If we consider just how devastating conditions had to become before the New Deal was possible, and how ultimately ineffective its programs were in resolving both ecological crises and unemployment—not to mention its failure to redress racial injustice and the continued oppression of indigenous peoples—we're forced to conclude that anyone who wants genuine socio-ecological transformation must look elsewhere.

From New Deal to Green Revolution

Moreover, in the case of agriculture, proponents of a Green New Deal should worry that the very architects of the New Deal, who in part intended to solve the Dust Bowl crisis, helped spur the Green Revolution that has given rise to the dominant global agricultural model of our era, with innumerable consequences. This model has increased crop yields, but at great costs, as ecologist David Tilman listed in *Nature*, including:

> contamination of groundwaters, release of greenhouse gases, loss of crop genetic diversity and eutrophication of rivers, streams, lakes and coastal marine ecosystems (contamination by organic and inorganic nutrients that cause oxygen depletion, spread of toxic species and changes in the structure of aquatic food webs) . . . loss of soil fertility, the erosion of soil, the increased incidence of crop and livestock diseases, and the high energy and chemical inputs associated with it.[36]

Henry A. Wallace, whom John Kenneth Galbraith cites as the second most important New Deal figure next to Roosevelt, was one of the primary figures who helped launch the global Green Revolution in agriculture.[37] Wallace was secretary of agriculture and then vice-president under Roosevelt. Later he ran as a progressive candidate for president against Harry S. Truman. Like many white progressives, Wallace was a champion of the poor, a proponent of technological fixes to socio-ecological crises, and at times ambiguous on questions of racial justice, especially when pushing for civil rights might put at risk other initiatives he supported by antagonizing extreme racists.[38]

Wallace was an Iowa agribusinessman and the founder of the Hi-Bred corn company specializing in hybrid seed varieties he helped develop, building on scientific research innovations that took place in the public sector. In 1936 Wallace's company changed its name to Pioneer Hi-Bred. It became one of the world's most important seed companies and was bought by Dupont in 1999. Puerto Rican journalist, researcher, and activist Carmelo Ruiz-Marrero writes, "Wallace promoted hybrid seed with evangelical zeal, and so helped transform the country's corn production. In 1933, around 1% of Iowa's corn came from hybrid seed, by 1943 the figure was almost 100%. By 1965, over 95% of the country's corn was from hybrid seed, to Pioneer's great profit."[39]

Internationally, Wallace was a major supporter of industrial agriculture and helped kick-start the Green Revolution while acting as Roosevelt's vice-president, using Mexico as a laboratory.[40] Ruiz-Marrero attributes the Mexican Agricultural Program (MAP) to Wallace. He writes,

> This program, a joint venture of the Rockefeller Foundation, the US government and the Mexican ministry of agriculture, introduced the Iowa model to the Mexican countryside: hybrid seeds, monocultures, agrochemical inputs, and mechanization. The changes—both technological and social—that this mode of farming effected on Mexico's agriculture were truly revolutionary.
>
> The MAP was the spearhead of Avila-Camacho's move against Cardenas' land reform. The Cardenista zeal for justice was replaced by the belief that rural hunger and poverty could be tackled and eradicated in an apolitical manner by applying American expertise and scientific technique, without any need for social critique or political activism, and especially without distributing lands to the poor.[41]

This model, modified in various ways, would be exported to Asia, Africa, and the rest of Latin America. Hybrid seeds trapped farmers in a cycle of debt and dependence on seed companies. Unlike open-pollinated varieties, yields decline if you collect hybrid seed, forcing farmers to keep buying them.[42] Their benefit primarily comes in the uniformity of the crop, which helps with mechanization, a key component of capitalist agriculture because it reduces labor costs and aids in other cost-saving measures.

"The 'machine-friendly' crop" pioneered by Wallace and developed to apply to a range of grain, fruits, and vegetables, writes James C. Scott, "was bred to incorporate a series of characteristics that made it easier to harvest it mechanically. Among the most important of these characteristics were resilience, a concentrated fruit set, uniformity of plant size and architecture, uniformity of fruit shape and size, dwarfing (in the case of tree crops especially), and fruits that easily break away from the plant. . . . Taste and nutritional quality were secondary to machine compatibility."[43] The constant pressure to expand profits "worked powerfully to transform and simplify both the field and the crop. Relatively inflexible, nonselective machines work best in flat fields with identical plants growing uniform fruits of perfectly even maturity. Agronomic science was deployed to approximate this ideal: large, finely graded fields; uniform irrigation and nutrients to regulate growth; liberal use of herbicides, fungicides, and insecticides to maintain uniform health; and, above all, plant breeding to create the ideal cultivar."[44]

The reliance on buying seeds and other inputs is one of the spurs, along with mechanization, promoting the concentration of land ownership. Most disturbing is the fact that there were other viable options that were better for the land and better for small farmers, but not as favorable for agribusiness profits. Biologist and geneticist Richard Lewontin writes, "Since the 1930's, immense effort has been put into getting better and better hybrids. Virtually no one has tried to improve the open-pollinated varieties, although scientific evidence shows that if the same effort had been put into such varieties, they would be as good [as] or better than hybrids by now."[45] The unfortunately named "Green" Revolution (considering that it required giant doses of fertilizer, pesticides, irrigation, and fossil-fuel use) had terrible consequences. According to physicist, activist, and author Vandana Shiva:

> In India alone, twenty years of Green Revolution agriculture have succeeded in destroying the fertility of Punjab's soils. These soils were maintained across centuries by generations of farming families and could have been indefinitely maintained if international "experts" and Indian followers had not mistakenly believed that technologies could substitute for land, and that chemicals could replace the organic fertility of soils.
>
> Today, 24 billion metric tons of fertile soils are lost from world agricultural systems each year. India is losing 6.6 billion metric tons of soil per year, China is losing 5.5 billion metric tons, and the United States is losing 3 billion metric tons. In fact, soil is being lost at ten to forty times the rate at which it can be replenished naturally. Soil nutrients lost to erosion cost $20 billion annually.[46]

Whether Wallace was motivated by social or entrepreneurial concerns, his example gets to the crux of the matter. There is always a problem—a hitch—when ostensibly progressive agendas are aligned with those of capital accumulation and become part of maintaining the system as a whole. Today this is happening with self-identified environmentalists positioning themselves as the architects of a new capitalism, promoting technological change, the Green New Deal, and the Green Economy. In other words, mainstream environmentalists have made maintenance of the status quo part of their own agenda.

In 2012, Greenpeace's chief policy advisor wrote, "Greens Can Build the New Capitalism."[47] A writer for the *Harvard Business Review* agrees, describing environmental NGOs as part of the third leg of a balanced stool, the other two being the government and private industry. Their shared purpose, like FDR's goal with the New Deal, is to "rescue capitalism from itself."[48] But if the right to profit remains sacrosanct, what happens when ecological, social, and economic priorities inevitably collide? Without a reversal of the power imbalances capitalism imposes and maintains, who decides what the trade-offs will be, which priorities will win the day? Even with liberal reforms and the expansion of democracy, the capitalist class remains intact and in power. As they have always done, elites as a group will, at the end of the day, attempt to stop or reverse efforts that threaten to truly redress injustice and inequality, and to end ecologically damaging practices, because such measures endanger their wealth and position—their very existence as elites.

Moreover, isn't the Green New Deal aiming rather low in comparison to the extremist path down which the global power elite are leading the planet? In the 1930s, elites had to be convinced that massive social upheaval, even revolution, was on the table before the best provisions of the New Deal could pass Congress. What can we possibly achieve if we take the New Deal as our starting point? While important reforms were achieved in the New Deal era, especially due to the hard work of organizers and activists pushing the reformist agenda of FDR's administration to the left, we must acknowledge the reality of an ever-growing ecological crisis—not only under conservative, but under liberal and "progressive" politics as usual—which all scientific projections show worsening absent more radical political action. As Naomi Klein puts it, "science is telling us all to revolt."[49]

At the global level, rather than revolt, mainstream environmental organizations are following the wealthiest countries and most powerful industries in advocating the "Inclusive Green Economy" and "Inclusive Green Growth"—helping prettify a historically unfounded defense of capital-friendly approaches to environmentalism. The UN, the Organisation for Economic Co-operation and Development, the African Development Bank, and the World Bank worked together in 2012–13 to provide the framework for initiatives under the heading "Green Growth."[50] Many environmental organizations reject the worst aspects of these proposals. But in framing their own goals in terms of the Green Economy and Green New Deal, rather than explicitly rejecting green capitalism, they lend such initiatives credibility, or at least plausibility. This represents a major shift and problem. As law professor and social scientist Paddy Ireland writes, "It used to be the left who emphasized the limits to capitalism and the right who told us of its adaptability. Now, however, it is the right, believing themselves liberated from the credible threat of class struggle worldwide, who candidly stress the incompatibility of workers rights, [environmental regulations,] and welfare states with the elementary laws of capital (presented, of course, as 'natural'), while the (erstwhile) left is reduced to insisting on the malleability and improvability of both capitalism and its corporations."[51]

Language matters, especially when the world is facing an ecological crisis of unprecedented proportions, because words can either make the situation and the possible solutions starkly clear, or they can obfuscate and obscure both the present reality and the future possibilities, facilitating harmful ecological denial. Today the dominant language, even within the environmental movement, is infected by *la langue de coton*, or "woolen language"—a term used by scholars to describe the veiled doublespeak of capitalism that "has an answer to everything because it says nothing."[52] Globally, agencies and organizations employ the *langue de coton* of capitalist environmental management in lieu of concrete actions to facilitate the transition of societies away from being life-destroying oligopolies and toward becoming democracies operating within ecological limits.

In this language, we are all "stakeholders," with access to the "knowledge products" that international agencies like UNEP make available for us to use in "innovative partnerships." To achieve sustainable development goals, they say, will require "overcoming sectoral and institutional boundaries" and "innovative partnership[s] to build synergies across silos of experience." No mention is made of the need for social struggle or social change. The language of the Green Economy has all the "hallmarks of neoliberalism's langue de coton," which, as scholar of rhetoric and composition Nancy Welch explains, includes "presupposition and effacement, tautological vagueness, and a tangled mix of metaphors."[53]

The Green New Deal and the Inclusive Green Economy

The original Global Green New Deal report commissioned by UNEP was prepared for its Green Economy Initiative in 2009.[54] Today, UN agencies refer less to the Global Green New Deal, instead emphasizing the Inclusive Green Economy as central to meeting Sustainable Development Goals (SDGs). As described on the UNEP webpage:

> Achieving the SDGs demands stronger, innovative and multi-stakeholder partnerships to mobilise and share knowledge, expertise, technology and financial resources. Both the UN system and national governments have recognized that achieving the goals and targets for the 2030 Agenda will require overcoming sectoral and institutional boundaries, and embracing a more integrated and coherent approach. . . .
>
> With the adoption of the 2030 Agenda for Sustainable Development and the success of the Paris Climate Summit in 2015, the GGKP's [Green Growth Knowledge Platform] objectives of encouraging widespread collaboration, addressing knowledge and data gaps, and supporting practitioners and policymakers with the latest analysis and data, are more relevant and necessary than ever. Furthermore, the

> GGKP web platform draws together over 2,000 knowledge products from more than 300 leading organisations, making it the largest existing source of green growth knowledge.[55]

According to this report, the Green Economy is an "everybody wins" economy. As the authors write, "Multiple benefits can stem from an integrated approach such as economic, health, security, social and environmental by maximizing, prioritizing and sequencing them to produce a healthy environment." Design principles of the program "are based on sharing, circularity, collaboration, solidarity, resilience, opportunity and interdependence." Further, "To create an Inclusive Green Economy these elements must speak to socio-ecological and economy-wide transitions."[56]

Who could object to a "healthy environment," "sharing," "collaboration," "solidarity," and "resilience"? This type of language—some adopted from progressive movements and some emerging from corporate management theory and doublespeak—trickled down to liberal politics, as illustrated by former British prime minister Tony Blair's declaration of Britain as a "stakeholder society." Welch writes of such language that, "it is precisely the generic and banal—an irenicism so complete . . . 'it suffocates meaning'—that woolen language aims for: ruffling no feathers, raising no hackles by offering no substantive statements at all." Welch goes on to explain that "woolen language . . . aims at consensus, though it is a consensus won" at the cost of genuine democratic engagement and debate. "Woolen language is thus fashioned to serve as 'a consensual language of power *par excellence*' " that depends "not just on the middling might of its metaphors, the soporific effects of its style. It depends also, above all, on the steady disavowal of any controversy as decisions are moved out of participatory, public, and accountable realms and as a public is trained to leave decision-making authority 'to the experts.' "[57]

Turning specifically to agriculture, two central components of the Green Economy related to agronomy, and central to the question of further dust-bowlification, are Climate-Smart Agriculture and the Paris Climate Agreement. In the language of these programs, as Welch puts it, "we find a further defining feature of neoliberal rhetoric: anti-performativity, where it matters little if something has been done as long as one says it has."[58]

Climate-Smart Agriculture

According to the UN's Food and Agriculture Organization (FAO), "Climate-smart agriculture is a pathway towards development and food security built on *three pillars:* increasing productivity and incomes, enhancing resilience of livelihoods and ecosystems and reducing and removing greenhouse gas emissions from the atmosphere."[59] The FAO provides a sourcebook to "help stakeholders to plan climate-smart production systems and landscapes," which is necessary because "agriculture policies are the basis for achieving food security and improving livelihoods. An effective combination of sustainable agriculture and climate change policies can boost green growth, protect the environment and contribute to the eradication of hunger and poverty." The report says that the "FAO works closely with many of the world's most vulnerable populations to help them increase their agricultural productivity, while ensuring that the natural resources they depend on are not exploited or depleted. FAO is working to support countries in transitioning to climate-smart agriculture in a number of ways."[60]

Old approaches to capitalist environmental management are now dressed up in new clothes like "climate-smart agriculture" (CSA), coopting the acronym long used to refer to "community-supported agriculture." Promoted in the name of "climate change resilience" by the FAO and governments and corporations around the world, the emphasis of climate-smart agriculture retains the familiar goal of recasting and modernizing local agriculture, as the glossy online guide, *Climate-Smart Agriculture* 101, reveals.[61]

This CSA approach ignores the stranglehold that agribusiness has on global croplands and ignores the established fact that the modern era's technologically advanced, but socially and ecologically destructive, farming for profit continues to generate massive global problems. As agronomist Miguel Altieri writes,

> Recently FAO along with other international organizations (i.e., CGIAR [formerly the Consultative Group on International Agricultural Research]) have embraced a version of agroecology, regarded as an option that can be practiced along with other approaches such as transgenic crops, conservation farming, microdosing of fertilizers and herbicides, and integrated pest management. They propose adjusting the ecological inefficiencies of industrial agriculture through "sustainable intensification," e.g., by increasing efficiency of water and fertilizer use, and confronting climate change by deploying "climate-smart" genetic varieties. Of course this vision renders the term agroecology meaningless, like sustainable agriculture, a concept devoid of meaning, and divorced from the reality of farmers, the politics of food and of the environment. In fact, these superficial technical adjustments are ideologically buttressed by intellectual projects to reframe and redefine agroecology by stripping it of its political and social content and promote the wrong notion that agroecological methods can co-exist alongside the aggressive expansion of industrial agriculture, transgenic crops and agrofuels. Agroecology does not need to be combined with other approaches.[62]

La Via Campesina, an international coalition of 168 (at the time of writing) peasant organizations advocating socially and ecologically sound agriculture and food sovereignty for communities, is one of a number of movement organizations that take a dim view of this rhetoric coming from the United Nations and elsewhere about the importance of "climate-smart" agricultural practices and the stakeholder model (or language) of inclusion.[63] They declare climate-smart agriculture a "false solution."[64] And, in denouncing the stakeholder model and rhetoric of "inclusiveness" that many environmental organizations have adopted, they call for a more radical approach to people's decision making. Similarly, Bob Goulais, speaking on behalf of the Union of Ontario Indians in their struggle against Nestle's bid for Great Lakes water, expressed the sentiments of people around the world when he declared, "We're not stakeholders but bonafide owners. . . . The Great Lakes are not for sale."[65]

Unfortunately, many environmentalists, rather than challenging the celebratory and conciliatory rhetoric of green capitalism, have succumbed to it. Never was this clearer than in the wake of the signing of the Paris Climate Agreement—viewed as a central pillar of the Green Economy.

Change We Can Believe In?

In February 2016 an international assemblage of scientists published a paper in *Nature Climate Change* titled "Consequences of Twenty-First Century Policy for Multi-Millennial Climate and Sea-Level Change."[66] The article's most breathtaking statement was that "policy decisions made in the next few years to decades will have profound impacts on global climate, ecosystems and human societies—not just for this century, but for the next ten millennia and beyond."[67] This statement appeared two months after the 2015 United Nations Climate Change Conference in Paris (otherwise known as the 21st Conference of the Parties [COP 21]), which the media widely described as representing a crossroads, or critical juncture, for civilization with respect to climate change.

Those bullish on the deal struck in Paris took their cues from U.S. president Barack Obama, German chancellor Angela Merkel, and French foreign minister Laurent Fabius, who all separately, but in unison, deemed the agreement a "turning point," while Chinese president Xi Jinping called it "a new starting point."[68] If Paris was a crossroads, leaders were eager to declare that they had "set the world on a new path, to a low-emissions, climate-resilient future," as then UN Secretary-General Ban Ki-Moon said. CEOs of major firms, the *Financial Times*, and OECD Secretary-General Angel Gurría also picked up the "turning point" phrase, and representatives of environmental organizations repeated it throughout the green media.[69] Michael Brune, executive director of the Sierra Club, called Paris "a turning point for humanity," and Kumi Naidoo, then Greenpeace International executive director, said that "the wheel of climate action turns slowly, but in Paris it has turned."[70]

However, even supporters of the agreement, like economist Nicholas Stern, president of the British Academy for the humanities and social sciences, who also referred to Paris as a "turning point," acknowledged that "current pledges for emissions limits in 2030 fall short of the collective ambition required" to bring them within a range that will avert catastrophe.[71] The UN *Report of the Conference of Parties* associated with the Paris agreement itself acknowledges that there is a "significant gap" between pledged emissions reductions and the goal of maintaining a safe level of warming.[72] Stern and other commentators are optimistic that countries will make up the difference later. But many of the world's leading scientists take a starkly different view, resulting in what an Associated Press article called a "clash of dueling climate realities: science and politics."[73]

As the climate deal took shape in Paris in December 2015, the *New York Times* reported, "Scientists See Catastrophe in the Latest Draft of Climate Deal."[74] Kevin Anderson, deputy director of the Tyndall Centre for Climate Change Research, wrote in *Nature*, "I was in Paris, and there was a real sense of unease among many scientists present. The almost euphoric atmosphere that accompanied the circulation of the various drafts could not be squared with their content. . . . It is pantomime season and the world has just gambled its future on the appearance in a puff of smoke of a carbon-sucking fairy godmother. The Paris agreement is a road map to a better future? Oh no it's not."[75] For the poorest people in the world, Anderson said, the Paris draft agreement was "somewhere between dangerous and deadly."[76]

Physicist and climate scientist Bill Hare writes, "even if warming this century is held to 1.5° C, many regions will still experience substantial damage from extreme heat waves, including severe damage to water resources and threats to food security. For example, coral reefs, already hit by the recent [2016] massive global bleaching event, will still be at grave risk of severe degradation and/or loss. Even just a further half degree warming, to 2° C above preindustrial levels, entails a stark increase in risks and damages that only become worse for even higher degrees of warming."[77] The UN's 2016 Emissions Gap report stipulates that if stronger action on emissions reductions is not taken before 2020—currently there is no evidence suggesting this will happen at the pace or scale necessary—"the door will close on the 1.5C warming limit."[78]

So why would figures like Nicholas Stern and Kumi Naidoo, who express concern for the poor and global injustice, praise the Paris pact, given the views of scientists like Anderson and Hare regarding its social implications?[79] Expressing such optimism, however cautiously and regardless of their intentions, helps sell the public a treacherous deal. Even if all the terms of the agreement are fulfilled, which would be unprecedented in the history of international climate pacts, communities and ecosystems around the world already are and increasingly will be, as the UN acknowledges, knowingly sacrificed: in the words of UNEP Executive Director Erik Solheim, an "avoidable human tragedy."[80]

Certainly, there are many serious problems with the Paris Climate Agreement from an ecological justice perspective and, more broadly, with current efforts to "green" capitalism—not least of which are their reinforcement of, and reliance upon, new forms of colonialism and imperialism. For all of these reasons, indigenous leaders have taken a stand in stark opposition to those celebrants of Paris.

In May 2016, the fifteenth session of the United Nations Permanent Forum on Indigenous Issues convened in New York City. Concern for issues related to the Paris agreement was a prominent theme in this series of meetings. Representatives from indigenous communities around the world decried ongoing violations of their rights to land, water, clean air, self-determination, and existence itself. In particular, indigenous leaders described the continuing struggles against incursions that were now routinely taking place under "green" cover. Calfin Lafkenche, a Mapuche leader from Chile, summarized points reiterated by other participants:

> We are here today in the UN to stop the offensive of the Green Economy and its market systems of carbon trading, carbon offsets, the Clean Development Mechanism, and REDD+, which constitute a new form of colonialism and have caused conflicts, forced relocation, threats to the cultural survival and violations of the rights of Indigenous peoples, especially the rights to life, to lands and territories, and to free, prior and informed consent.[81]

Representatives protested the 2015 Paris Climate Agreement as an embodiment of this new colonialism. Alberto Saldamando, human and indigenous rights expert and attorney with the Indigenous Environmental Network, said:

> The Paris Agreement is a trade agreement, nothing more. It promises to privatize, commodify and sell forest and agriculture lands as carbon offsets in fraudulent schemes. . . . These offset scams provide financial laundering mechanisms for developed countries to launder their carbon pollution in the Global South. Case-in-point, the United States' climate change plan includes 250 million megatons to be absorbed by oceans and forest offset markets. Essentially, those responsible for the climate crisis not only get to buy their way out of compliance but they also get to profit from it as well.[82]

Moreover, the Paris decision document explicitly states that while recognizing uneven responsibilities for climate change and the need for collaborative approaches to address climate-related problems, "Article 8 of the Agreement [addressing loss and damages] does not involve or provide a basis for any liability or compensation."[83]

This is quite a diplomatic coup for the wealthier countries most responsible for climate change. First, the agreement absolves them from legal obligations to curtail emissions at rates that would reduce warming to levels scientists suggest could avert disaster. Second, it ensures the wealthier countries cannot be held liable when disaster hits as a result of insufficient action. Finally, approval from leaders of some environmental organizations lends the whole scheme credibility at the same time as an alliance of indigenous and climate justice organizations from North America and Canada with a delegation at the COP 21 negotiations call the Paris agreement a "dangerous distraction that threatens all of us."[84]

Altogether, the Paris agreement keeps the status quo intact while giving the impression that significant change is on the way.

Significant change *is* on the way. But it looks very different to climate scientists and frontline communities than it does to mainstream environmentalists and politicians. Indeed, the coming change appears so harrowing that to understand it and how it will affect people, prominent scientists are looking back to the Dust Bowl, one of the most dramatic social and ecological disasters in history. Two months before the Paris agreement took shape, NASA's chief scientist, Ellen Stofan, likened the current period to the 1930s and warned that a new Dust Bowl era is on the horizon for regions around the world.[85] As physicist and author Joseph Romm put it in an article in *Nature*, "A 2007 analysis of 19 climate projections estimated that levels of aridity comparable to those in the Dust Bowl could stretch from Kansas to California by mid-century. . . . Recent studies have projected 'extreme drought' conditions by mid-century over some of the most populated areas on Earth—southern Europe, south-east Asia, Brazil, the US Southwest, and large parts of Australia and Africa. These dust-bowl conditions are projected to worsen for many decades and be 'largely irreversible for 1,000 years after emissions stopped.' "[86]

This alarming prospect raises many important issues and questions. Despite all of the scientific research, knowledge, analysis, and forewarning, delegates from nearly 200 nations signed an agreement that condemns a large portion of their populations and environments. And they celebrated!

How can the environmental movement find a way forward when so many people in power and with green credentials are proclaiming that society has already made the crucial turn at the crossroads and is now moving in the right direction (with some hiccups, such as the Trump administration)? How do we redress the injustice faced by communities that are, as Indigenous Environmental Network executive director Tom B. K. Goldtooth puts it, "on the frontlines of climate change and false solutions to climate change."[87]

So far this book has investigated how we arrived at this particular crossroads, where we now confront another distressing incongruence between mainstream politics and economics on the one hand, and ecology and justice on the other. The previous chapters make clear that this is not the first time in modern history the world system has reached a breaking point. It is not the first time scientists and activists have warned that human and ecological catastrophe was imminent, and then watched in horror as their predictions came true. Nor is it the first time influential environmentalists have taken politics at face value and put their faith in an imperial political-economic system that can never accomplish what it claims—ultimately finding themselves on the wrong side of history and justice. Finally, it is not the first time that indigenous communities were on the front lines of both ecological crises and false solutions to crises that reinforced the colonial status quo. The 1930s represent just such a moment, an earlier crossroads, when fateful decisions determined the future of generations, including ours. What are the lessons of this past for the current crossroads at which we still stand?

NO EMPIRES, NO DUST BOWLS: TOWARD A DEEPER ECOLOGICAL SOLIDARITY

> A red line is a point of no return or a limit past which safety can no longer be guaranteed. Frontline communities are not only waging fights to stop extraction at the source. We are holding the uncompromising line of collective survival, and demonstrating real solutions that are within our grasp.
>
> We join the call for System Change, Not Climate Change because we know that the fundamental driving force behind the climate crisis is capitalism, and the very nature of the extractive economy as a whole. Climate justice is not only about the environment. It is tied to peace, jobs, housing, poverty, migration, food sovereignty, gender equality, and access to health care. System Change requires fundamental respect for human rights, particularly the rights of Indigenous Peoples, as well as the rights of future generations and Mother Earth.
>
> —#ItTakesRoots to #GrowtheResistance, *We Are Mother Earth's Red Line: Frontline Communities Lead the Climate Justice Fight Beyond the Paris Agreement*, 2016

Learning the Real Lessons of the Dust Bowl

If we are to extricate ourselves from the current planetary socio-ecological crises, it is essential that we understand fully the dynamics of the first anthropogenic global environmental crisis, which are still at work today. The 1930s crisis involved the destruction and erosion of the living material beneath our feet on a then-unprecedented scale. Prairies, woodlands, pampas, and forests, nourished by the vibrant underworld of soil, in turn provide the soil's protection. During the "heyday of colonialism and imperialism," which included the consolidation of the first global agricultural market and food regime, fertile lands around the world were stripped of their profuse beauty and life.

The soil of these rich ecologies—necessary to support every terrestrial living creature, including humans—was shorn of its protective layer and the landscape was flattened to make way for the desolate monoculture of capitalist agriculture. Many lives were simply discarded and displaced to make way for the global land grab from the late 1800s to the early 1900s. The areas impacted and the lives mutilated were sacrifices. The worshipped gods were capital and profit. The religion was white supremacy.

The ecological crisis of the new imperialism, predicated upon the domination of peoples and attempted decimation of entire cultures, reached its apogee by the 1930s. In wetter parts of the world, massive quantities of eroded soil flushed into rivers, silting them to the point that river ecologies were disrupted and human navigation often became difficult.[1] In arid regions the soil's desiccated remains took flight, as in the plains of North America where, as Steinbeck wrote, "the wind felt over the earth, loosened the dust, and carried it away."[2] With their origins in the counties of southwest Kansas, west Texas and Oklahoma, northeast New Mexico, and southeast Colorado, towering dust clouds moved across the continent, precipitating the flight of poor farmers, themselves scattered to the wind.

For all their power, classic fictional and popular depictions of the Dust Bowl do not capture its broader context and dynamics. As discussed in the preceding chapters, neither do standard scholarly or official accounts. While rooted in sociological analyses, the chapters of this book present an integrated, interdisciplinary approach to resituating the Dust Bowl within the global historical development of the modern world system. In so doing, the links between the past and present are clarified, revealing the continuity of capitalism's racialized division of humanity and the rest of nature, as well as ongoing consequences of this division for the biosphere, people, and environmental politics.

This direct line connecting the Dust Bowl era to today means we must move beyond using the case as an analog, and instead understand it as antecedent to our current Epoch of Ecological Extremes. The imperial policies, practices, and ideological justifications that led to the global problem of soil erosion created the social conditions for expanded destruction since the Second World War, shaped the modern character of environmental policy and "politics as usual," and informed hegemonic notions of "sustainable development."

Some of the colonial dynamics that drove the crisis of erosion to its dramatic pitch in the 1930s, and shaped the early environmental movement, have changed—due especially to the massive struggles for national liberation, civil rights, the rights of peasants and rural workers, women's rights, indigenous sovereignty, and environmental justice. However, many of these dynamics, especially with respect to the capacity of the world system for ecological destructiveness, state violence and social control (via military, police, the judiciary, and surveillance), and ease with which foreign investors and companies drive ecological destruction around the world, are amplified in the present.

Attacks on indigenous sovereignty continue to this day as a new ethno-racial caste system has emerged on a world scale, with efforts to enforce it reflected overtly in the anti-immigrant, anti-refugee, anti-Muslim, pro-police and -imprisonment, and pro-military platforms of political parties throughout the recent decades of austerity, growing inequality, globalization, and financial crises. The persistence of ethno-racial caste also is reflected in the statistics on global inequality between and within nations. Wealth and political power continue to be disproportionately held by white men in Britain, Europe, and the white settler colonial states like the United States and Canada—though elites everywhere have benefited in an outsized fashion from developments over the past few decades. As Oxfam reports, we have entrenched a political and economic system only "working for the few."[3] The rise of China hasn't significantly altered this reality. Rather, evidence of anti-black racism and an imperial attitude toward non-Han peoples reflects, in part, the adoption of capitalist colonial ideological trappings as Chinese investors and the Chinese state extend their own imperial reach and find their place in the Eurocentric global economic culture.[4] Communities of color, ethnic minorities, and the poor, on the other hand, continue disproportionately to bear the burdens of industrial production, social control efforts (such as imprisonment and police brutality), wars for resources, climate change, and ecological deterioration—in other words, the flip side of the massive accumulation of wealth in the late twentieth and early twenty-first centuries.

The links between social domination and ecological degradation persist in the new ecological imperialism of our time, wherein all of these dynamics merge. As I write in July 2017, the year is set to be the bloodiest since UN record-keeping began for environmental defenders and indigenous activists. The UN special rapporteur on human rights and the environment, John Knox, stated just this month: "There is now overwhelming incentive to wreck the environment for economic reasons. The people most at risk are people who are already marginalized and excluded from politics and judicial redress, and are dependent on the environment. The countries do not respect the rule of law. Everywhere in the world, defenders are facing such threats."[5] Explaining the uptick in attacks, Knox said, "There is an epidemic now, a culture of impunity, a sense that anyone can kill environmental defenders without repercussions, eliminate anyone who stands in the way. It [comes from] mining, agribusiness, illegal logging and dam building."[6] What Max Weber wrote during his 1904 visit to Indian Territory (part of what is now the state of Oklahoma) is true today: "everything that stands in the way of capitalist culture is being crushed."[7]

Such dynamics help explain the ongoing desecration of the land and the inability of environmental "politics as usual" to keep pace. Nowhere is this clearer than in the trends that are leading scientists to declare we are entering a New Dust Bowl period. The interconnected problems of land degradation, freshwater scarcity, and climate change are unimaginable at their current scale without the persistence of ecological imperialism. The New Dust Bowl period has many of the reprehensible hallmarks of the first, with vast consequences for the land and people.

The New Land Rush

In a throwback to an earlier age of overt colonialism and marking its reappearance in a different guise, in November 2009 the *New York Times Magazine* ran an article titled "Is There Such a Thing as Agro-Imperialism?"[8] In it, author Andrew Rice examines how governments, corporations, and wealthy individuals are dealing with continued land degradation, climate change, and freshwater scarcity. The dwindling availability of good, well-watered agricultural land as a result of these problems has led to a new land rush in supposedly less exploited parts of the globe. Land acquisition is pursued as an investment that will pay off when times get harder and land and food are more expensive, or as a way to guarantee food sources for home countries. These modern day land grabbers are honing in, as did their predecessors, on the African continent. Rice explains,

> Because much of the world's arable land is already in use—almost 90 percent, according to one estimate, if you take out forests and fragile ecosystems—the search has led to the countries least touched by development, in Africa. According to a recent study by the World Bank and the United Nations Food and Agriculture Organization, one of the earth's last large reserves of underused land is the billion-acre Guinea Savannah zone, a crescent-shaped swath that runs east across Africa all the way to Ethiopia, and southward to Congo and Angola.[9]

Rice quotes Susan Payne, CEO of Emergent Asset Management, saying that "Africa is the Final Frontier. . . . It's the one continent that remains relatively unexploited." In Africa, the reporter adds, "land and labor come so cheaply that she [Payne] calculates that the risks are worthwhile."[10]

As this new land grab unfolds, Rice takes keen note of the contradiction between the humanitarian rhetoric of UN officials and the actual role of international agencies in promoting what activists around the world have decried as neocolonialism: "The Food and Agriculture Organization, for instance, co-sponsored a report calling for a major expansion of commercial agriculture in Africa, but the organization's director-general has simultaneously been warning of the 'neocolonial' dangers of land deals."[11] As director-general of the

FAO, Jacques Diouf said in 2008, at the height of the increase in food prices and food riots in twenty-eight countries, "The risk is of creating a neo-colonial pact for the provision of non-value-added raw materials in the producing countries and unacceptable work conditions for agricultural workers."[12] Yet since that time land acquisitions in Africa and elsewhere by global investors and governments, encouraged by international agencies and institutions, have continued unabated.[13]

The *Financial Times* in 2016 published an investigative series on the heady investment atmosphere associated with what they termed the new "Great Land Rush."[14] One highlighted region was a rural area in the Ethiopian lowlands: "This remote spot is a frontier in a contest for land that stretches from Myanmar to Saskatchewan. Investors are betting billions on an asset that is both more abundant and fiercely contested than any other." With climate change, drought and more extreme and unpredictable weather events disrupting agricultural production, the *Financial Times* expects the phenomenon to expand further and projects that "the struggle playing out in the Ethiopian lowlands is a glimpse of others to come in a crowded, warming world."[15]

Affirming these accounts, a 2015 report by the Worldwatch Institute stated that "over half of the global land grabbed is in Africa, especially in water-rich countries like the Congo," while "the largest area acquired from a single country is in Papua New Guinea."[16] While the *New York Times* article focused on land grabs by countries in the Middle East and by China, the Worldwatch report explains that globally "the largest investor country is the United States." Even though the United States is already a major agricultural producer, it "has acquired about 7 million hectares worldwide."[17]

Activists Edward Loure and Fred Nelson warned about another aspect of the struggle for land in their 2016 *Guardian* article "The Global Land Rights Struggle Is Intensifying."[18] Loure describes his family's eviction from land in Tanzania to make way for a wildlife reserve. Indigenous groups continue to find themselves up against investors and environmental organizations, reflecting the history of conservation in the United States when national parks were created by forcefully evicting indigenous communities, while white settlers and investors were encouraged to claim and exploit the rest of western indigenous lands newly opened by conquest.[19]

Despite the highly problematic declaration of the FAO and World Bank that the African continent contains the "earth's last large reserves of underused land," a modern version of the colonial conception of *terra nullius*, a 2017 *New York Times* article describes how "the loss of fertile land fuels 'looming crisis' across Africa."[20] The author, Pulitzer Prize–winning journalist, and former *New York Times* East Africa Bureau Chief Jeffrey Gettleman, writes, "Data from NASA satellites reveals an overwhelming degradation of agricultural land throughout Africa, with one recent study showing that more than 40 million Africans are trying to survive off land whose agricultural potential is declining."[21] The basic situation is that "the quality of farmland in many areas is getting worse, and the number of people squeezed onto that land is rising fast."[22] This is on a continent where more people still make a living through agriculture than on any other.

Gettleman goes on to describe the scene on the continent in terms that might have come straight out of British or U.S. colonial administrative or soil science writing. There is a nod to the impact of white settlers and foreign investment, but the problem, in the end, centers on the natives, echoing earlier colonial narratives. There are too many people; they are misusing and degrading the land; they are consuming more; and the plague of drought means the international community will have to come to the rescue as times get worse and the inevitable famine settles over the land. The author describes class and racial conflict between the white, Anglo-European settlers and conservationists and the native population. Foreign investment in land is causing the eviction of small landholders in order to make way for "big commercial farms." And this time the old, familiar story has a twist: climate change is added to the cocktail of drivers that leave the soil "so dried out and exhausted that there is little solace even when the prayed-for rains finally come. The ground is as hard as concrete and the rain just splashes off, like a hose, spraying the driveway."[23] Rather than highlight the fact that the wealthy are most responsible for climate change and that the local people try to make a living on marginal lands as a result of the history of colonialism and neocolonialism, Gettleman hones in on overpopulation and fertility rates, as well as on the native "invaders" attempting to access privately owned land to graze their herds. He is also sure to point out that in Zimbabwe, when land previously owned by wealthy whites under the colonial regime was redistributed to indigenous people, "in many cases, the farms were run into the ground."[24]

For students of Dust Bowl history, and especially for readers of this book, such descriptions and events should ring a bell. The old imperialists are still at it in the United States and Europe, and empire builders from the Middle East and Asia have now joined suit. Much of the familiar terminology and scenery associated with the heyday of colonialism are still there: the "frontier," the "land rush" for "virgin soils" (as one author put it), the conflict between the hapless, too numerous natives and white settlers. If scientists already project a grim future with respect to the soil, climate, and water, what do these additional trends portend?

Back in the United States, there are even renewed calls to privatize remaining tribal lands and make their resources available for exploitation. For example, right-wing columnist and author Naomi Schaefer Riley published an article in the *Atlantic* called "One Way to Help Native Americans: Property Rights" and wrote a book on the topic, *The New Trail of Tears*, published in 2016.[25] The idea was a major part of President Donald Trump's agenda just after the 2016 elections. Headlines read: "Trump Advisors Aim to Privatize Oil-Rich American Indian Reservations" (Reuters, December 5, 2016); "Trump Advisers' Plan to 'Privatize' Indian Lands: Limited Potential" (*Forbes*, December 6, 2016); "A Misguided Plan to 'Privatize' Native Nations Lands?" (*Indian Country Today*, December 26, 2016).

While all of these developments raise again the ugly specter of the "white man's burden" and ecological imperialism, soil scientists are exposing the ways in which the earth is taking a hit and efforts to conserve the world's soils are failing.

The State of Global Soils

In 2013 the first plenary session of the Global Soil Partnership, initiated by the UN's Food and Agriculture Organization, met at the FAO headquarters in Rome.[26] It established the Intergovernmental Technical Panel on Soils (ITPS), comprised of twenty-seven soil experts representing all regions of the world.[27] One of the panel's primary responsibilities was to produce the first *Status of the World's Soils Report (SWSR)* for publication in 2015. Scientists involved concluded that "while there is cause for optimism in some regions, the overwhelming conclusion from the report is that the majority of the world's soils are in only fair, poor, or very poor condition."[28] Furthermore, "the current outlook is for the situation to worsen—unless concerted action is taken by individuals, the private sector, governments, and international organizations."[29]

The section of the main report on the "drivers of global soil change" begins with a discussion of population growth and urbanization; in other words, in line with decades-old colonial and elite discourse and reports cited in previous chapters, it focuses on poor people.[30] The rural poor, the report states, "often farm marginal lands of low agricultural productivity, typically employing traditional farming methods. This may aggravate soil degradation and biodiversity decline, with resulting yield losses and food insecurity."[31]

Proximate causes cited for the current crisis are industrial agriculture, farming on marginal lands, increased production of biofuels, economic development, military conflict, population growth, and lack of education of farmers, among other factors. When the report's authors discuss commercial agriculture, they are careful to point out that soil erosion is caused by "inappropriate agricultural practices in both subsistence and large-scale high-input commercial agriculture" on the steeper lands in Latin America and the Caribbean.[32] They note that the poor countries will have to make "difficult decisions on the trade-offs between preserving natural ecosystems and economic development."[33]

Some of the report's diagnoses echo the ahistorical and seemingly (though impossibly) apolitical Dust Bowl narratives that focus on the ill-suited techniques of uneducated plainsmen operating on vulnerable lands. Nevertheless, the warning of the ITPS scientists is clear enough: "If soil is managed poorly, it is impossible to be optimistic about the future. . . . The current trajectories in soil condition have potentially catastrophic consequences that will affect millions of people in some of the most vulnerable regions over coming decades. More importantly, the global community is presently ill-prepared and ill-equipped to mount a proportionate response."[34]

That the global community is ill-prepared to mount a "proportionate response" to the crisis is both unsurprising—given the international responses to climate change, the Syrian refugee crisis, and the attempted ethnic cleansing of the Rohingya people in Myanmar—but still devastating to consider, especially in light of the history detailed in this book and the known consequences for communities around the world. While the warning in the report is clear, the manner in which it is delivered is very troubling. Similar reports on a range of topics neutralize any possible feeling regarding these issues, which are life and death to so many, by following professional standards of technical dispassion as they sound a death knell to the earth's soil. In the face of catastrophe, the most we can feel is that "it is impossible to be optimistic." But, why can we not accomplish the goals set out by the authors—who are some of the world's top soil scientists—and implement the measures so many already know would allow us to avoid catastrophe? What are the barriers to change? They offer no observations on this point that approach the clarity and forthrightness of colonial soil scientists Graham Vernon Jacks and Robert Orr Whyte in the 1930s, who wrote plainly, "So long as the land yielded fat profits, the restrictive measures which were already recognized as necessary if the soil were to be saved had no chance of being applied."[35]

A key to understanding the FAO panel's politically limited universe may be found in its glossary, which includes the definition of soil degradation for the purposes of the report. This entry reads, "Soil degradation: the diminishing capacity of the soil to provide ecosystem goods and services as desired by its stakeholders."[36] This isn't an ecological or even scientific definition, but a political one that reduces human communities and the rest of nature to ecosystem services and an unclear set of stakeholders. Are stakeholders the world's most powerful institutions, such as corporations? Are they subsistence farmers? Rice plants? Worms? Can you imagine the same definition in relation to climate change? Who are the stakeholders of the world's land, air, and water other than every living being on the planet, each of which is dependent upon all three? Which stakeholders get to decide how much degradation is too much and what we do about it?

Whether the global scientists of ITPS do not understand the systemic nature of the problems, or global environmental politics and cultural norms of contemporary science have limited what may be studied and included in such reports, the apolitical tone with respect to a very political topic is dismaying and only serves to reinforce the political status quo and leave the barriers to implementation of their suggested actions to address erosion a mystery. Moreover, the most recent World Soil Compact, informed by the work of this panel of scientists and signed in 2015, has no more teeth than the Paris Climate Agreement.

The Red Line or the Bottom Line?

One of the major limitations of environmental politics today, evident in policymaking and official reporting at the national and international levels, as well as in mainstream environmental organizations, is that the ahistorical worldview they promote limits the understanding both of past socio-ecological changes and of possibilities for the future. The consequence is a hegemonic environmental politics that reinforces, rather than challenges, the social status quo and contributes to the social organization of irresponsibility and forms of ecological denial. This despite a century's worth of evidence that shows these politics are ineffectual in addressing ecological crises on the scale necessary to avoid devastating impacts on life on earth. Such politics cannot really make the connections "between the guns that take black lives on the streets of US cities and in police custody and the much larger forces that annihilate so many black lives on arid land and in precarious boats around the world."[37] If they did, it would be clear that the direct links between such issues imply the need for a dramatically different kind of environmentalism.

In previous chapters I have discussed the historical factors contributing to the development of mainstream approaches to ecological change. In sum, the imperial origins of modern mainstream environmentalism resulted in a segregated environmental movement worldwide, and led to a stark divide between what activists and scholars refer to as "the environmentalism of the rich" and "the environmentalism of the poor."[38] Political and economic elites have an outsized influence and control over government and international environmental agencies.[39] Mainstream environmental organizations are supported by, and dependent upon, the patronage of the wealthy, which impacts their priorities and strategies.

Decision makers within major environmental institutions tend to be economically privileged and therefore do not necessarily have the lived experience of oppression under capitalism informing their perspective. They are therefore more susceptible to the ideological developments that celebrate green capitalism and reinforce Eurocentric ideas, and less likely to search for alternatives. Because of their backgrounds, they are also more likely to identify with political and economic elites and view them as primary partners in social change, rather than with oppressed communities struggling for more significant social change. They accept the ideological flattening of power imbalances and gloss over the reality of conflict to adopt the "stakeholder" model of inclusion and decision making. Environmental agencies and organizations tend to hire people with backgrounds similar to those of the employees already there, reproducing their organizational culture.[40]

It is not surprising, under these circumstances, that environmentalists in leadership positions, whether they work for the United Nations or the World Wildlife Fund, don't see the conflict between holding the red line—as described by the It Takes Roots delegation report on Paris from which the epigraph for this chapter comes—and satisfying the bottom line of corporate financial reports. They usually have not lived, or do not have to live, where the deeper conflict plays out. They are not people forced to live on the front lines in Arctic communities, in the sacrifice zones of fossil-fuel and mineral extraction, in the Dust-Bowlified wastes where the waving wheat once softened and vivified the harder edges of the landscape. They don't have to live as either a fish or a local fisherman where the plastic is multiplying faster than the living beings, in bodies of water overfished by industrial trawlers, to the extent that scientists expect there to be more plastic in the ocean by weight than fish by 2050.[41]

However, no matter the specific class background or experience with racism or sexism, all of us have been raised under the "social gravity" of the racialized capitalist system—though it shapes our lives in very different ways.[42] Most of us think about the social system of which we are a part as much as we think about the air we breathe, or gravity itself. Hence, even if we are from frontline communities, we may have narrowed our vision of the possible, probable, or desirable. Sometimes we accept the unacceptable limitations of the current social order, internalizing them in our hearts and minds, or we accept them pragmatically to keep a job, maintain patronage, keep a "seat at the table," or otherwise not rock the corporate boat (or yacht) from which we can be thrown overboard.

Sociologist and activist Herbert Docena has written how the past several decades of environmentalists aligning with mainstream environmentalism—promoting a greener version of capitalism rather than a more radically democratic society—have weakened the global climate justice movement and narrowed its vision. He tells the story of how liberal elites have worked, as did the New Deal coalition, "to change the heart and soul" of the environmental movement by working to change the system in order to keep it the same—pushing a reformist agenda while coopting the more radical rhetoric of environmental or climate justice.[43]

However, because this agenda and the mechanisms that it puts in place, including international climate negotiations, have failed to ensure the "collective survival" defended by the It Takes Roots Alliance and many more today, there is a new resurgence of activism geared toward forging a deeper ecological solidarity to protect the planet and fight for justice. These are models from which to draw to move beyond the imperial legacy of green capitalist versions of environmentalism.

Docena writes that activists have often made a distinction between the people in the conference rooms and those in the streets, but that "whether and how the 'people in the streets' will build the 'power to change the world' and prevail over 'the people in the conference rooms' will likely depend on who wins the streets"—in other words, who wins the heart and soul of the environmental movement.[44]

Healing the Ecological Rift, Avoiding Global Dust Bowls

The authors of the *Status of the World's Soil Resources* wrote in 2015: "History will record whether this generation of decision makers responded with sufficient zeal to ensure that soil did indeed remain as humanity's silent ally."[45]

But who do we want as our decision makers? Under what conditions should they make decisions? In whose interests? These are the bigger questions that must be answered to address our current crises. We cannot continue to lump the rich and well-resourced with the poor, or to group the oppressor and the oppressed—those fighting against the liberation of others and those fighting for their own liberation—together as "stakeholders" in environmental conflicts. We cannot encourage mainstream environmental organizations—those on the privileged side of the segregated environmental movement and therefore more linked to power—to diversify their staff and memberships, without also challenging them to articulate a platform and practice of deeper ecological justice.

We must realize, as Naomi Klein said in her Edward Said Lecture delivered in London in 2016 titled "Let Them Drown: The Violence of Othering in a Warming World":

> A culture that places so little value on black and brown lives that it is willing to let human beings disappear beneath the waves, or set themselves on fire in detention centres, will also be willing to let the countries where

> black and brown people live disappear beneath the waves, or desiccate in the arid heat. When that happens, theories of human hierarchy—that we must take care of our own first—will be marshalled to rationalise these monstrous decisions. We are making this rationalisation already, if only implicitly. Although climate change will ultimately be an existential threat to all of humanity, in the short term we know that it does discriminate, hitting the poor first and worst, whether they are abandoned on the rooftops of New Orleans during Hurricane Katrina or whether they are among the 36 million who according to the UN are facing hunger due to drought in Southern and East Africa.[46]

Understanding that imperialism and the ethno-racial caste system it engenders are at the heart of our contemporary ecological and social crises points to the necessity of tackling the imperial system of capital head on.

The mainstream environmental movement has been hamstrung by disorienting claims that capitalism can solve the ecological crisis, and by misplaced faith in the "good capitalists" who will transform the world with technology and green or fairly traded products, or in international climate agreements such as the one presented in Paris in 2015.

Looking toward political and economic elites for salvation, and often relying on them for funding, significant segments of the movement are cut off from those with the greatest interest in transforming the system, the global working and dispossessed classes. This means they are not engaged in the arduous task of overcoming the historical divisions imposed by the racialized division of humanity and the rest of nature at the heart of the ecological rift of capitalism.

To break out of this cycle of historical violence, achieve genuine justice, and heal the ecological rift, we must add to the three R's of mainstream environmentalism—reduce, reuse, recycle—a more fundamental four: restitution (of lands and sovereignty, of power to the people), reparations (for slavery, stolen labor, genocide, and other past injustices), restoration (of earth systems), and revolution (moving away from capitalism).

Environmentalists cannot continue to defend or make peace with the status quo, without expecting the same results this has engendered in the past, but on a larger scale with respect to ecological crises and human trauma. The importance of learning from our history cannot be overstated. Debates over solutions to global ecological crises like climate change, soil degradation, and water scarcity too often proceed as if we have no historical evidence to help us understand what works and what doesn't work. The case of the Dust Bowl of the 1930s, which, as I have shown, was one dramatic regional manifestation of a global social and ecological crisis generated by settler colonialism and imperialism, illustrates the enormous consequences of relying on imperial "politics as usual" to attempt a change in "business as usual."

Similar to the ineffective (from a social and ecological standpoint) climate conferences held for decades by the UN, world leaders and mainstream environmentalism could not ultimately prevent or resolve the crisis of soil erosion in the 1930s because of their commitment to maintaining the global social and economic status quo—the racialized class system in which we still live today. The Dust Bowl did not arise because there was a lack of awareness of the issue or the technical means to address it. Like dust-bowlification today, the ultimate source of the crisis was social, not technological, thus requiring massive social change to address. At the heart of the matter is that allowing the "accumulation of injustice" makes inevitable the "accumulation of catastrophe." We must struggle within our movements, scientific communities, educational institutions, and broader policy worlds to transcend what Dr. Martin Luther King, Jr., saw as Western society's "proneness to adjust to injustice" and break free from what Karl Marx called "the tradition of all the dead generations" that in times of change "weighs like a nightmare on the brain of the living."[47] Our approach should be unapologetically *radical*—which simply means, from the Latin, that we must get *to the root* of things.

NOTES

Introduction

Epigraph. Transcript of interview with Melt White, "Surviving the Dustbowl," PBS *American Experience*, http://www.pbs.org/wgbh/americanexperience/features/interview/dustbowl-witness-white/, accessed September 25, 2016.

1. Joseph Romm, "Desertification: The Next Dust Bowl," *Nature* 478 (October 2011): 450–451, 450, doi: 10.1038/478450a; Joe Romm, "My Nature Piece on Dust-Bowlification and the Grave Threat It Poses to Food Security," *ThinkProgress*, May 24, 2012, https://thinkprogress.org/my-nature-piece-on-dust-bowlification-and-the-grave-threat-it-poses-to-food-security–6eeb25eaef20.
2. Romm, "Desertification," 450.
3. Matt Simon, "Fantastically Wrong: American Greed and the Harebrained Theory of 'Rain Follows the Plow,' " *Wired*, August 25, 2014, https://www.wired.com/2014/06/fantastically-wrong-rain-follows-the-plow/; Howard Berkes, "The Vision of John Wesley Powell: Explorer Foresaw Water Issues That Would Plague the West," NPR, August 26, 2003, http://www.npr.org/programs/atc/features/2003/aug/water/part1.html?a_aid=3598aabf.

   Manifest Destiny was an idea promoted by U.S. elites to recast white territorial expansion as both spreading democracy and following the will of God. See Julius W. Pratt, "The Origin of 'Manifest Destiny,' " *American Historical Review* 32, no. 4 (1927): 795–798, https://www.jstor.org/stable/pdf/1837859.pdf?refreqid=excelsior%3Acdc52e00136b7a83333934db6d9f5cef.
4. William Bryant Logan, *The Ecstatic Skin of the Earth* (New York: Norton, 2007 [1995]).
5. "Labor Unionism in American Agriculture," Bulletin No. 836, United States Department of Labor, Bureau of Labor Statistics (Washington, DC: U.S. Government Printing Office, 1945), esp. pp. 39–41 and 282–338.
6. "The Great Okie Migration," Smithsonian American Art Museum, http://americanexperience.si.edu/wp-content/uploads/2015/02/The-Great-Okie-Migration.pdf.

7. Indigenous peoples whose sovereignty and communities were attacked in the late 1800s had fought and survived earlier policies of extermination and forced relocation. Many of the indigenous nations represented in what became the Dust Bowl states had been forced onto reservations there by the U.S. military via the Trail of Tears and other episodes of violent removal from various regions of what is now the United States. During the late 1800s reservation land was targeted by allotment, which privatized indigenous lands and transferred lands deemed surplus to white settlers (see Chapter Three). There are many books on the opening of the West; see, for example, Dee Brown, *Bury My Heart at Wounded Knee: An Indian History of the American West* (New York: Henry Holt, 2000 [1970]).
8. National Drought Mitigation Center, "Drought in the Dust Bowl Years," http://drought.unl.edu/droughtbasics/dustbowl/droughtinthedustbowlyears.aspx, accessed April 15, 2016.
9. William Lockeretz, "The Lessons of the Dust Bowl: Several Decades Before the Current Concern with Environmental Problems, Dust Storms Ravaged the Great Plains, and the Threat of More Dust Storms Still Hangs Over Us," *American Scientist* 66 (September–October 1978): 560–569, 560.
10. Donald Worster, *Dust Bowl: The Southern Plains in the 1930s* (New York: Oxford University Press, 2004), 4. Given the extensive number of man-made ecological disasters in world history, it is unclear to me what valid criteria for ranking might be. The point here is that the Dust Bowl is significant both culturally and academically, as it helps us understand the modern social forces that contribute to ecological crises and act as barriers to their prevention and resolution.
11. Worster, *Dust Bowl*, 4.
12. William Riebsame, "The Dust Bowl: Historical Image, Psychological Anchor, and Ecological Taboo," *Great Plains Quarterly* 6, no. 2 (Spring 1986): 127–136, 127–128.
13. Worster, *Dust Bowl*, 25, 4.
14. Romm, "Desertification," 450–451; Romm, "My Nature Piece on Dust-Bowlification and the Grave Threat It Poses to Food Security."
15. Steve Cole and Leslie McCarthy, "NASA Study Finds Carbon Emissions Could Dramatically Increase Risk of U.S. Megadroughts," NASA, February 12, 2015, http://www.nasa.gov/press/2015/february/nasa-study-finds-carbon-emissions-could-dramatically-increase-risk-of-us.
16. Julia Calderon, "NASA Scientists Are Comparing Climate Change to the Dust Bowl," *Business Insider*, October 20, 2015.

17. Robert A. McLeman et al., "What We Learned from the Dust Bowl: Lessons in Science, Policy, and Adaptation," *Population and Environment* 35 (2014): 417–440, 436.
18. McLeman et al., "What We Learned from the Dust Bowl," 435.
19. Pare Lorentz, *The Plow That Broke the Plains*, Resettlement Administration, United States Farm Security Administration, 1936, http://plainshumanities.unl.edu/encyclopedia/doc/egp.fil.055.
20. Gilbert C. Fite, "Review of *The Dust Bowl: An Agricultural and Social History* by R. Douglas Hurt," *Great Plains Quarterly* 3, no. 4 (1983): 243–244, 244. Reference to: R. Douglas Hurt, *The Dust Bowl: An Agricultural and Social History* (Chicago: Nelson-Hall, 1981).
21. Carolyn Merchant, Preface to the Second Edition, *Ecological Revolutions: Nature, Gender, and Science in New England* (Chapel Hill: University of North Carolina Press, 2010 [1989]), xiii–xxii, xiv.
22. William Cronon, "A Place for Stories: Nature, History, and Narrative," *Journal of American History* 78, no. 4 (1992): 1347–1376, 1347.
23. Bonnifield as quoted in Cronon, "A Place for Stories," 1348.
24. Worster as quoted in Cronon, "A Place for Stories," 1348.
25. Steinbeck's book was made into a widely popular film and, along with his subsequent work, contributed to multiple nominations for the Nobel Prize in Literature, which he eventually won in 1962.
26. Worster, *Dust Bowl*, 96–97.
27. Dr. Ellen Stofan, "The Future We Can See: What the Earth Is Telling Us," speech at James Beard Foundation Future of Food Conference, October 19–20, 2015, http://livestream.com/jamesbeardfoundation/FoodConference2015/videos/10236969.
28. Barack Obama, "This Is Your Victory," speech, Grant Park, Chicago, November 4, 2008, CNN, http://edition.cnn.com/2008/POLITICS/11/04/obama.transcript/. The person he is referring to is Ann Nixon Cooper, an African-American woman who, being 106 years old, had lived to see women and African-Americans win the vote and, as President Obama says in this quote, witness Americans conquer the Dust Bowl.
29. David Anderson, "Depression, Dust Bowl, Demography, and Drought: The Colonial State and Soil Conservation in East Africa during the 1930's," *African Affairs* 83, no. 332 (July 1984): 321–343, 327.
30. W. E. B. DuBois, "The Souls of White Folk" [1920], *Monthly Review* 55, no. 6 (2003): 44–58, 55.
31. Branko Milanovic, "The Two Faces of Globalization: Against Globalization as We Know It," *World Development* 31, no. 4 (2003): 668.

32. Will Steffen, Wendy Broadgate, Lisa Deutsch, Owen Gaffney, and Cornelia Ludwig, "The Trajectory of the Anthropocene: The Great Acceleration," *Anthropocene Review* 2, no. 1 (2015): 81–98.
33. William H. McNeill, *The Global Condition* (Princeton: Princeton University Press, 1992), 135–149; William H. McNeill, "The Conservation of Catastrophe," *New York Review of Books*, December 20, 2001, http://www.nybooks.com/articles/2001/12/20/the-conservation-of-catastrophe/. Sociologist John Bellamy Foster developed McNeill's political economy in "Capitalism and the Accumulation of Catastrophe," *Monthly Review* 67, no. 7 (December 2011), http://monthlyreview.org/2011/12/01/capitalism-and-the-accumulation-of-catastrophe.
34. Ulrich Beck, "Climate for Change, or How to Create a Green Modernity?" *Theory, Culture and Society* 27, nos. 2–3 (2010): 254–266, 261.
35. Peter U. Clark et al., "Consequences of Twenty-First-Century Policy for Multi-millennial Climate and Sea-Level Change," *Nature Climate Change* 6 (February 2016): 360–369, http://www.nature.com/nclimate/journal/v6/n4/full/nclimate2923.html.
36. W. E. B. DuBois, "*The World and Africa*" *and* "*Color and Democracy*," ed. Henry Louis Gates, Jr. (New York: Oxford University Press, 2007); John Bellamy Foster and Hannah Holleman, "Weber and the Environment: Classic Foundations for a Postexemptionalist Sociology," *American Journal of Sociology* 117, no. 6 (May 2012): 1625–1673; Radhakamal Mukerjee, "The Ecological Outlook in Sociology," *American Journal of Sociology* 38, no. 3 (November 1932): 349–355, http://www.jstor.org/stable/2767475?seq=1#page_scan_tab_contents; Erin Murphy, "Women's Anti-Imperialism, 'The White Man's Burden,' and the Philippine-American War," *Asia-Pacific Journal* 7, no. 27 (July 6, 2009), http://apjjf.org/-Erin-Murphy/3182/article.html.
37. The Department of Sociology at KU today boasts renowned scholars in environmental sociology and social theory such as Joane Nagel and Robert J. Antonio.
38. Dorceta E. Taylor, "The Rise of the Environmental Justice Paradigm: Injustice Framing and the Social Construction of Environmental Discourses," *American Behavioral Scientist* 43, no. 4 (2000): 508–580, http://journals.sagepub.com/doi/abs/10.1177/0002764200043004003#articleCitationDownloadContainer.
39. Dorceta E. Taylor, *The Rise of the American Conservation Movement: Power, Privilege, and Environmental Protection* (Durham, NC: Duke University Press, 2016); Dorceta E. Taylor, *Race, Class, Gender, and American*

Environmentalism, United States Department of Agriculture, General Technical Report, PNW-GTR–534, April 2002, https://www.fs.fed.us/pnw/pubs/gtr534.pdf; Dorceta E. Taylor, *The State of Diversity in Environmental Organizations*, prepared for Green 2.0, July 2014, https://orgs.law.harvard.edu/els/files/2014/02/FullReport_Green2.0_FINALReducedSize.pdf.

40. John Bellamy Foster, Brett Clark, and Richard York, *The Ecological Rift: Capitalism's War on the Earth* (New York: Monthly Review Press, 2011).

41. Foster, Clark, and York, *The Ecological Rift*, 47.

42. Stefano Longo, Rebecca Clausen, and Brett Clark, *The Tragedy of the Commodity* (Brunswick, NJ: Rutgers University Press, 2015); Philip Mancus, "Nitrogen Fertilizer Dependency and Its Contradictions," *Rural Sociology* 72, no. 2 (June 2007), http://onlinelibrary.wiley.com/doi/10.1526/003601107781170008/full; Foster, Clark, and York, *The Ecological Rift*.

For a compendium of examples of some of the great work in this tradition, please see the metabolic rift bibliography published online by *Monthly Review*; it is a wonderful resource for scholars and activists alike: Ryan Wishart, R. Jamil Jonna, and Jordan Besek, "The Metabolic Rift: A Selected Bibliography," https://monthlyreview.org/commentary/metabolic-rift/. The "Environment & Science" section of the Haymarket Books online catalogue also lists important contributions in this area: Haymarket Books, "Environment & Science," http://haymarketbooks.org.

43. Mathew R. Sanderson and Scott R. Frey, "From Desert to Breadbasket . . . to Desert Again? A Metabolic Rift in the High Plains Aquifer," *Journal of Political Ecology* 21 (2014): 516–532.

44. David Naguib Pellow, *Total Liberation: The Power and Promise of Animal Rights and the Radical Earth Movement* (Minneapolis: University of Minnesota Press, 2014); David Naguib Pellow, *Resisting Global Toxics: Transnational Movements for Environmental Justice*, Urban and Industrial Environments series (Cambridge, MA: MIT Press, 2007); David Naguib Pellow and Robert J. Brulle, *Power, Justice and the Environment: A Critical Appraisal of the Environmental Justice Movement* (Cambridge, MA: MIT Press, 2005); David Naguib Pellow, "Toward a Critical Environmental Justice Studies: Black Lives Matter as an Environmental Justice Challenge," *DuBois Review* 2016: 1–16.

45. Kimberlé W. Crenshaw, "Mapping the Margins: Intersectionality, Identity Politics, and Violence against Women of Color," *Stanford Law Review* 43, no. 6 (July 1991): 1241–1299, http://www.jstor.org/stable/1229039?seq=1#page_scan_tab_contents; Kimberlé W. Crenshaw,

"Demarginalizing the Intersection of Race and Sex: A Black Feminist Critique of Antidiscrimination Doctrine, Feminist Theory and Antiracist Politics," *University of Chicago Legal Forum* 1989, no. 1: 139–167, http://chicagounbound.uchicago.edu/cgi/viewcontent.cgi?article=1052&context=uclf; Kimberlé Crenshaw et al., eds., *Critical Race Theory: The Key Writings that Formed the Movement* (New York: New Press, 1996).

46. Kari Marie Norgaard, *Living in Denial: Climate Change, Emotions, and Everyday Life* (Cambridge, MA: MIT Press, 2011); Kari Marie Norgaard, *Cognitive and Behavioral Challenges in Responding to Climate Change*, World Bank background paper to the 2010 World Development Report, http://documents.worldbank.org/curated/en/289171468331269847/pdf/WPS4940.pdf.
47. Evelyn Nakano Glenn, "Settler Colonialism as Structure: A Framework for Comparative Studies of U.S. Race and Gender Formation," *Sociology of Race and Ethnicity* 1, no. 1 (January 1, 2015): 52–72, 52, http://journals.sagepub.com/doi/abs/10.1177/2332649214560440; Arghiri Emmanuel, "White-Settler Colonialism and the Myth of Investment Imperialism," *New Left Review* 73 (May–June 1972), https://newleftreview.org/I/73/arghiri-emmanuel-white-settler-colonialism-and-the-myth-of-investment-imperialism; Patrick Wolfe, *Settler Colonialism and the Transformation of Anthropology: The Politics and Poetics of an Ethnographic Event*, Writing Past Colonialism series (London: Bloomsbury Academic, 1998).
48. Fred Magdoff and Harold van Es, *Building Soils for Better Crops*, 3rd ed. (College Park, MD: SARE Outreach, 2010); Fred Magdoff and Brian Tokar, *Agriculture and Food in Crisis: Conflict, Resistance and Renewal* (New York: New York University Press, 2010); Fred Magdoff, John Bellamy Foster, and Frederick H. Buttel, *Hungry for Profit: The Agribusiness Threat to Farmers, Food, and the Environment* (New York: Monthly Review Press, 2000); Fred Magdoff, "A Rational Agriculture Is Incompatible with Capitalism," *Monthly Review* 66, no. 10 (March 2015), https://monthlyreview.org/2015/03/01/a-rational-agriculture-is-incompatible-with-capitalism/.
49. Fred Magdoff and Chris Williams, *Creating an Ecological Society: Toward a Revolutionary Transformation* (New York: Monthly Review Press, 2017); see also Chris Williams, *Ecology and Socialism: Solutions to Capitalist Ecological Crisis* (Chicago: Haymarket Books, 2010).
50. Hannah Holleman and Rebecca Clausen, "Biofuels, BP-Berkeley, and the New Ecological Imperialism," *MR Online*, January 15, 2008, https://mronline.org/2008/01/15/biofuels-bp-berkeley-and-the-new-ecological-imperialism/; John Bellamy Foster and Hannah Holleman, "Weber and the Environment: Classical Foundations for a Postexemptionalist Sociology,"

American Journal of Sociology 117, no. 6 (May 2012): 1625–1673; Hannah Holleman, "Energy Policy and Environmental Possibilities: Biofuels and Key Protagonists of Ecological Change," *Rural Sociology* 77, no. 2 (June 2012): 280–307, http://onlinelibrary.wiley.com/doi/10.1111/j.1549-0831.2012.00080.x/abstract; Hannah Holleman and John Bellamy Foster, "The Theory of Unequal Ecological Exchange: A Marx-Odum Dialectic," *Journal of Peasant Studies* 41, no. 2 (2014): 199–233; Hannah Holleman, "Denaturalizing Ecological Disaster: Colonialism, Racism and the Global Dust Bowl of the 1930s," *Journal of Peasant Studies* 44, no. 1 (2017): 234–260, http://www.tandfonline.com/doi/abs/10.1080/03066150.2016.1195375.

One. Dust to Dust

Epigraph. Edward W. Said, *Culture and Imperialism* (New York: Vintage Books, 1993), 6.

1. Eric Hobsbawm, *The Age of Extremes, 1914–1991* (London: Abacus, 1995).
2. UNESCO, International Social Science Council, 2013 World Social Science Report, *Changing Global Environments* (Paris: OECD Publishing and UNESCO Publishing, 2013), www.unesco.org/new/en/social-and-human-sciences/resources/reports/world-social-science-report–2013/, accessed July 24, 2017.
3. Cheryl Dybas, "Life Underground Critical to Earth's Ecosystems," National Science Foundation, July 29, 2009, https://www.nsf.gov/discoveries/disc_summ.jsp?cntn_id=115253.
4. Dybas, "Life Underground Critical to Earth's Ecosystems."
5. Susan S. Lang, " 'Slow, Insidious' Soil Erosion Threatens Human Health and Welfare as Well as the Environment, Cornell Study Asserts," *Cornell Chronicle*, March 20, 2006, http://www.news.cornell.edu/stories/2006/03/slow-insidious-soil-erosion-threatens-human-health-and-welfare.
6. Ronald Amundson et al., "Soil and Human Security in the 21st Century," *Science* 348, no. 6235 (May 8, 2015): 648, doi: 10.1126/science.1261071.
7. Charles Darwin, *The Formation of Vegetable Mould through the Action of Worms, with Observations on their Habits* (London: John Murray, 1904).
8. UN Food and Agriculture Organization, "International Year of Soils 2015: Frequently Asked Questions," http://www.fao.org/soils–2015/faq/en/, accessed April 1, 2016.
9. UN Food and Agriculture Organization, "Soil Is a Non-renewable Resource: Its Preservation Is Essential for Food Security and Our Sustainable Future," http://www.fao.org/3/a-i4373e.pdf, accessed April 1, 2016.

10. James B. Nardi, *Life in the Soil: A Guide for Naturalists and Gardeners* (Chicago: University of Chicago Press, 2007), 240.
11. "Soil Erosion and Degradation," World Wildlife Fund, http://www.worldwildlife.org/threats/soil-erosion-and-degradation, accessed April 1, 2016.
12. Hubert W. Kelley, *Keeping the Land Alive: Soil Erosion—Its Causes and Cures* (Rome: Food and Agriculture Organization of the United Nations, 1990), http://www.fao.org/docrep/t0389e/T0389E02.htm#The%20worst%20threat%20is%20erosion, accessed April 1, 2016.
13. European Commission, Standing Committee on Agricultural Research (SCAR), *The Scope and Role of the "New" SCAR*, https://ec.europa.eu/research/scar/index.cfm?pg=home, last modified September 10, 2015.
14. Amundson et al., "Soil and Human Security in the 21st Century."
15. David Pimentel, "Soil Erosion: A Food and Environmental Threat," *Environment, Development and Sustainability* 8, no. 1 (February 2006): 119–137, 123.
16. Amundson et al., "Soil and Human Security in the 21st Century."
17. Fred Magdoff and Harold van Es, *Building Soils for Better Crops* (College Park, MD: SARE, 2009), 173–186.
18. Magdoff, *Building Soils for Better Crops*, 98.
19. Oliver Milman, "Earth Has Lost a Third of Arable Land in Past 40 Years, Scientists Say," *Guardian*, December 2, 2015, http://www.theguardian.com/environment/2015/dec/02/arable-land-soil-food-security-shortage. "Arable land includes land defined by the FAO as land under temporary crops (double-cropped areas are counted once), temporary meadows for mowing or for pasture, land under market or kitchen gardens, and land temporarily fallow. Land abandoned as a result of shifting cultivation is excluded." Definition from World Bank, http://data.worldbank.org/indicator/AG.LND.ARBL.ZS.
20. David Pimentel, "Soil Erosion: A Food and Environmental Threat," *Environment, Development and Sustainability* 8 (2006): 119–137, 123.
21. John Crawford, "What If the World's Soil Runs Out?," interview by World Economic Forum, *Time*, December 14, 2012, http://world.time.com/2012/12/14/what-if-the-worlds-soil-runs-out/.
22. Lang, " 'Slow, Insidious' Soil Erosion Threatens Human Health and Welfare as Well as the Environment, Cornell Study Asserts."
23. George Monbiot, "We're Treating Soil Like Dirt. It's a Fatal Mistake, as Our Lives Depend on It," *Guardian*, March 25, 2015, http://www.theguardian.com/commentisfree/2015/mar/25/treating-soil-like-dirt-fatal-mistake-human-life.

24. Tim Radford, "Soil Erosion as Big a Problem as Global Warming, Say Scientists," *Guardian*, February 14, 2004, http://www.theguardian.com/world/2004/feb/14/science.environment.
25. Pimentel, "Soil Erosion," 131.
26. David Montgomery, *Dirt: The Erosion of Civilizations* (Berkeley and Los Angeles: University of California Press, 2007).
27. *Status of the World's Soil Resources (SWSR)*, Main Report, Food and Agriculture Organization of the United Nations and Intergovernmental Technical Panel on Soils, Rome, Italy, 2015, p. 103. The report explains, "Estimated rates of soil erosion of arable or intensively grazed lands have been found to be 100–1000 times higher than natural background erosion rates. These erosion rates are also much higher than known soil formation rates which are typically well below 1 tonnes ha–1 yr–1 with median values of ca. 0.15 tonnes ha–1 yr–1."
28. UN Convention to Combat Desertification, *Land Degradation Neutrality*, September 25, 2015, http://www.unccd.int/en/programmes/RioConventions/RioPlus20/Pages/Land-DegradationNeutralWorld.aspx.
29. Mark Anderson and Arthur Neslen, "Land Degradation Costs the World up to $10.6tn a Year, Report Says," *Guardian*, September 15, 2015, https://www.theguardian.com/global-development/2015/sep/15/land-degradation-costs-word-trillions-dollars-year-report-says.
30. Anderson, "Land Degradation Costs the World up to $10.6tn a Year, Report Says."
31. Lynne Peeples, "Dust Storms' Health Risks: Asthma Triggers, Chemicals, Bacteria May Be in the Wind," *Huffington Post*, August 11, 2012, http://www.huffingtonpost.com/2012/08/11/dust-storms-health-disease_n_1764246.html.
32. Berta Acero, "Sandstorm Causes Health Problems," United Nations Office for Disaster Risk Reduction, September 14, 2015, https://www.unisdr.org/archive/45756; Peeples, "Dust Storms' Health Risks."
33. Subhash Mehta, "Re: The Future of Family Farming: Providing Resources for Women and Young Farmers," Global Forum on Food Security and Nutrition, http://www.fao.org/fsnforum/comment/5909.
34. Eric Holt Gimenez, "We Already Grow Enough Food for 10 Billion People—and Still Can't End Hunger," *Huffington Post*, May 2, 2012, http://www.huffingtonpost.com/eric-holt-gimenez/world-hunger_b_1463429.html.
35. World Health Organization, "Children: Reducing Mortality," http://www.who.int/mediacentre/factsheets/fs178/en/, last modified January 2016.

36. Global Nutrition Report, *From Promise to Impact: Ending Malnutrition by 2030* (Global Nutrition Report Stakeholder Group, 2016), 1, http://ebrary.ifpri.org/utils/getfile/collection/p15738coll2/id/130354/filename/130565.pdf; International Food Policy Research Institute, *Global Nutrition Report 2015, Actions and Accountability to Advance Nutrition & Sustainable Development* (Washington, DC: International Food Policy Research Institute, 2015), doi: 10.2499/9780896298835.
37. U.S. Department of Agriculture Economic Research Service, *Food Security in the U.S.*, https://www.ers.usda.gov/topics/food-nutrition-assistance/food-security-in-the-us/key-statistics-graphics.aspx#children, last modified October 11, 2016.
38. USDA, *Food Security in the U.S.*; Tracie McMillan, "The New Face of Hunger," *National Geographic*, August 2014, http://www.nationalgeographic.com/foodfeatures/hunger/.
39. U.S. Department of Labor, Bureau of Labor Statistics, *Occupational Outlook Handbook: Agricultural Workers*, December 17, 2015, https://www.bls.gov/ooh/farming-fishing-and-forestry/agricultural-workers.htm; U.S. Department of Labor, National Agricultural Workers Survey, *Agricultural Worker Tables: Earnings, Income, and Public Assistance*, 2013–2014, https://naws.jbsinternational.com/table/4/5; U.S. Census Bureau, *Income and Poverty in the United States: 2015*, report prepared by Bernadette D. Proctor, Jessica L. Semega, and Melissa A. Kollar, Report Number: P60–256, September 13, 2016, https://www.census.gov/library/publications/2016/demo/p60–256.html.
40. Edward H. Ip, Santiago Saldana, Thomas A. Arcury, Joseph G. Grzywacz, Grisel Trejo, and Sara A. Quandt, "Profiles of Food Security for U.S. Farmworker Households and Factors Related to Dynamic of Change," *American Journal of Public Health* 105, no. 10 (October 2015), doi: 10.2105/AJPH.2015.302752.
41. Centers for Disease Control and Prevention, National Institute for Occupational Safety and Health (NIOSH), *NIOSH Pesticide Poisoning Monitoring Program Protects Farmworkers*, DHHS (NIOSH) Publication Number 2012–108, December 2011, https://www.cdc.gov/niosh/docs/2012–108/; Farmworker Justic, "Exposed and Ignored: How Pesticides Are Endangering Our Nation's Farmworkers" (2013), 14, https://www.farmworkerjustice.org/sites/default/files/aExposed%20and%20Ignored%20by%20Farmworker%20Justice%20singles%20compressed.pdf; Catherine Ward, "Six Solutions to Lifting the World's Farm Workers Out of Poverty," *Christian Science Monitor*, September 5, 2017, https://www.

csmonitor.com/World/Making-a-difference/Change-Agent/2012/0905/Six-solutions-to-lifting-the-world-s-farm-workers-out-of-poverty.

42. United Nations General Assembly, *Report of the Special Rapporteur on the Right to Food*, Human Rights Council Thirty-Fourth Session, February 27–March 24, 2017, 3–6, http://reliefweb.int/sites/reliefweb.int/files/resources/1701059.pdf.
43. U.S. Department of Labor, Bureau of Labor Statistics, *National Census of Fatal Occupational Injuries in 2015*, news release: 10:00 a.m. (EST) Friday, December 16, 2016, http://www.bls.gov/news.release/pdf/cfoi.pdf.
44. Mareesa Nicosia, "The Forgotten Students of California's Drought," *Atlantic*, September 10, 2015, https://www.theatlantic.com/education/archive/2015/09/the-students-of-the-california-drought/404572/; Eric Holthaus, "Photos from the Front Lines of California's Agriculture Decline," October 26, 2014, http://www.slate.com/articles/technology/future_tense/2014/10/california_central_valley_agriculture_drought_and_climate_change_photos.html; Diane Nelson, "Protecting California's Farmworkers as Temperatures Climb," August 31, 2017, http://www.washingtonpost.com/sf/brand-connect/ucdavis/protecting-californias-farmworkers-as-temperatures-climb/.
45. Michael Marois, "California Drought Threatens 50% Farm Town Unemployment," *Bloomberg*, February 13, 2014, http://www.bloomberg.com/news/articles/2014–02–14/california-drought-threatens–50-farm-town-unemployment; "Unemployment Rates in California, Mendota, and Parlier, 2003–2009," *Rural Migration News* 15, no. 3 (July 2009), https://migration.ucdavis.edu/rmn/more.php?id=1477.
46. Marois, "California Drought Threatens 50% Farm Town Unemployment."
47. UNESCO World Water Assessment Programme, *Water and Jobs: Facts and Figures*, United Nations World Water Development Report 2016, 3, http://unesdoc.unesco.org/images/0024/002440/244041e.pdf; World Bank, *Water in Agriculture*, February 27, 2017, http://www.worldbank.org/en/topic/water/brief/water-in-agriculture.
48. U.S. Department of Agriculture, Economic Research Service, *Irrigation and Water Use, Overview*, https://www.ers.usda.gov/topics/farm-practices-management/irrigation-water-use/, last modified April 28, 2017.
49. Sid Perkins, "Is Agriculture Sucking Fresh Water Dry?" *Science*, February 13, 2012, http://www.sciencemag.org/news/2012/02/agriculture-sucking-fresh-water-dry; Arjen Y. Hoekstra and Mesfin M. Mekonnen, "The Water Footprint of Humanity," *PNAS* 109, no. 9 (2012): 3232–3237, 3232, doi: 10.1073/pnas.1109936109, http://www.pnas.org/content/109/9/3232.

50. UNESCO, *Water and Jobs,* 6; Todd C. Frankel, "New NASA Data Show How the World Is Running Out of Water," June 16, 2015, https://www.washingtonpost.com/news/wonk/wp/2015/06/16/new-nasa-studies-show-how-the-world-is-running-out-of-water/.
51. Richard A. Kerr, "The Greenhouse Is Making the Water-Poor Even Poorer," *Science* 336, no. 405 (2012): 405.
52. Kerr, "The Greenhouse Is Making the Water-Poor Even Poorer."
53. Martin Wild and Beate Liepert, "The Earth Radiation Balance as Driver of the Global Hydrological Cycle," *Environmental Research Letters* 5, no. 2 (April 2010): 1, doi: 10.1088/1748–9326/5/2/025203.
54. Steve Graham, Claire Parkinson, and Mous Chahine, "The Water Cycle and Climate Change," NASA Earth Observatory, October 1, 2010, http://earthobservatory.nasa.gov/Features/Water/page3.php.
55. NASA, "Water Cycle," http://science.nasa.gov/earth-science/oceanography/ocean-earth-system/ocean-water-cycle/, accessed July 20, 2016.
56. Heather Rogers, "Erasing Mossville: How Pollution Killed a Louisiana Town," *Intercept,* November 4, 2015, https://theintercept.com/2015/11/04/erasing-mossville-how-pollution-killed-a-louisiana-town/; David Briggs, "Environmental Pollution and the Global Burden of Disease," *British Medical Bulletin* 68 (2003), doi: 10.1093/bmb/ldg019; World Bank, "Statement from World Bank China Country Director on 'Cost of Pollution in China' Report," press release, July 11, 2007, http://www.worldbank.org/en/news/press-release/2007/07/11/statement-world-bank-china-country-director-cost-pollution-china-report.
57. "Freshwater Threats," *National Geographic Reference,* http://www.nationalgeographic.com/environment/habitats/freshwater-threats/.
58. "Freshwater Threats," *National Geographic Reference.*
59. World Wildlife Fund, *Living Planet Report 2016: Risk and Resilience in a New Era* (Gland, Switzerland: WWF International, 2016), 30.
60. Benjamin S. Halpern et al., "A Global Map of Human Impact on Marine Ecosystems," *Science* 15, no. 319 (2008): 948, doi: 10.1126/science.1149345.
61. UN World Water Assessment Program, *United Nations World Water Development Report,* vol. 1, *Water and Energy* (Paris: UNESCO, 2014), 2.
62. Mesfin M. Mekonnen and Arjen Y. Hoekstra, "Four Billion People Facing Severe Water Scarcity," *Science Advances* 2, no. 2 (February 2016): e1500323, http://advances.sciencemag.org/content/advances/2/2/e1500323.full.pdf.
63. Jamie Linton and Jessica Budds, "The Hydrosocial Cycle: Defining and Mobilizing a Relational-Dialectical Approach to Water," *Geoforum* 57 (2013): 170–180, 176–179.

64. Will Steffen, Paul J. Crutzen, and John R. McNeill, "The Anthropocene: Are Humans Now Overwhelming the Great Forces of Nature?" *Ambio* 26, no. 8 (December 2007): 614–621; John Bellamy Foster, Richard York, and Brett Clark, *The Ecological Rift: Capitalism's War on the Earth* (New York: Monthly Review Press, 2011); James Syvitski et al., "Changing the History of the Earth: The Role of Water in the Anthropocene," *Global Water News*, no. 12 (October 2012): 6–7.
65. Paul Milly et al., "Stationarity Is Dead: Whither Water Management?" *Science* 319, no. 5863 (February 1, 2008): 573–574, 573.
66. Kerr, "The Greenhouse Is Making the Water-Poor Even Poorer."
67. Joseph Romm, "Desertification: The Next Dust Bowl," *Nature* 478 (October 27, 2011): 450–451, doi: 10.1038/478450a.
68. Richard Seager, "An Imminent Transition to a More Arid Climate in Southwestern North America," Lamont-Doherty Earth Observatory, The Earth Institute at Columbia University, http://ocp.ldeo.columbia.edu/res/div/ocp/drought/science.shtml; Richard Seager et al., "Model Projections of an Imminent Transition to a More Arid Climate in Southwestern North America," *Science* 316, no. 5828 (May 2007): 1181–1184, doi: 10.1126/science.1139601.
69. Marlena Baldacci and Mariano Castillo, "Oklahoma Quakes This Year Top Tremors in California," *CNN*, June 19, 2014, http://www.cnn.com/2014/06/19/us/oklahoma-earthquakes-wastewater-wells/; Joe Wertz, "Exploring the Link Between Earthquakes and Oil and Gas Disposal Wells," *StateImpact Oklahoma*, https://stateimpact.npr.org/oklahoma/tag/earthquakes/.
70. Eric Levitz, "Oklahoma Now No. 1 in Earthquakes," *New York*, November 11, 2015, http://nymag.com/daily/intelligencer/2015/11/oklahoma-now-no–1-in-earthquakes.html; Jessica Miller, "Oklahoma World's No. 1 Earthquake Area," *Enid News & Eagle*, November 10, 2015, http://www.enidnews.com/news/local_news/oklahoma-world-s-no-earthquake-area/article_69b145b8-c180–5065–8f99-b2a7ec7ce913.html.
71. Morgan Brennan, "Oklahoma Goes from Two 3.0 Quakes a Year to Two a Day," *CNBC*, April 21, 2015, http://www.cnbc.com/2015/04/21/oklahoma-goes-from-two–30-earthquakes-a-year-to-two-a-day.html.
72. Cole Mellino, "70 More Earthquakes Hit Oklahoma, Averaging Nearly Three a Day in 2015," *EcoWatch*, January 11, 2016, http://ecowatch.com/2016/01/11/fracking-earthquakes-oklahoma/.
73. U.S. Geological Survey, "Induced Earthquakes," https://earthquake.usgs.gov/research/induced/overview.php; https://earthquake.usgs.gov/research/induced/myths.php, accessed February 20, 2018.

74. Susan Phillips, "Burning Question: What Would Life Be Like Without the Halliburton Loophole?" *StateImpact Pennsylvania*, December 5, 2011, https://stateimpact.npr.org/pennsylvania/2011/12/05/burning-question-what-would-life-be-like-without-the-halliburton-loophole/.
75. Congressional Research Service, *An Overview of Unconventional Oil and Natural Gas: Resources and Federal Actions*, by Michael Ratner and Mary Tiemann, Congressional Research Service, April 22, 2015, https://www.fas.org/sgp/crs/misc/R43148.pdf.
76. U.S. Geological Survey, "Hydraulic Fracturing and Induced Seismicity," http://energy.usgs.gov/OilGas/UnconventionalOilGas/HydraulicFracturing.aspx#3892235-overview, last modified April 1, 2016; U.S. Geological Survey, "Induced Earthquakes."
77. Wastewater includes both "flowback" and what the industry calls "produced water." For definitions, see U.S. Environmental Protection Agency, "The Hydraulic Fracturing Water Cycle," http://www.epa.gov/hfstudy/hydraulic-fracturing-water-cycle#ftn6, last modified June 1, 2015; James Conca, "Thanks to Fracking, Earthquake Hazards in Parts of Oklahoma Now Comparable to California," *Forbes*, September 7, 2016, https://www.forbes.com/sites/jamesconca/2016/09/07/the-connection-between-earthquakes-and-fracking/#576bbb3c6d68.
78. Anna Kuchment, "Drilling for Earthquakes," *Scientific American*, March 28, 2016, https://www.scientificamerican.com/article/drilling-for-earthquakes/.
79. Robert Rapier, "The Irony of President Obama's Oil Legacy," *Forbes*, January 15, 2016, https://www.forbes.com/sites/rrapier/2016/01/15/president-obamas-petroleum-legacy/#50710704c10f; John M. Broder, "Obama to Open Offshore Areas to Oil Drilling for First Time," *New York Times*, March 31, 2010, http://www.nytimes.com/2010/03/31/science/earth/31energy.html.
80. U.S. Environmental Protection Agency, "Deepwater Horizon—BP Gulf of Mexico Oil Spill," https://www.epa.gov/enforcement/deepwater-horizon-bp-gulf-mexico-oil-spill.
81. Peter Moskowitz, "Louisiana Five Years after BP Oil Spill: 'It's Not Going Back to Normal No Time Soon,'" *Guardian*, April 18, 2015, https://www.theguardian.com/environment/2015/apr/18/lousiana-bp-oil-spill-five-years-not-going-back-to-normal.
82. Tom Zeller, Jr., "Estimates Suggest Spill Is Biggest in U.S. History," *New York Times*, May 27, 2010, http://www.nytimes.com/2010/05/28/us/28flow.html; Michael T. Klare, "The Relentless Pursuit of Extreme Energy," *Nation*, May 18, 2010, http://www.thenation.com/article/relentless-pursuit-extreme-energy/.

83. Bryan Walsh, "Government Report Blames BP on Oil Spill. But There's Plenty of Fault," *Time*, September 14, 2011, http://science.time.com/2011/09/14/government-report-blames-bp-on-oil-spill-but-theres-plenty-of-fault/.
84. Fred Magdoff and John Bellamy Foster, *What Every Environmentalist Needs to Know About Capitalism: A Citizen's Guide to Capitalism and the Environment* (New York: Monthly Review Press, 2011), 102–107.
85. Arthur Neslen, "BP Tops the List of Firms Obstructing Climate Action in Europe," *Guardian*, September 21, 2015, https://www.theguardian.com/environment/2015/sep/21/bp-tops-the-list-of-firms-obstructing-climate-action-in-europe.
86. Matthew Daly and Josh Boak, "Trump Plan Would Expand Oil Drilling in Arctic and Atlantic," *PBS Newshour*, June 29, 2017, http://www.pbs.org/newshour/rundown/trump-plan-expand-oil-drilling-arctic-atlantic/.
87. Clifford Krauss, "New Technologies Redraw the World's Energy Picture," *New York Times*, October 25, 2011, http://www.nytimes.com/2011/10/26/business/energy-environment/new-technologies-redraw-the-worlds-energy-picture.html.
88. "Leave Tar Sands Oil in Ground: 110 Scientists Invoke First Nation Treaty Rights," Indian Country Today Media Network (NY), June 15, 2015, http://indiancountrytodaymedianetwork.com/2015/06/15/leave-tar-sands-oil-ground–110-scientists-invoke-first-nation-treaty-rights–160735.
89. Aldo Orellana Lopez and Sian Cowman, "How Extreme Energy Leads to Extreme Politics," *Foreign Policy in Focus*, August 31, 2015, http://fpif.org/how-extreme-energy-leads-to-extreme-politics/.
90. Jaeah Lee and James West, "The Great Frack Forward," *Mother Jones*, September 2014, http://www.motherjones.com/environment/2014/09/china-us-fracking-shale-gas.
91. Eduardo Porter, "Innovation Sputters in Battle against Climate Change," *New York Times*, July 21, 2015, http://www.nytimes.com/2015/07/22/business/energy-environment/innovation-to-stanch-climate-change-sputters.html?_r=0.
92. Maria van der Hoeven, foreword to *Tracking Clean Energy Progress 2015*, International Energy Agency (Paris: International Energy Agency, 2015), 4.
93. Andrea Thompson, "Climate Scientist: 2 Degrees of Warming Too Much," *LiveScience*, December 4, 2014, http://www.livescience.com/41690–2-degrees-of-warming-too-much.html.

94. Brian Eckhouse, "Wall Street Sours on $9 Billion Mechanism for Green Projects," *Bloomberg*, July 10, 2017, https://www.bloomberg.com/news/articles/2017–07–10/wall-street-sours-on–9-billion-mechanism-for-green-projects.
95. Porter, "Innovation Sputters in Battle against Climate Change."
96. Richard York, "Do Alternative Energy Sources Displace Fossil Fuels?" *Nature Climate Change* 2 (2012): 441–443, 441, doi: 10.1038/nclimate1451.
97. Naomi Klein, *This Changes Everything: Capitalism vs. the Climate* (New York: Simon & Schuster, 2014).
98. Ben Stein, "In Class Warfare, Guess Which Class Is Winning," *New York Times*, November 26, 1006, http://www.nytimes.com/2006/11/26/business/yourmoney/26every.html?_r=0.
99. Credit Suisse Research Institute, *Global Wealth Report 2013* (October 2013), https://publications.credit-suisse.com/tasks/render/file/?fileID=BCDB1364-A105–0560–1332EC9100FF5C83; Food and Agriculture Organization of the United Nations, *Water-Energy-Food-Nexus*, http://www.fao.org/energy/water-food-energy-nexus/en/.
100. Credit Suisse Research Institute, *Global Wealth Report 2015* (October 2015), 11, https://publications.credit-suisse.com/tasks/render/file/?fileID=F2425415-DCA7–80B8-EAD989AF9341D47E.
101. Credit Suisse Research Institute, *Global Wealth Report 2016* (November 2016), 11, http://publications.credit-suisse.com/tasks/render/file/index.cfm?fileid=AD783798-ED07-E8C2–4405996B5B02A32E.
102. Credit Suisse, *Global Wealth Report* 2016, 6.
103. Larry Elliott, "Inequality Gap Widens as 42 People Hold Same Wealth as 3.7bn Poorest," *Guardian*, January 21, 2018, https://www.theguardian.com/inequality/2018/jan/22/inequality-gap-widens-as–42-people-hold-same-wealth-as–37bn-poorest; Noah Kirsch, "The 3 Richest Americans Hold More Wealth Than the Bottom 50% of the Country, Study Finds," *Forbes*, November 9, 2017, https://www.forbes.com/sites/noahkirsch/2017/11/09/the–3-richest-americans-hold-more-wealth-than-bottom–50-of-country-study-finds/#4a681b8d3cf8.
104. Oxfam, "World's Richest 10% Produce Half of Carbon Emissions While Poorest 3.5 Billion Account for Just a Tenth," press release, December 2, 2015, https://www.oxfam.org/en/pressroom/pressreleases/2015–12–02/worlds-richest–10-produce-half-carbon-emissions-while-poorest–35.
105. NASA, "NASA, NOAA Data Show 2016 Warmest Year on Record Globally," January 18, 2017, https://www.nasa.gov/press-release/nasa-noaa-data-show–2016-warmest-year-on-record-globally.

106. Justin Gillis, "2014 Breaks Heat Record, Challenging Global Warming Skeptics," *New York Times*, January 16, 2015, http://www.nytimes.com/2015/01/17/science/earth/2014-was-hottest-year-on-record-surpassing–2010.html; Chris Mooney and Joby Warrick, "It's Official: 2015 'Smashed' 2014's Global Temperature Record. It Wasn't Even Close," *Washington Post*, January 20, 2016, https://www.washingtonpost.com/news/energy-environment/wp/2016/01/20/its-official–2015-smashed–2014s-global-temperature-record-it-wasnt-even-close/; Climate Central, "Ten Hottest Years: All since 1998," February 16, 2017, http://www.climatecentral.org/gallery/graphics/10-hottest-years-on-record; Jugal K. Patel, "How 2016 Became Earth's Hottest Year on Record," *New York Times*, January 18, 2017, https://www.nytimes.com/interactive/2017/01/18/science/earth/2016-hottest-year-on-record.html?_r=0.
107. John Bellamy Foster, "Capitalism and the Accumulation of Catastrophe," *Monthly Review* 63, no. 7 (December 2011), https://monthlyreview.org/2011/12/01/capitalism-and-the-accumulation-of-catastrophe/.
108. Rick Gladstone, "Unicef Calls 2014 One of Worst Years for Children," *New York Times*, December 8, 2014, http://www.nytimes.com/2014/12/09/world/unicef-calls–2014-one-of-worst-years-on-record-for-worlds-children.html?_r=0.
109. UN High Commissioner for Refugees, "Worldwide Displacement Hits All-Time High as War and Persecution Increase," news release, June 18, 2015, http://www.unhcr.org/558193896.html.
110. Adrian Edwards, "Forced Displacement Worldwide at Its Highest in Decades," UN High Commissioner for Refugees, news release, June 19, 2017, http://www.unhcr.org/afr/news/stories/2017/6/5941561f4/forced-displacement-worldwide-its-highest-decades.html.
111. Elliot Negin, "Think Today's Refugee Crisis Is Bad? Climate Change Will Make It a Lot Worse," *Huffington Post*, June 30, 2015, http://www.huffingtonpost.com/elliott-negin/think-todays-refugee-cris_b_7691330.html.
112. Negin, "Think Today's Refugee Crisis Is Bad?"

Two. The First Global Environmental Problem

This chapter is adapted from Hannah Holleman, "De-naturalizing Ecological Disaster: Colonialism, Racism and the Global Dust Bowl of the 1930s," *Journal of Peasant Studies* 44, no. 1 (2016): 234–260, http://www.tandfonline.com/doi/full/10.1080/03066150.2016.1195375.

Epigraph. Edward W. Said, *Culture and Imperialism* (New York: Vintage Books, 1993), xii–xiii.

1. Louis R. Baumhardt, "Dust Bowl Era," in *Encyclopedia of Water Science*, ed. Bobby A. Stewart and Terry Howell (New York: Marcel Dekker, 2003), 187–191, 187.
2. Great Plains Drought Area Committee, *Report of the Great Plains Drought Area Committee* (Washington, DC, 1936), 4.
3. Great Plains Drought Area Committee, *Report of the Great Plains Drought Area Committee*, 6.
4. William Lockeretz, "The Lessons of the Dust Bowl: Several Decades before the Current Concern with Environmental Problems, Dust Storms Ravaged the Great Plains, and the Threat of More Dust Storms Still Hangs over Us," *American Scientist* 66, no. 5 (September–October 1978): 560–569, 560.
5. Paul Bonnifield, *The Dust Bowl: Men, Dirt, and Depression* (Albuquerque: University of New Mexico Press, 1979); William Cronon, "A Place for Stories: Nature, History, and Narrative," *Journal of American History* 78, no. 4 (1992): 1347–76; Geoff Cunfer, *On the Great Plains: Agriculture and Environment* (College Station: Texas A & M University Press, 2005); Timothy Egan, *The Worst Hard Time: The Untold Story of Those Who Survived the Great American Dust Bowl* (New York: Houghton Mifflin Harcourt, 2006); James N. Gregory, *American Exodus: The Dust Bowl Migration and Okie Culture in California* (New York: Oxford University Press, 1991); R. Douglas Hurt, *The Dust Bowl: An Agricultural and Social History* (Chicago: Nelson-Hall, 1981); William E. Riebsame, "The Dust Bowl: Historical Image, Psychological Anchor, and Ecological Taboo," *Great Plains Quarterly* 6, no. 2 (Spring 1986): 127–136; Donald Worster, *Dust Bowl: The Southern Plains in the 1930s* (New York: Oxford University Press, 2004 [1979]); Philippe C. Baveye, David Rangel, Astrid R. Jacobson, Magdeline Laba, Christophe Darnault, Wilfred Otten, Ricardo Radulovich, and Flavio A. O. Camargo, "From Dust Bowl to Dust Bowl: Soils Still Very Much a Frontier of Science," *Soil Science Society of America Journal* 75 (November, 2011): 2037–48, doi: 10.2136/sssaj2011.0145; John R. Borchert, "The Dust Bowl in the 1970s," *Annals of the American Association of Geographers* 61, no. 1 (March 1971): 1–22; Robert A. McLeman, Juliette Dupre, Lea Berrang Ford, James Ford, Konrad Gajewski, and Gregory Marchildon, "What We Learned from the Dust Bowl: Lessons in Science, Policy, and Adaptation," *Population and Environment* 35, no. 4 (June 2014): 417–440, doi: 10.1007/s11111-013-0190-z; Zeynep K. Hansen and Gary D. Libecap, "Small Farms, Externalities, and the Dust Bowl of the 1930s," *NBER Working Paper* No. 10055, *Journal of Political Economy* 112 (June 2014): 665–694; Richard Hornbeck, "The Enduring Impact of the American

Dust Bowl: Short- and Long-Run Adjustments to Environmental Catastrophe," *American Economic Review* 102, no. 4 (2012): 1477–1507, doi: 10.1257/aer.102.4.1477; Siegfried D. Schubert, Max J. Suarez, Philip J. Pegion, Randal D. Koster, and Julio T. Bacmeister, "On the Cause of the 1930s Dust Bowl," *Science* 303, no. 5665 (2004): 1855–1859; Lockeretz, *The Lessons of the Dust Bowl;* S. Brönnimann, A. Stickler, T. Griesser, T. Ewen, A. N. Grant, A. M. Fischer, M. Schraner, T. Peter, E. Rozanov, and T. Ross, "Exceptional Atmospheric Circulation During the 'Dust Bowl,' " *Geophysical Research Letters* 36, no. 8 (2009); Benjamin I. Cook, Ron L. Miller, and Richard Seager, "Amplification of the North American 'Dust Bowl' Drought through Human-Induced Land Degradation," *PNAS* 106, no. 13 (2009): 4997–5001; Matthew R. Sanderson and R. Scott Frey, "From Desert to Bread Basket . . . to Desert Again? A Metabolic Rift in the High Plains Aquifer," *Journal of Political Ecology* 21 (2014): 516–532.

6. Discussions of the precise boundaries of the Dust Bowl appear in: Harry C. McDean, "Dust Bowl Historiography," *Great Plains Quarterly* 6 (1986): 117–126; Jess C. Porter and Allen G. Finchum, "Redefining the Dust Bowl Region via Popular Perception and Geotechnology," *Great Plains Research* 19 (2009): 201–214. The particular cultural, economic, soil, and climatological characteristics contributing to the Dust Bowl are emphasized in: Lockeretz, *The Lessons of the Dust Bowl*, 560–569; Paul Bonnifield, *The Dust Bowl: Men, Dirt, and Depression* (Albuquerque: University of New Mexico Press, 1979); Harry C. McDean, "Dust Bowl Historiography," *Great Plains Quarterly* 6 (Spring 1986): 117–126; Schubert et al., "On the Cause of the 1930s Dust Bowl," 1855–1859.
7. R. Douglas Hurt, "Federal Land Reclamation in the Dust Bowl," *Great Plains Quarterly* 6 (1986): 94–106, 99.
8. Worster, *Dust Bowl*, 96.
9. Geoff Cunfer, "Scaling the Dust Bowl," in *Placing History: How Maps, Spatial Data, and GIS Are Changing Historical Scholarship*, ed. Anne Kelly Knowles and Amy Hillier (Redlands, CA: ESRI Press, 2008), 96.
10. Cunfer, "Scaling the Dust Bowl," 102.
11. Cunfer, *On the Great Plains.*
12. Schubert et al., "On the Cause of the 1930s Dust Bowl," 1855–1859, 1855.
13. Worster, *Dust Bowl*, 196.
14. Worster, *Dust Bowl*, 96–97.
15. Worster, *Dust Bowl*, 97.
16. Worster, *Dust Bowl*, 97.
17. Worster, *Dust Bowl*, 63.
18. Worster, *Dust Bowl*, 6.

19. Worster, *Dust Bowl*, 5.
20. Worster, *Dust Bowl*, 7.
21. Matthew R. Sanderson and R. Scott Frey, "From Desert to Breadbasket . . . to Desert Again? A Metabolic Rift in the High Plains Aquifer," *Journal of Political Ecology* 21 (2014): 516–532, 519.
22. Sanderson and Frey, "A Metabolic Rift in the High Plains Aquifer," 516.
23. Sanderson and Frey, "A Metabolic Rift in the High Plains Aquifer," 516.
24. Cronon, "A Place for Stories," 1356–1357.
25. Cronon, "A Place for Stories," 1357.
26. Lockeretz, "The Lessons of the Dust Bowl," 564.
27. Lockeretz, "The Lessons of the Dust Bowl," 565.
28. Worster, *Dust Bowl*, 96.
29. Worster, *Dust Bowl*, 247.
30. Worster, *Dust Bowl*, 247–248.
31. David Naguib Pellow, *Resisting Global Toxics: Transnational Movements for Environmental Justice* (Cambridge, MA: MIT Press, 2007), 46.
32. Richard H. Grove, *Green Imperialism* (Cambridge: Cambridge University Press, 1995); Will Gray Brechin, "Conserving the Race: Natural Aristocracies, Eugenics, and the US Conservation Movement," *Antipode* 28, no. 3 (1996): 229–245; Joseph Murphy, "Environment and Imperialism: Why Colonialism Still Matters," *SSRI Papers*, No. 20 (2009).
33. "Erosion a World Problem," *Springfield Republican* (Massachusetts), May 25, 1939, 1.
34. "Erosion a World Problem," *Springfield Republican.*
35. "Dust Bowls of the Empire," *Round Table* 29, no. 114 (1939): 338–351, 346–350.
36. "Dust Bowls of the Empire," 338.
37. "Dust Bowls of the Empire," 340.
38. "Dust Bowls of the Empire," 349.
39. "Dust Bowls of the Empire," 346.
40. "Dust Bowls of the Empire," 349–350.
41. "Dust Bowls of the Empire," 348.
42. "Dust Bowls of the Empire," 338–339.
43. "Dust Bowls of the Empire," 339.
44. "Dust Bowls of the Empire," 347.
45. "Dust Bowls of the Empire," 339.
46. Sir Albert Howard, "Soil Erosion and Surface Drainage," Superintendent of Government Printing, India, February 5, 1915, 1–24, 6.
47. "Dr. Chatley Sees Erosion as Threat to China's Land," *China Press*, January 27, 1937: 9.

48. H. A. Tempany, G. M. Roddan, and L. Lord, "Soil Erosion and Soil Conservation in the Colonial Empire," *Empire Forestry Journal* 23, no. 2 (1944): 142–159.
49. Tempany, Roddan, and Lord, "Soil Erosion," 143.
50. "Supplement: Land Usage and Soil Erosion in Africa," *Journal of the Royal African Society* 37, no. 146 (January 1938): 3–19, 10.
51. Gorrie R. Maclagan, "The Problem of Soil Erosion in the British Empire with Special Reference to India," *Journal of the Royal Society of Arts* 86, no. 4471 (July 29, 1938): 901–926, 902.
52. Elspeth Huxley, "Fighting Soil Erosion Problem," *Japan Times*, July 1, 1937: 1.
53. Graham Vernon Jacks and Robert Orr Whyte, *The Rape of the Earth: A World Survey of Soil Erosion* (London: Faber and Faber, 1939), 17.
54. Jacks and Whyte, *The Rape of the Earth*, 211.
55. Jacks and Whyte, *The Rape of the Earth*, 20, 26.
56. Jacks and Whyte, *The Rape of the Earth*, 47–48.
57. Jacks and Whyte, *The Rape of the Earth*, 36.
58. Jacks and Whyte, *The Rape of the Earth*, 173.
59. Jacks and Whyte, *The Rape of the Earth*, 54.
60. David Anderson, "Depression, Dust Bowl, Demography, and Drought: The Colonial State and Soil Conservation in East Africa during the 1930s," *African Affairs* 332, no. 83 (July 1984): 321–343.
61. Jacks and Whyte, *The Rape of the Earth*, 262.
62. Jacks and Whyte, *The Rape of the Earth*, 262.
63. Jacks and Whyte, *The Rape of the Earth*, 262.
64. Jacks and Whyte, *The Rape of the Earth*, 249.
65. "Erosion a World Problem," 1.
66. A. M. Champion, "The Reconditioning of Native Reserves in Africa," *Journal of the Royal African Society* (October 1939): 442–464, 452.
67. E. P. Stebbing, "The Man-Made Desert in Africa: Erosion and Drought," *Journal of the Royal African Society* (January 1938): 3–40, 26–27.
68. Isaiah Bowman, "Science and Social Effects: Three Failures," *Scientific Monthly* 50, no. 4 (April 1940): 289–298, 297–298.
69. Tempany, Roddan, and Lord, "Soil Erosion," 159.

Three. Imperialism, White Settler Colonialism, and the Ecological Rift

This chapter is adapted from Hannah Holleman, "De-naturalizing Ecological Disaster: Colonialism, Racism and the Global Dust Bowl of the 1930s," *Journal of Peasant Studies* 44, no. 1 (2016): 234–260, http://www.tandfonline.com/doi/full/10.1080/03066150.2016.1195375.

Epigraph 1. Adam Smith, *An Inquiry into the Nature and Causes of the Wealth of Nations*, 11th ed., vol. 2 (Hartford, CT: Oliver D. Cooke, 1811 [1776]), 60.

Epigraph 2. Rudolf Hilferding, *Finance Capital: A Study of the Latest Phase of Capitalist Development* (London: Routledge and Kegan Paul, 1981 [1910]), 335.

1. Max Weber, "A Letter from Indian Territory" [1904], *Free Inquiry in Creative Sociology* 16, no. 2 (1988): 133–136, 135.
2. John Bellamy Foster and Hannah Holleman, "Weber and the Environment: Classical Foundations for a Postexemptionalist Sociology," *American Journal of Sociology* 117, no. 6 (May 2012): 1625–1673.
3. John Bellamy Foster, *The Vulnerable Planet: A Short Economic History of the Environment* (New York: Monthly Review Press, 1999), 121; Brett Clark and John Bellamy Foster, "Marx's Ecology in the 21st Century," *World Review of Political Economy* 1, no. 1 (2010): 142–156. In the words of John Bellamy Foster (1999), the "division of nature" refers to the "the disconnection of natural processes from each other and their extreme simplification . . . an inherent tendency of capitalist development" (121). Clark and Foster (2010) explain: "Capital accumulation requires the continual expansion of the division of nature as well as the division of labor. The division of nature is no longer, however, a social division of nature, in which the earth's different landscapes and species are utilized by human beings within a context that maintains the reproduction of nature itself. Instead, it is a detailed/alienated division of nature that breaks the circle of natural processes, creating ecological rifts. Nature is remade in such a way as to promote a single end: the accumulation of capital, irrespective of the lessons of rational science and conditions of sustainability" (152). Here I am illustrating the ways in which this process was racialized, along with the increasingly global division of labor and the broader society. Lands and people were identified as the natural property of white people, and modes of land tenure that differed from capitalist property relations, like the people practicing them, were treated as backward, with the people dehumanized. Ideas of *terra nullius* and the Doctrine of Discovery develop to justify the racialized division of nature and humanity—each side of which requires the other. See Roxanne Dunbar-Ortiz, *An Indigenous Peoples' History of the United States* (Boston: Beacon Press, 2014), 2–3.
4. W. E. B. DuBois, "The Souls of White Folk" [1920], *Monthly Review* 55, no. 6 (2003): 44–58, 54.
5. DuBois, "The Souls of White Folk," 55. "The Souls of White Folk," appeared in *Darkwater* in 1920, but was based on two earlier essays published in 1910 and 1917.

6. Magdoff, *Imperialism*, 34.
7. Magdoff, *Imperialism*, 35.
8. Magdoff, *Imperialism*, 35.
9. Roxanne Dunbar-Ortiz, *An Indigenous Peoples' History of the United States* (Boston: Beacon Press, 2014), 37.
10. DuBois, "The Souls of White Folk," 55.
11. Dubois, "The Souls of White Folk," 45–46.
12. Dunbar-Ortiz, *An Indigenous Peoples' History*, 163.
13. Edward W. Said, *Culture and Imperialism* (New York: Vintage Books, 1993), xii.
14. John Bellamy Foster, *Naked Imperialism: The US Pursuit of Global Dominance* (New York: Monthly Review Press, 2006). Today many children become familiar with Kipling's work *The Jungle Book*.
15. Foster, *Naked Imperialism*, 124; "The Philippine-American War, 1899–1902," *Milestones in American History*, U.S. Office of the Historian, https://history.state.gov/milestones/1899–1913/war, accessed February 18, 2018. The Trump administration posted a notice on May 9, 2017, explaining that " 'Milestones in the History of U.S. Foreign Relations' has been retired and is no longer maintained," though the material cited here was still available on the date of access. The atrocities of the war committed by the U.S. military included brutality and torture using techniques such as the "water cure" (which should sound familiar to contemporary readers), resettling communities in concentration camps, massacres of defenseless civilians, burning villages to the ground, and systematic rape of women and girls. See Foster, *Naked Imperialism*, 121–131.
16. Kansas Historical Society, "Kiowa-Lone Wolf v. Hitchcock," Kansapedia, http://www.kshs.org/kansapedia/kiowa-lone-wolf-v-hitchcock/19287 commission, last modified December 2017.
17. David Naguib Pellow, *Resisting Global Toxics: Transnational Movements for Environmental Justice* (Cambridge, MA: MIT Press, 2007), 50.
18. Sven Beckert, *Empire of Cotton: A Global History* (New York: Knopf, 2014), xv.
19. Karl Marx, *Capital* (London: Penguin Books, 1990 [1867]), vol. 1, 873–940; Foster, *Marx's Ecology: Materialism and Nature*, 173.
20. Beckert, *Empire of Cotton*, 244. Beckert notes that European economic power was based on the fact that European capitalists and statesmen "built a comparative advantage with a willingness and ability to use force to extend their interests" (30).
21. Marx, *Capital*, vol. 1, 918.
22. Magdoff, *Imperialism*, 108–109.

23. Beckert, *Empire of Cotton*, 250.
24. Beckert, *Empire of Cotton*, 308.
25. Harry Magdoff, *Imperialism: From the Colonial Age to the Present* (New York: Monthly Review Press, 1978), 37, 108; Beckert, *Empire of Cotton*, chapters 9, 12.
26. Magdoff, *Imperialism*, 37.
27. Magdoff, *Imperialism*, 37.
28. James Bryce, *Impressions of South Africa* (London: Macmillan, 1897), 577–578, 581–582.
29. J. A. Hobson, *Imperialism: A Study* (Ann Arbor: University of Michigan Press, 1965 [1898]), 78.
30. John Bellamy Foster, Brett Clark, and Richard York, *The Ecological Rift: Capitalism's War on the Earth* (New York: Monthly Review Press, 2011), 349–350.
31. Foster, Clark, and York, *The Ecological Rift*, 350.
32. Foster, *The Vulnerable Planet*, 121.
33. Foster, Clark, and York, *The Ecological Rift*, 350.
34. Marx, *Capital*, vol. 1, 579–580.
35. John C. Weaver, *The Great Land Rush and the Making of the Modern World, 1650–1900* (Montreal: McGill-Queen's University Press, 2003), 329–330.
36. Edward D. Melillo, "The First Green Revolution: Debt Peonage and the Making of the Nitrogen Fertilizer Trade, 1840–1930," *American History Review* 117, no. 4 (2012): 1028–1060; Foster, Clark, and York, *The Ecological Rift*, 350.
37. Harriet Friedmann, "From Colonialism to Green Capitalism: Social Movements and Emergence of Food Regimes," in *New Directions in the Sociology of Global Development*, Research in Rural Sociology and Development, vol. 11, ed. Frederick H. Buttel and Philip McMichael (Amsterdam and London: Elsevier, 2005), 227–264.
38. Philip McMichael, "A Food Regime Genealogy," *Journal of Peasant Studies* 36, no. 1 (2009): 139–169, 141, doi: 10.1080/03066150902820354.
39. George L. Beckford, *Persistent Poverty: Underdevelopment in Plantation Economies of the Third World* (New York: Oxford University Press, 1972).
40. Beckert, *Empire of Cotton*, 309.
41. Carolyn Merchant, *Ecological Revolutions: Nature, Gender, and Science in New England* (Chapel Hill: University of North Carolina Press, 1989).
42. Peter Hudis and Kevin B. Anderson, eds., *The Rosa Luxemburg Reader* (New York: Monthly Review Press, 2004), 110.

43. Melvin E. Page and Penny M. Sonnenberg, eds., *Colonialism: An International Social, Cultural, and Political Encyclopedia*, vol. 1 (Oxford: ABC-CLIO, 2003), 199–200.
44. Mitch Keller, "The Scandal at the Zoo," *New York Times*, August 6, 2006, http://www.nytimes.com/2006/08/06/nyregion/thecity/06zoo.html. This was the same world's fair where Max Weber gave a lecture before visiting Indian Territory.
45. Sara Shahriari, "Human Zoo: For Centuries, Indigenous Peoples Were Displayed as Novelties: An Interview with Nancy Egan," *Indian Country Today*, August 30, 2011, http://indiancountrytodaymedianetwork.com/2011/08/30/human-zoo-centuries-indigenous-peoples-were-displayed-novelties–48239.
46. BBC journalist Hugh Schofield writes that "the climax of the story comes with the imperialist high noon of the late nineteenth and early twentieth centuries." Hugh Schofield, "Human Zoos: When Real People Were Exhibits," BBC News, December 27, 2011, http://www.bbc.com/news/magazine–16295827.
47. Keller, "The Scandal at the Zoo"; Timothy Ryback, "A Disquieting Book from Hitler's Library," *New York Times*, December 7, 2011, http://www.nytimes.com/2011/12/08/opinion/a-disquieting-book-from-hitlers-library.html.
48. Dunbar-Ortiz, *An Indigenous Peoples' History*, 1–2.
49. Beckert, *Empire of Cotton*, 350–354.
50. Beckert, *Empire of Cotton*, 238–241.
51. Dunbar-Ortiz, *An Indigenous Peoples' History*, 133.
52. Dunbar-Ortiz, *An Indigenous Peoples' History*, 139.
53. Dunbar-Ortiz, *An Indigenous Peoples' History*, 144; Boyd Cothran and Ari Kelman, "How the Civil War Became the Indian Wars," *New York Times*, May 25, 2015, http://opinionator.blogs.nytimes.com/2015/05/25/how-the-civil-war-became-the-indian-wars/?_r=0.
54. Ted Steinberg, *Down to Earth: Nature's Role in American History* (New York: Oxford University Press, 2009 [2002]), 127.
55. Dunbar-Ortiz, *An Indigenous Peoples' History*, 144.
56. G. William Rice, "25 U.S.C. Sec. 71: The End of Indian Sovereignty or a Self-limitation of Contractual Ability?" *American Indian Law Review* 5 (1977): 239–253, 240.
57. Dunbar-Ortiz, *An Indigenous Peoples' History*, 145.
58. Dunbar-Ortiz, *An Indigenous Peoples' History*, 153.
59. Scott L. Malcomson, *One Drop of Blood: The American Misadventure of Race* (New York: Farrar, Straus, and Giroux, 2000), 15.

60. Judith Royster, "The Legacy of Allotment," *Arizona State Law Journal* 27, no. 1 (1995): 1–78.
61. David A. Chang, *The Color of the Land: Race, Nation, and the Politics of Land Ownership in Oklahoma, 1832–1929* (Chapel Hill: University of North Carolina Press, 2010).
62. Dunbar-Ortiz, *An Indigenous Peoples' History*, 159.
63. Walter LaFeber, *The New Empire: An Interpretation of American Expansion 1860–1898* (Ithaca, NY: Cornell University Press, 1998 [1963]), 13.
64. R. J. Thompson and B. M. Nicholls, "The Glen Grey Act: Forgotten Dimensions in an Old Theme," *South African Journal of Economic History* 8, no. 2 (1993): 58–70.
65. Friedmann, "From Colonialism to Green Capitalism."
66. Roxanne Dunbar-Ortiz, "One or Two Things I Know about Us: Rethinking the Image and Role of the Okies," *Monthly Review* 54, no. 3 (2002), http://monthlyreview.org/2002/07/01/one-or-two-things-i-know-about-us/.
67. Dunbar-Ortiz, *An Indigenous Peoples' History*, 37.
68. Michelle Alexander, *The New Jim Crow: Mass Incarceration in the Age of Colorblindness* (New York: New Press, 2010), 25.
69. Frederick Douglass, *Life and Times of Frederick Douglass* (Hartford, CT: Park Publishing, 1882), 468.
70. Matthew R. Sanderson and R. Scott Frey, "From Desert to Breadbasket . . . to Desert Again? A Metabolic Rift in the High Aquifer," *Journal of Political Ecology* 21 (2014): 516–532; Great Plains Drought Area Committee, *Report of the Great Plains Drought Area Committee* (Washington, DC: U.S. Government Printing Office, 1936), 4.
71. Sanderson and Frey, "From Desert to Breadbasket."
72. Friedmann, "From Colonialism to Green Capitalism," 231–232.
73. William Beinart and Peter A. Coates, *Environment and History: The Taming of Nature in the USA and South Africa* (London: Routledge, 1995), 7–8.
74. Beinart and Coates, *Environment and History*, 59.
75. Bonnie G. Colby, John E. Thorson, and Sarah Britton, *Negotiating Tribal Water Rights: Fulfilling Promises in the Arid West* (Tucson: University of Arizona Press, 2005).
76. On segregation in the environmental movement, see Dorceta E. Taylor, *The State of Diversity in Environmental Organizations* (Washington, DC: Green 2.0 Working Group, 2014). On the implications for movement efficacy, see Angela Park, *Everybody's Movement: Environmental Justice and Climate Change* (Washington, DC: Environmental Support Center, 2009).

77. Evelyn Nakano Glenn, "Settler Colonialism as Structure: A Framework for Comparative Studies of US Race and Gender Formation," *Sociology of Race and Ethnicity* 1, no. 1 (2015): 54–74.
78. Dunbar-Ortiz, *An Indigenous Peoples' History*, 5. Dunbar-Ortiz explains the predominant simplistic and ahistorical understandings of race as the result of a dehistoricized "multiculturalism," acting as "an insidious smoke screen meant to obscure the fact that the very existence of the country is a result of the looting of an entire continent and its resources." With such multiculturalism, Dunbar-Ortiz writes, "manifest destiny won the day."

Four. The White Man's Burden, Soil Erosion, and the Origins of Green Capitalism

Epigraph. Graham Vernon Jacks and Robert Orr Whyte, *The Rape of the Earth: A World Survey of Soil Erosion* (London: Faber and Faber, 1939), 38.

1. Jacks and Whyte, *The Rape of the Earth*, 38.
2. Theodore Roosevelt, "Opening Address by the President," *Proceedings of a Conference of Governors* (Washington, DC: U.S. Government Printing Office, 1909), 9. Conference of Governors on the Conservation of Natural Resources held in Washington, DC, May 13–15, 1908.
3. David W. Orr and David Ehrenfeld, "None So Blind: The Problem of Ecological Denial," *Conservation Biology* 9, no. 5 (October 1995): 985–987; Stanley Cohen, *States of Denial: Knowing about Atrocities and Suffering* (Cambridge, MA: Polity Press, 2001); Kari Marie Norgaard, *Living in Denial: Climate Change, Emotions, and Everyday Life* (Cambridge, MA: MIT Press, 2011).
4. Cohen, *States of Denial*, 107–109.
5. Cohen, *States of Denial*, quoted in Norgaard, *Living in Denial*, 10–11.
6. Cohen, *States of Denial*, quoted in Norgaard, *Living in Denial*, 10–11.
7. Cohen's emphasis is not "ecological denial," though environmental issues are used as illustrations in his work. The study of ecological denial more specifically is an important area of research in environmental sociology.
8. John Bellamy Foster, "Capitalism and the Accumulation of Catastrophe," *Monthly Review* 63, no. 7 (December 2011), https://monthlyreview.org/2011/12/01/capitalism-and-the-accumulation-of-catastrophe/.
9. Norgaard, *Living in Denial*, 226.
10. Marcel Mazoyer and Laurence Roudart, *A History of World Agriculture: From the Neolithic Age to the Current Crisis*, trans. James H. Membrez (London and Sterling, VA: Earthscan, 2006), 124; Verena Winiwarter,

"Prolegomena to a History of Soil Knowledge in Europe," in *Soils and Societies: Perspectives from Environmental History*, ed. John Robert McNeill and Verena Winiwarter (Cambridgeshire, UK: White Horse Press, 2010), 177–215; Eric Brevik and Alfred Hartemink, "Early Soil Knowledge and the Birth and Development of Soil Science," *Catena* 83 (2010): 23–33; Terrence J. Toy, George R. Foster, and Kenneth G. Renard, *Soil Erosion: Processes, Prediction, Measurement, and Control* (Hoboken, NJ: Wiley, 2002), 16; Hugh Hammond Bennett, "Erosion and Civilization," in Hugh Hammond Bennett, ed., *Soil Conservation* (New York: McGraw-Hill, 1939), 16–54.

11. John R. McNeill and Verena Winiwarter, "Breaking the Sod: Humankind, History, and Soil," *Science* 304 (2004): 1627–1629, 1627, doi: 10.1126/science.1099893; Markus Dotterweich, "The History of Human-Induced Soil Erosion: Geomorphic Legacies, Early Descriptions and Research, and the Development of Soil Conservation—A Global Synopsis," *Geomorphology* 201 (2013): 1–34, 10–21.
12. Eric Brevik and Alfred Hartemink, "History, Philosophy, and Sociology of Soil Sciences," in *Soils, Plant Growth and Crop Production*, ed. Willy H. Verheye (UK: EOLSS, 2010); Dotterweich, "The History of Human-Induced Soil Erosion," 4–5.
13. David R. Montgomery, *Dirt: The Erosion of Civilization* (Berkeley: University of California Press, 2007), 95–96.
14. USDA, *Report of the Commissioner of Agriculture for the Year 1862* (Washington, DC: U.S. Government Printing Office, 1863), 5–6.
15. Richard Grove, "Climatic Fears," *Harvard International Review*, January 6, 2002, http://hir.harvard.edu/article/?a=955.
16. John Wesley Powell, *Report on the Lands of the Arid Region of the United States* (Washington, DC: U.S. Government Printing Office, 1878).
17. *Documentary Chronology of Selected Events in the Development of the American Conservation Movement, 1847–1920*, in Library of Congress Conservation Collection, *The Evolution of the Conservation Movement*, https://memory.loc.gov/ammem/amrvhtml/cnchron2.html.
18. Richard H. Grove, *Green Imperialism* (Cambridge: Cambridge University Press, 1995), 72.
19. McNeill and Winiwarter, "Breaking the Sod: Humankind, History, and Soil," 1628.
20. McNeill and Winiwarter, "Breaking the Sod: Humankind, History, and Soil," 1627.
21. McNeill and Winiwarter, "Breaking the Sod: Humankind, History, and Soil," 1627.

22. McNeill and Winiwarter, "Breaking the Sod: Humankind, History, and Soil," 1627. It was the mold-board plow that made possible the inversion of the sod. Without it, crops in furrows could not compete with grass. It made "breaking" the grasslands possible and was, at the time, a relatively new invention. See: "Agriculture Milestones," *Scientific American*, https://www.scientificamerican.com/article/agriculture-milestones/.
23. Vimbai C. Kwashirai, "Dilemmas in Conservationism in Colonial Zimbabwe, 1890–1930," *Conservation and Society* 4, no. 4 (December 2006): 541–561, 541.
24. Grove, *Green Imperialism*, 71–72 and 309–379.
25. Sven Beckert, *Empire of Cotton: A Global History* (New York: Knopf, 2014), 101, 115, 125.
26. Hugh Hammond Bennett, "Early Efforts toward Erosion Control," in Hugh Hammond Bennett, ed., *Soil Conservation* (New York: McGraw-Hill, 1939), 868–898.
27. Bennett, "Early Efforts toward Erosion Control," 870.
28. Joseph Scott III, "A Geographical Description of the States of Maryland and Delaware: Also of the Counties, Towns, Rivers, Bays and Islands: With a List of the Hundreds in Each County" (Philadelphia, 1807), 22–23, quoted in *Soil Conservation*, ed. Hugh Hammond Bennett, 873.
29. Arthur R. Hall, "Early American Erosion-Control Practices in Virginia," U.S. Department of Agriculture Miscellaneous Publication 256 (Washington, DC: U.S. Government Printing Office, 1937), 2.
30. Russell Lord, "Progress of Soil Conservation in the United States," *Geographical Journal* 105, nos. 5–6 (May–June 1945): 159–166, 164.
31. Douglas Helms, "Two Centuries of Soil Erosion," *OAH Magazine of History*, Winter 1991: 24–28, 24.
32. Bennett, *Soil Conservation*, 869.
33. "Southern Land-Murder," *Friends' Review: A Religious, Literary and Miscellaneous Journal*, January 19, 1856.
34. "Soil of Palestine," *Episcopal Recorder*, July 15, 1837.
35. Alexander Del Mar, "The Map of Europe Fifty Years Hence," *Independent*, April 1, 1875.
36. Wayne D. Rasmussen, "Lincoln's Agricultural Legacy," USDA National Agricultural Library, https://www.nal.usda.gov/lincolns-agricultural-legacy.
37. USDA, *Report of the Commissioner of Agriculture for the Year 1862*, 13.
38. USDA, *Report of the Commissioner of Agriculture for the Year 1862*, 13.
39. George Perkins Marsh, *Man and Nature* (Seattle and London: University of Washington Press, 2003 [1864]), 186–187.
40. Marsh, *Man and Nature*, 186–187.

41. David Lowenthal, Introduction to George Perkins Marsh, *Man and Nature* (Cambridge, MA: Harvard University Press, 1965 [1864]), xxii.
42. Char Miller, *Gifford Pinchot and the Making of Modern Environmentalism* (Washington, DC: Island Press, 2001), 55.
43. Theodore Roosevelt, *The Winning of the West: An Account of the Exploration and Settlement of Our Country from the Alleghenies to the Pacific* (New York: Putnam, 1917 [1889]), vol. 2, 57–58.
44. USDA Forest Service, *The Beginning Era of Concern about Natural Resources, 1873–1905*, http://www.foresthistory.org/ASPNET/Publications/first_century/sec1.htm; U.S. Department of State, *Papers Relating to Foreign Affairs*, 1898, 904–908, https://www.mtholyoke.edu/acad/intrel/mkinly3.htm.
45. Gary Brechin, "Conserving the Race: Natural Aristocracies, Eugenics, and the U.S. Conservation Movement," *Antipode* 28, no. 3 (July 1996): 229–245, 234. Ancient Chinese and Vedic texts address soils and erosion, and evidence of agricultural practices to reduce erosion is found throughout Africa, the Middle East, South America, Asia, North America, and beyond, testament to extensive historical experience and knowledge.
46. Bennett, *Soil Conservation*, 894–895.
47. "Washed Soils: How to Prevent and Reclaim Them," USDA Farmer's Bulletin No. 20 (Washington, DC: U.S. Government Printing Office, October 27, 1894).
48. Nathaniel Southgate Shaler, "The Economic Aspects of Soil Erosion," *National Geographic* 7 (January 1896): 328–338, 328.
49. Shaler, "The Economic Aspects of Soil Erosion," 338.
50. Shaler, "The Economic Aspects of Soil Erosion," 337.
51. Shaler, "The Economic Aspects of Soil Erosion," 338.
52. "How to Prevent Washing Away of Soil," *Topeka Weekly Capital*, May 10, 1898: 6.
53. Bennett, *Soil Conservation*, 895.
54. Roosevelt, "Opening Address by the President," 8.
55. Roosevelt, "Opening Address by the President," 8.
56. Roosevelt, "Opening Address by the President," 9.
57. "Final Declaration of the Governors," Conference on the Conservation of Natural Resources, Washington, DC, May 13–15, 1908, USDA Farmer's Bulletin No. 340 (Washington, DC: U.S. Government Printing Office, December 1908), 6.
58. Governor of Hawaii Walter F. Frear, "Conservation in Hawaii," *Proceedings of a Conference of Governors* (Washington, DC: U.S. Government Printing Office, 1909), 338.

59. "Conference on Conservation of Natural Resources," *Science* 27, no. 700 (May 29, 1908): 867–869, 867.
60. "Conference on Conservation of Natural Resources," *Science*, 868.
61. "Conference on Conservation of Natural Resources," *Science*, 868.
62. "Warn Governors of the Danger in Our Wanton Waste," *Philadelphia Inquirer*, May 15, 1908: 1.
63. *Daily Oklahoman*, October 31, 1908: 7.
64. E. E. Free and J. M. Westgate, "The Control of Blowing Soils," USDA Farmer's Bulletin No. 421 (Washington, DC: U.S. Government Printing Office, 1910), image on p. 6.
65. Edward Marshall, "We Are the Richest, But Most Wasteful People, Gifford Pinchot Says," *New York Times*, February 26, 1911: SM6.
66. Marshall, "We Are the Richest, But Most Wasteful People, Gifford Pinchot Says," SM6.
67. Marshall, "We are the Richest, But Most Wasteful People, Gifford Pinchot Says," SM6.
68. Stefan Bechtel, *Mr. Hornaday's War: How a Peculiar Victorian Zookeeper Waged a Lonely Crusade for Wildlife That Changed the World* (Boston: Beacon Press, 2012).
69. Mitch Keller, "The Scandal at the Zoo," *New York Times*, August 6, 2006, http://www.nytimes.com/2006/08/06/nyregion/thecity/06zoo.html?pagewanted=all&_r=0.
70. William T. Hornaday, *Our Vanishing Wild Life: Its Extermination and Preservation* (New York: Scribner, 1913), 248–249.
71. Hornaday, *Our Vanishing Wild Life*, 364–365.
72. John Bellamy Foster, *Marx's Ecology: Materialism and Nature* (New York: Monthly Review Press, 2000).
73. Marsh, George Perkins, *Man and Nature; or, Physical Geography as Modified by Human* Action (New York: Charles Scribner & Co., 1867), vii; Robert Lionel Sherlock, *Man as a Geological Agent: An Account of His Action on Inanimate Nature* (Washington, DC: U.S. Government Printing Office, 1922).
74. Sherlock, *Man as a Geological Agent*, 316.
75. Sherlock, *Man as a Geological Agent*, 333.
76. Sherlock, *Man as a Geological Agent*, 23.
77. Sherlock, *Man as a Geological Agent*, 333.
78. Sherlock, *Man as a Geological Agent*, 343.
79. Sherlock, *Man as a Geological Agent*, 310.
80. Sherlock, *Man as a Geological Agent*, 309.
81. Sherlock, *Man as a Geological Agent*, 310.

82. Sherlock, *Man as a Geological Agent*, 311.
83. Sherlock, *Man as a Geological Agent*, 308.
84. Sherlock, *Man as a Geological Agent*, 308.
85. South Africa, Drought Investigation Commission, *Final Report of the Drought Investigation Commission* (Cape Town: Cape Times Limited, Government Printer, 1923), 5.
86. Gary Brechin, "Conserving the Race: Natural Aristocracies, Eugenics, and the U.S. Conservation Movement," *Antipode* 28, no. 3 (July 1996): 229–245, doi: 10.1111/j.1467–8330.1996.tb00461.x.
87. Peder Anker, *Imperial Ecology: Environmental Order in the British Empire, 1895–1945* (Cambridge, MA: Harvard University Press, 2002).
88. Greg Bankoff, "Conservation and Colonialism: Gifford Pinchot and the Birth of Tropical Forestry in the Philippines," in Alfred W. McCoy and Francisco A. Scarano, eds., *Colonial Crucible: Empire in the Making of the Modern American State* (Madison: University of Wisconsin Press, 2009), 479–488, 479. Bankoff writes with respect to the Philippines: "The question of the wilderness and national forest reserves that proved so divisive in late-nineteenth-century and early-twentieth-century U.S. politics had its counterpart in America's erstwhile colony across the Pacific. In the Philippines, however, the colonial context somewhat simplified matters: the conservation movement was not rent apart by any semblance of the acrimonious dissension between preservationists who wished to set aside certain landscapes and those who advocated a more utilitarian or planned use of resources . . . far from facilitating unrestricted access to all this timber by its own citizens and newly acquired subjects, the nascent colonial administration had already been captured by proponents of the creed of utilitarian conservation. It was in America's Asian colony that the Progressive era state was able to implement its reformist agenda virtually unopposed, providing a testing ground for many of the programs later enacted in the continental United States."
89. Paul S. Sutter, "Tropical Conquest and the Rise of the Environmental Management State: The Case of U.S. Sanitary Efforts in Panama," in McCoy and Scarano, eds., *Colonial Crucible*, 317–326, 321.
90. Sutter, "Tropical Conquest and the Rise of the Environmental Management State," 321. On the origins of U.S. colonial forestry practices and Gifford Pinchot's role in their development, see Greg Bankoff, 2009, "Breaking New Ground? Gifford Pinchot and the Birth of 'Empire Forestry' in the Philippines, 1900–05," *Environment and History* 15, no. 3 (August 2009): 369–393; and Bankoff, "Conservation and Colonialism," in McCoy and Scarano, eds., *Colonial Crucible*, 479.

91. USDA NRCS, "Hugh Hammond Bennett, 'Father of Soil Conservation,' " https://www.nrcs.usda.gov/wps/portal/nrcs/detail/national/about/history/?cid=stelprdb1044395, reprinted with permission of the American Council of Learned Societies from "Hugh Hammond Bennett," *American National Biography* (New York: Oxford University Press, 1999), vol. 2, 582–583; Hugh Hammond Bennett, "Some Geographic Aspects of Cuban Soils," *Geographical Review* 18, no. 1 (January 1928): 62–82, https://www.jstor.org/stable/208763?seq=1#page_scan_tab_contents.
92. Hugh Hammond Bennett et al., *The Soils of Cuba* (Washington, DC: Tropical Plant Research Foundation, 1928), xx.
93. Dorceta E. Taylor, *The Rise of the American Conservation Movement: Power, Privilege, and Environmental Protection* (Durham, NC: Duke University Press, 2016), 394.
94. Taylor, *The Rise of the American Conservation Movement*, 394–395.
95. Tom Griffiths and Libby Robin, eds., *Ecology and Empire: Environmental History of Settler Societies* (Seattle: University of Washington Press, 1997); William Beinart and Lotte Hughes, *Environment and Empire* (New York: Oxford University Press, 2007); Kate Barger Showers, *Imperial Gullies: Soil Erosion and Conservation in Lesotho* (Athens: Ohio University Press, 2005); Peder Anker, *Imperial Ecology: Environmental Order in the British Empire* (Cambridge, MA: Harvard University Press, 2002); Joachim Radkau, *Nature and Power: A Global History of the Environment* (Cambridge: Cambridge University Press, 2008); Taylor, *The Rise of the American Conservation Movement*; Carolyn Merchant, *Ecological Revolutions: Nature, Gender, and Science in New England* (Chapel Hill: University of North Carolina Press, 1989).
96. Taylor, *The Rise of the American Conservation Movement*, 395, 397.
97. Taylor, *The Rise of the American Conservation Movement*.

Five. Ecological Rifts and Shifts

Epigraph. Russell Lord, "Progress of Soil Conservation in the United States," *Geographical Journal* 105, nos. 5–6 (May–June 1945): 159–166, 162.

1. Marx, Economic and Philosophical Manuscripts, in John Bellamy Foster, ed., "Marx's Theory of Metabolic Rift: Classical Foundations for Environmental Sociology," *American Journal of Sociology* 105, no. 2 (September 1999): 366–405, 381.
2. Marx as quoted in Foster, "Marx's Theory of Metabolic Rift," 380.
3. Marx as quoted in Foster, "Marx's Theory of Metabolic Rift," 380.

4. David Naguib Pellow, *Total Liberation: The Power and Promise of Animal Rights and the Radical Earth Movement* (Minneapolis: University of Minnesota Press, 2014), 6.
5. See, for example, the goals of the Obama administration's President's Advisory Council on Doing Business in Africa, *Recommendation Report*, April 8, 2015, https://www.trade.gov/pac-dbia/docs/PAC-DBIA-Report_Final.pdf.
6. Max Ehrenfreund, "A Majority of Millennials Now Reject Capitalism, Poll Shows," *Washington Post*, April 26, 2016, https://www.washingtonpost.com/news/wonk/wp/2016/04/26/a-majority-of-millennials-now-reject-capitalism-poll-shows/?utm_term=.8c1713a54057; "Emerging and Developing Economies Much More Optimistic Than Rich Countries about Future," *Pew Research Center: Global Attitudes and Trends*, October 9, 2014, http://www.pewglobal.org/2014/10/09/emerging-and-developing-economies-much-more-optimistic-than-rich-countries-about-the-future/.
7. Peter Whoriskey, "Your Favorite Organic Brand Is Actually Owned by a Multinational Food Company," *Washington Post*, May 6, 2015, https://www.washingtonpost.com/news/wonk/wp/2015/05/06/your-favorite-organic-brand-is-actually-owned-by-a-multinational-food-company/?utm_term=.4b4e46ad070c.
8. John Mackey and Raj Sisodia, *Conscious Capitalism: Liberating the Heroic Spirit of Business* (Cambridge, MA: Harvard Business School Press, 2013).
9. Brett Clark and Richard York, "Rifts and Shifts: Getting to the Root of Environmental Crises," *Monthly Review* 60, no. 6 (November 2008), https://monthlyreview.org/2008/11/01/rifts-and-shifts-getting-to-the-root-of-environmental-crises/.
10. Benjamin Keen and Keith Haynes, *A History of Latin America*, 9th ed. (Boston: Wadsworth Cengage Learning, 2010), 263–266.
11. Millard Fillmore, "State of the Union 1850—2 December 1850," *American History from Revolution to Reconstruction and Beyond*, http://www.let.rug.nl/usa/presidents/millard-fillmore/state-of-the-union–1850.php.
12. Gregory T. Cushman, *Guano and the Opening of the Pacific World: A Global Ecological History* (New York: Cambridge University Press, 2013), 82.
13. J. Rockstrom et al., "A Safe Operating Space for Humanity," *Nature* 461, no. 7263 (2009): 472–475, 474.
14. Rockstrom et al., "A Safe Operating Space for Humanity," 472.
15. J. Rockstrom et al., "Planetary Boundaries—an Update," Stockholm Resilience Center (2015), http://www.stockholmresilience.org/research/research-news/2015–01–15-planetary-boundaries-an-update.html, accessed February 20, 2018.

16. Karl Marx, *Capital* (London: Penguin Books, 1990 [1867]), vol. 1, 638.
17. William H. McNeill and Charles P. Kindleberger, "Control and Catastrophe in Human Affairs [with Comments]," *Daedalus* 118, no. 1 (1989): 1–15, 12.
18. William H. McNeill, "The Conservation of Catastrophe," *New York Review of Books*, December 20, 2001: 86–88, http://www.nybooks.com/articles/2001/12/20/the-conservation-of-catastrophe/.
19. John Bellamy Foster, "Capitalism and the Accumulation of Catastrophe," *Monthly Review* 63, no. 7 (December 2011), https://monthlyreview.org/2011/12/01/capitalism-and-the-accumulation-of-catastrophe/.
20. Lord, "Progress of Soil Conservation in the United States," 162.
21. "Gale, The Library of Michigan and CIVICTechnologies Partner to Make Business Resources Available for the Michigan Business Community," Cengage, June 10, 2013, https://news.cengage.com/library-research/gale-the-library-of-michigan-and-civictechnologies-partner-to-make-business-resources-available-for-the-michigan-business-community/; "Dust Bowl 1931–1939," in Richard C. Hanes and Sharon M. Hanes, eds., *Historic Events for Students: The Great Depression*, vol. 1 (Detroit: Gale, 2002), 168–185; *World History in Context*, link.galegroup.com/apps/doc/CX3424800020/WHIC?u=nysl_ro_ironhs&xid=d7a081c6, accessed March 17, 2017.
22. E. E. Free and J. M. Westgate, "The Control of Blowing Soils," USDA Farmer's Bulletin No. 421 (Washington, DC: U.S. Government Printing Office, 1910).
23. Lord, "Progress of Soil Conservation in the United States," 162.
24. National Drought Mitigation Center, "The Great Depression," University of Nebraska-Lincoln, http://drought.unl.edu/DroughtBasics/DustBowl/TheGreatDepression.aspx, last modified 2017.
25. Thorstein Veblen, *Absentee Ownership and Business Enterprise in Recent Times: The Case of America* (New York: A. M. Kelley, 1964 [1923]); David E. Conrad, "Tenant Farming and Sharecropping," *The Encyclopedia of Oklahoma History and Culture*, http://www.okhistory.org/publications/enc/entry.php?entry=TE009, accessed June 14, 2017; Olaf F. Larson, "Farm Population Mobility in the Southern Great Plains," *Social Forces* 18, no. 4 (May 1940): 514–520.
26. Otis T. Osgood, "Some Observations on the Relation of Farm Land Tenure to Soil Erosion and Depletion," *Journal of Land and Public Utility Economics* 17, no. 4 (November 1941): 410–422; USDA, *Soils & Men: Yearbook of Agriculture 1938* (Washington, DC: U.S. Government Printing Office, 1938).

27. O. E. Baker, Address, *Proceedings of the First International Congress of Soil Science* (Washington, DC: U.S. Government Printing Office, 1927), 91–93.
28. H. H. Bennett and W. R. Chapline, *Soil Erosion a National Menace*, USDA Circular No. 33 (Washington, DC: U.S. Government Printing Office, 1928), 22.
29. "81 Percent of Soil Damaged," *Daily Oklahoman*, July 13, 1930: 17.
30. Kendrick A. Clements, "Herbert Hoover and Conservation, 1921–33," *American Historical Review* 89, no. 1 (February 1984): 67–88, 81; Joan Hoff Wilson, "Hoover's Agricultural Policies, 1921–1928," *Agricultural History* 51, no. 2 (April 1977): 335–361; Elizabeth Hoffman and Gary D. Libecap, "Institutional Choice and the Development of U.S. Agricultural Policies in the 1920s," *Journal of Economic History* 51, no. 2 (June 1991): 397–411.
31. Herbert Hoover as quoted in Clements, "Herbert Hoover and Conservation, 1921–33," 81.
32. "The World Wheat Situation, 1931–32: A Review of the Crop Year," *Wheat Studies* 9, no. 3 (December 1932): 63–136.
33. Donald Worster, *Dust Bowl: The Southern Plains in the 1930s* (New York: Oxford University Press, 2004 [1979]), 24. Worster wrote this before the major socio-ecological crises of recent years, such as Hurricane Katrina.
34. Donald A. Wilhite, "Government Response to Drought in the United States: With Particular Reference to the Great Plains," *Journal of Climate and Applied Meteorology* 22 (January 1983): 40–50, 44.
35. Wilhite, "Government Response to Drought in the United States," 42.
36. George F. Garcia, "Herbert Hoover and the Issue of Race," *Annals of Iowa* 44, no. 7 (Winter 1979): 507–515; Worster, *Dust Bowl*, 35.
37. Herbert Hoover, "Public vs. Private Financing of Relief Efforts," President's News Conference, February 3, 1931, *The American Presidency Project*, http://www.presidency.ucsb.edu/ws/?pid=22932; History.com Staff, *Herbert Hoover*, 2009, http://www.history.com/topics/us-presidents/herbert-hoover, accessed February 20, 2018; "Drought of 1930–1931," *The Encyclopedia of Arkansas History and Culture*, http://www.encyclopediaofarkansas.net/encyclopedia/entry-detail.aspx?entryID=4344, last modified March 31, 2010.
38. Worster, *Dust Bowl*, 35–38; "Summary of 71st Congress Shows It a Record Breaker," *Chicago Tribune*, March 4, 1931: 2, http://archives.chicagotribune.com/1931/03/04/page/2/article/summary-of–71st-congress-shows-it-a-record-breaker.
39. Alex Wagner, "America's Forgotten History of Illegal Deportations," *Atlantic*, March 6, 2017, https://www.theatlantic.com/politics/archive/2017/03/americas-brutal-forgotten-history-of-illegal-deportations/517971/; Francisco E. Balderrama and Raymond Rodríguez, *A Decade of*

Betrayal: Mexican Repatriation in the 1930s (Albuquerque: University of New Mexico Press, 2006).

40. Adrian Florido, "Mass Deportation May Sound Unlikely, But It's Happened Before," NPR, September 8, 2015, http://www.npr.org/sections/codeswitch/2015/09/08/437579834/mass-deportation-may-sound-unlikely-but-its-happened-before; "INS Records for 1930s Mexican Repatriations," U.S. Citizenship and Immigration Services, March 3, 2014, https://www.uscis.gov/history-and-genealogy/our-history/historians-mailbox/ins-records–1930s-mexican-repatriations.
41. Nan E. Woodruff, "The Failure of Relief during the Arkansas Drought of 1930–1931," *Arkansas Historical Quarterly* 39, no. 4 (Winter 1980): 301–313, 311, http://www.encyclopediaofarkansas.net/encyclopedia/entry-detail.aspx?entryID=4344.
42. Worster, *Dust* Bowl, 38.
43. Ta-Nehisi Coates, "The Case for Reparations," *Atlantic*, June 2014, https://www.theatlantic.com/magazine/archive/2014/06/the-case-for-reparations/361631/.
44. Anne Bonds and Joshua Inwood, "Beyond White Privilege: Geographies of White Supremacy and Settler Colonialism," *Progress in Human Geography* 40, no. 6 (2016): 715–733, 720.
45. Malcolm X, "Selected Speeches and Statements," in George Breitman, ed., *Malcolm X Speaks* (New York: Pathfinder Press, 1965), 69.
46. Fred Magdoff and Harold Van Es, "Erosion: A Short-Term Memory Problem?" *Building Soils for Better Crops*, 3rd ed. (Washington, DC: USDA, 2009), 154–155.
47. Sarah T. Phillips, "Lessons from the Dust Bowl: Dryland Agriculture and Soil Erosion in the United States and South Africa, 1900–1950," *Environmental History* 4, no. 2 (April 1999): 245–266, 256–257.
48. Lord, "Progress of Soil Conservation in the United States," 164.
49. Lord, "Progress of Soil Conservation in the United States," 164.
50. John Bellamy Foster and Robert W. McChesney, "A New New Deal under Obama?" *Monthly Review* 60, no. 9 (February 2009), https://monthlyreview.org/2009/02/01/a-new-new-deal-under-obama/.
51. Puakev, "How Franklin Roosevelt and the New Deal Were Pulled to the Left," *Daily Kos*, January 20, 2016, http://www.dailykos.com/story/2016/1/20/1464281/-How-Franklin-Roosevelt-and-the-New-Deal-Were-Pulled-to-the-Left; "The Second New Deal," BBC, http://www.bbc.co.uk/schools/gcsebitesize/history/mwh/usa/secondnewdealrev1.shtml; David Greenberg, "The Populism of the FDR Era," *Time*, June 24, 2009, http://content.time.com/time/specials/packages/article/0,28804,

1906802_1906838_1908686,00; Foster and McChesney, "A New New Deal under Obama?"

52. David Greenberg, "The Populism of the FDR Era."
53. Lord, "Progress of Soil Conservation in the United States," 162.
54. Benjamin I. Cook, Richard Seager, and Jason E. Smerdon, "The Worst North American Drought Year of the Last Millennium: 1934," *Geophysical Research Letters* 41, no. 20 (October 2014): 7298–7305, 7298, doi: 10.1002/2014GL061661, http://onlinelibrary.wiley.com/doi/10.1002/2014GL061661/abstract.
55. Cook, "The Worst North American Drought," 7298.
56. Cook, "The Worst North American Drought," 7298.
57. Cook, "The Worst North American Drought," 7299; Worster, *Dust Bowl*, 41–43.
58. Worster, *Dust Bowl*, 40.
59. Worster, *Dust Bowl*, 41–42.
60. Olaf F. Larsen, "Farm Population Mobility in the Southern Great Plains," *Social Forces* 18, no. 4 (May 1940): 514–520, doi: 10.2307/2570628; Donald Worster, *Nature's Economy: A History of Ecological Ideas*, 2nd ed. (New York: Cambridge University Press, 1994), 224.
61. Olaf F. Larsen, "Farm Population Mobility in the Southern Great Plains," 516–517.
62. Jon S. Blackman, *Oklahoma's Indian New Deal* (Norman: University of Oklahoma Press, 2013), 40–41, 146.
63. Meriam Report, Institute for Government Research, *The Problem of Indian Administration* (Baltimore: Johns Hopkins University Press, 1928), 3.
64. Meriam Report, *The Problem of Indian Administration*, 94.
65. Meriam Report, *The Problem of Indian Administration*, 5, 4.
66. Blackman, *Oklahoma's Indian New Deal*, 118–119.
67. Jim Bissett, *Agrarian Socialism in America: Marx, Jefferson, and Jesus in the Oklahoma Countryside, 1904–1920* (Norman: University of Oklahoma Press, 2002), xiii; Roxanne Dunbar-Ortiz and John Womack, Jr., "Dreams of Revolution: Oklahoma 1917," *Monthly Review* 62, no. 6 (November 2010), https://monthlyreview.org/2010/11/01/dreams-of-revolution-oklahoma-1917/; James Green, *Grass-Roots Socialism: Radical Movements in the Southwest, 1895–1943* (Baton Rouge: Louisiana State University Press, 1978).
68. Patrick E. McGinnis, *Oklahoma's Depression Radicals: Ira M. Finley and the Veterans of Industry of America* (New York: Peter Lang, 1991), 71–93; Bissett, *Agrarian Socialism in America*, 179, 182; Green, *Grass-Roots Socialism*, 53–86.

69. Franklin D. Roosevelt, "Address at Chicago, Ill., October 14, 1936," *American Presidency Project*, http://www.presidency.ucsb.edu/ws/?pid=15185.
70. Puakev, "How Franklin Roosevelt and the New Deal Were Pulled to the Left."
71. Juan F. Perea "The Echoes of Slavery: Recognizing the Racist Origins of the Agricultural and Domestic Worker Exclusion from the National Labor Relations Act," *Ohio State Law Journal* 72, no. 1 (2011): 96–138, 116.
72. Perea, "The Echoes of Slavery," 107.
73. Sitkoff cited in Perea, "The Echoes of Slavery," 108.
74. "More Than 80 Years Helping People Help the Land: A Brief History of NRCS," USDA Natural Resources Conservation Service, https://www.nrcs.usda.gov/wps/portal/nrcs/detail/national/about/history/?cid=nrcs143_021392.
75. Robert A. McLeman et al., "What We Learned from the Dust Bowl: Lessons in Science, Policy, and Adaptation," *Population and Environment* 35, no. 4 (2014): 417–440, 427, doi: 10.1007/s11111-013-0190-z.
76. Neil M. Maher, *Nature's New Deal: The Civilian Conservation Corps and the Roots of the American Environmental Movement* (New York: Oxford University Press, 2008), 124.
77. Maher, *Nature's New Deal*, 124.
78. Franklin D. Roosevelt, "Letter to All State Governors on a Uniform Soil Conservation Law," February 26, 1937, http://www.presidency.ucsb.edu/ws/?pid=15373.
79. Roosevelt, "Letter to All State Governors on a Uniform Soil Conservation Law."
80. Jess Gilbert, *Planning Democracy: Agrarian Intellectuals and the Intended New Deal* (New Haven, CT: Yale University Press, 2015).
81. Gilbert, *Planning Democracy*, 100.
82. Gilbert, *Planning Democracy*, 258. Antonio Gramsci was an Italian Communist, elected member of parliament, social theorist, and labor activist imprisoned by the Fascists when they took power in Italy in 1926. He introduced the concept of "organic intellectuals" to explain the diverse intellectual formations inherent to the development of distinct social groups. He writes, "Every social group, coming into existence on the original terrain of an essential function in the world of economic production, creates together with itself, organically, one or more strata of intellectuals which give it a homogeneity and an awareness of its own function not only in the economic but also in the social and political

fields." Antonio Gramsci, "The Intellectuals," Chapter 3 in Roger S. Gottlieb, ed., *An Anthology of Western Marxism* (Oxford: Oxford University Press, 1989), 112–119, 113. In other words, Gilbert here is referring to "home-grown" intellectuals emerging from agrarian regions and classes of the United States, as distinct from outsider or elite intellectuals whose ideas do not reflect local conditions or experiences, even if their ideas are privileged and imposed on local contexts and peoples.

83. Gilbert, *Planning Democracy*, 8; James C. Scott, *Seeing Like a State: How Certain Schemes to Improve the Human Condition Have Failed* (New Haven, CT: Yale University Press, 1998).
84. Gilbert, *Planning Democracy*, 241.
85. Gilbert, *Planning Democracy*, 258.
86. Gilbert, *Planning Democracy*, 258.
87. Worster, *Dust Bowl*, 28.
88. Worster, *Dust Bowl*, 28.
89. Gilbert, *Planning Democracy*, 258.
90. David Anderson, "Depression, Dust Bowl, Demography, and Drought: The Colonial State and Soil Conservation in East Africa during the 1930s," *African Affairs* 80, no. 332 (1984): 321–343, 339–340, https://www.jstor.org/stable/722351?seq=1#page_scan_tab_contents.
91. Anderson, "Depression, Dust Bowl, Demography, and Drought."
92. Worster, *Dust Bowl*, 229.
93. Quoted in R. Douglas Hurt, "The Dust Bowl: An Agricultural and Social History" (Chicago: Nelson-Hall, 1981), 140.
94. Matthew R. Sanderson and R. Scott Frey, "From Desert to Bread Basket . . . to Desert Again? A Metabolic Rift in the High Plains Aquifer," *Journal of Political Ecology* 21 (2014): 516–532.
95. Robert Mitchum, "Dust Bowl Would Devastate Today's Crops, Study Finds," *UChicago News*, December 19, 2016, https://news.uchicago.edu/article/2016/12/19/dust-bowl-would-devastate-todays-crops-study-finds; Michael Glotter and Joshua Elliott, "Simulating US Agriculture in a Modern Dust Bowl Drought," *Nature Plants* 3, article no. 16193 (2016).
96. Mitchum, "Dust Bowl Would Devastate Today's Crops."
97. Harry L. Henderson and David B. Woolner, eds., *FDR and the Environment* (New York: Palgrave Macmillan, 2005), acknowledgments.

Six. "We're Not Stakeholders"

Epigraph 1. Audre Lorde, *Sister Outsider* (New York: Ten Speed Press, 2007 [1984]), 123. The chapter from which this epigraph is taken was originally a paper delivered as part of a colloquium at Amherst College in Massachusetts in 1980.

Epigraph 2. Samir Amin, "Can Environmental Problems Be Subject to Economic Calculations?" *Monthly Review* 45, no. 7 (December 1993): 27.

1. The acting assistant secretary of the U.S. Bureau of Oceans and International Environmental and Scientific Affairs, Kenneth C. Brill, was referring to the Dust Bowl, which he explained this way: "Farmers moving onto the fragile Plains persisted in using agricultural methods that were inappropriate for the environment." Kenneth C. Brill, *The US Commitment to Combating Desertification*, U.S. Department of State Archive, Washington, DC, June 20, 2001, https://20012009.state.gov/g/oes/rls/rm/4005.htm.
2. James Ferguson, *Expectations of Modernity: Myths and Meanings of Urban Life on the Zambian Copperbelt* (Berkeley: University of California Press, 1999), 48.
3. John Bellamy Foster, "The Planetary Rift and the New Human Exemptionalism: A Political Economic Critique of Ecological Modernization Theory," *Organization and Environment* 25, no. 3 (2010): 211–237.
4. Ulrich Beck, "Climate for Change, or How to Create a Green Modernity?" *Theory, Culture and Society* 27, nos. 2–3 (2010): 254–266, 261; C. S. A. van Koppen, A. P. J. Mol, and J. P. M. Tatenhove, "Coping with Extreme Climate Events: Institutional Flocking," *Futures* 42, no. 7 (September 2010): 749–758, 750, https://doi.org/10.1016/j.futures.2010.04.024; Amory B. Lovins, L. Hunter Lovins, and Paul Hawken, "A Road Map for Natural Capitalism," *Harvard Business Review*, July–August 2007, https://hbr.org/2007/07/a-road-map-for-natural-capitalism; Paul Hawken, Amory Lovins, and L. Hunter Lovins, *Natural Capitalism: Creating the Next Industrial Revolution* (Boston: Little, Brown and Company, 1999).
5. Lovins, Lovins, and Hawken, "A Road Map for Natural Capitalism."
6. Arthur P. J. Mol and Martin Jänicke, "The Origins and Theoretical Foundations of Ecological Modernisation Theory," in *The Ecological Modernisation Reader*, ed. Arthur P. J. Mol, David A. Sonnenfield, and Gert Spaargaren (London: Routledge, 2009), 23. Arthur P. J. Mol and Gert Spaargaren, "Ecological Modernisation Theory in Debate: A Review," in *Ecological Modernisation around the World: Perspectives and Critical Debates*," ed. Arthur P. J. Mol and David A. Sonnenfield (New York: Routledge, 2000), 22.
7. Ulrich Beck, "Climate for Change, or How to Create a Green Modernity?" 261.

8. Arthur P. J. Mol, "The Environmental Movement in an Era of Ecological Modernisation," *Geoforum* 31, no. 1 (February 2000): 46–56, 48.
9. Mol, "The Environmental Movement," 48.
10. Fred Block, "The Future of Economics, New Circuits for Capital, and Re-Envisioning the Relation of State and Market," in *Markets on Trial: The Economic Sociology of the US Financial Crisis: Part B*, ed. Michael Lounsbury and Paul M. Hirsch (Somerville, MA: Emerald Group, 2010), 379–388, 384.
11. Edward Barbier, "Needed: A Global Green New Deal," *Forbes*, June 9, 2010, https://www.forbes.com/sites/davos/2010/06/09/needed-a-global-green-new-deal/#6c2ffc7e578c.
12. UN Department of Economic and Social Affairs, *A Global Green New Deal for Climate, Energy, and Development* (New York: United Nations, December 2009), https://sustainabledevelopment.un.org/content/documents/cc_global_green_new_deal.pdf.
13. Edward Barbier, "How Is the Global Green New Deal Going?" *Nature* 468, no. 8 (April 8, 2010): 832–833, 832, doi: 10.1038/464832a, https://www.nature.com/nature/journal/v464/n7290/full/464832a.html#a1.
14. UN Department of Economic and Social Affairs, *Global Green New Deal: An Update for the G20 Pittsburgh Summit* (New York: United Nations, September 2009), https://wedocs.unep.org/rest/bitstreams/11748/retrieve.
15. Barbier, "How Is the Global Green New Deal Going?" 832.
16. UN Environment Programme, *Rethinking the Economic Recovery: A Global Green New Deal*, report by Edward B. Barbier prepared for the Economics and Trade Branch, Division of Technology, Industry and Economics, April 2009, http://www.sustainable-innovations.org/GE/UNEP%20%5B2009%5D%20A%20global%20green%20new%20deal.pdf.
17. UN Department of Economic and Social Affairs, *A Global Green New Deal for Climate, Energy, and Development*, 10; Barbier, "How Is the Global Green New Deal Going?"
18. Barbier, "How Is the Global Green New Deal Going?" 832; Greenpeace Press Release, "G20 Outcome: Where's the Green?" April 2, 2009, http://www.greenpeace.org/international/en/press/releases/2009/g20-outcome-where-s-the-green/.
19. Timothy Luke, "A Green New Deal: Why Green, How New and What Is the Deal?" in *After Sustainable Cities? 2014*, ed. Mike Hodson and Simon Marvin (New York and London: Routledge, 2014), 32; Jomo Kwame Sundaram, "The UN and Global Economic Stagnation," *Inter Press Service News Agency*, July 7, 2016, http://www.ipsnews.net/2016/07/the-un-and-global-economic-stagnation/.

20. Gabriel Kolko, "The New Deal Illusion," *Counter Punch*, August 29, 2012, https://www.counterpunch.org/2012/08/29/the-new-deal-illusion/.
21. Don Fitz, "How Green Is the Green New Deal?" *Counter Punch*, July 11, 2014, https://www.counterpunch.org/2014/07/11/how-green-is-the-green-new-deal/; Greenpeace, "Tackling the Climate Crisis Will Help Resolve Financial Crisis," November 2008, http://www.greenpeace.org/international/Global/international/planet–2/report/2008/11/tackling-the-climate-crisis-wi.pdf; Mohamed Abdallah Youness, "How Climate Change Contributed to the Conflicts in the Middle East and North Africa," World Bank, December 12, 2015, http://blogs.worldbank.org/arabvoices/climate-change-conflict-mena; Caitlin E. Werrell, Francesco Femia, and Anne-Marie Slaughter, "The Arab Spring and Climate Change: A Climate and Security Correlations Series," Center for American Progress, posted February 28, 2013, https://www.americanprogress.org/issues/security/reports/2013/02/28/54579/the-arab-spring-and-climate-change/.
22. Anneleen Kenis and Matthias Lievens, *The Limits of the Green Economy: From Reinventing Capitalism to Repoliticising the Present* (New York: Routledge, 2015), 72–74.
23. Green Party of the United States, "The Green New Deal," 2015, http://gpus.org/organizing-tools/the-green-new-deal/.
24. Naomi Klein, "Labor Leaders' Cheap Deal with Trump," *New York Times*, February 7, 2017, https://www.nytimes.com/2017/02/07/opinion/labor-leaders-cheap-deal-with-trump.html?mcubz=0. From the article: " 'We must make the transition to a clean energy economy now in order to create millions of good jobs, rebuild the American middle class, and avert catastrophe,' George Gresham, president of 1199 S.E.I.U., the largest health care union in the nation, said in a statement two days after Mr. Trump's pipeline executive orders."

    George Gresham, "Largest Healthcare Union in the Nation, 1199SEIU, Calls for Clean Energy Jobs Instead of Dirty Fuel Pipelines," 1199SEIU United Healthcare Workers East, January 26, 2017, https://www.1199seiu.org/news/largest-healthcare-union-nation–1199seiu-calls-clean-energy-jobs-instead-dirty-fuel-pipelines.
25. Monica Frassoni, "Democracy and the Green New Deal: Opportunity in a Time of Populism," *Equal Times*, March 2, 2017, https://www.equaltimes.org/democracy-and-the-green-new-deal#.WVkoDzOZNBz.
26. Thomas Piketty, "A New Deal for Europe," *New York Review of Books*, February 25, 2016, http://www.nybooks.com/articles/2016/02/25/a-new-deal-for-europe/.

27. John Mulgrew, "Election 2017: Stormont 'Must Secure Solid Budget in Wake of Election to Ensure Economic Stability in Northern Ireland,' " *Belfast Telegraph*, February 21, 2017, http://www.belfasttelegraph.co.uk/business/news/election–2017-stormont-must-secure-solid-budget-in-wake-of-election-to-ensure-economic-stability-in-northern-ireland–35466833.html.
28. Frédéric Lemaître, "Aux Pays-Bas et en Autriche, les Verts ont su incarner l'opposition à l'extrême droite," *Le Monde*, March 16, 2017, http://www.lemonde.fr/international/article/2017/03/16/aux-pays-bas-comme-en-autriche-les-verts-ont-su-incarner-l-opposition-a-l-extreme-droite_5095554_3210.html; Anneleen Kenis and Matthias Lievens, *The Limits of the Green Economy*, 72–74.
29. Oscar Kimanuka, "Why Africa Should Champion the Crusade on Green Economy," *New Times*, January 30, 2015, http://www.newtimes.co.rw/section/article/2015–01–30/185451/.
30. "A National Plan for the UK: From Austerity to the Age of the Green New Deal," fifth anniversary report of the Green New Deal Group, http://www.greennewdealgroup.org/wp-content/uploads/2013/09/Green-New-Deal–5th-Anniversary.pdf; The Green New Deal Group, https://www.greennewdealgroup.org/?page_id=2. From "About the Group" on the website:

> As in past times of crises, disparate groups have come together to propose a new solution to an epochal challenge. The Green New Deal Group drew inspiration from the tone of President Roosevelt's comprehensive response to the Great Depression to propose a modernised version, a 'Green New Deal' designed to power a renewables revolution, create thousands of green-collar jobs and rein in the distorting power of the finance sector while making more low-cost capital available for pressing priorities.

Meeting since early 2007, the membership of the Green New Deal Group is drawn to reflect a wide range of expertise relating to the current financial, energy and environmental crises. The views and recommendations of the Green New Deal report, published in July 2008, are those of the group writing in their individual capacities.

The Green New Deal Group comprises, in alphabetical order: Larry Elliott, economics editor of the *Guardian;* Colin Hines, codirector of Finance for the Future, former head of Greenpeace International's Economics Unit; Tony Juniper, former director of Friends of the Earth;

Jeremy Leggett, founder and chairman of Solarcentury and SolarAid; Caroline Lucas, Green Party MEP; Richard Murphy, codirector of Finance for the Future and director, Tax Research LLP; Ann Pettifor, former head of the Jubilee 2000 debt relief campaign, campaign director of Operation Noah; Charles Secrett, advisor on sustainable development, former director of Friends of the Earth; and Andrew Simms, policy director, nef (the new economics foundation).

31. Rupert Read, "In the Corbyn Era, Greens Must Move from Socialism to Ecologism," *Ecologist*, May 10, 2016, http://www.theecologist.org/News/news_analysis/2987663/in_the_corbyn_era_greens_must_move_from_socialism_to_ecologism.html; "UK Needs a 'Green New Deal,' " Green Party, July 21, 2008, https://www.greenparty.org.uk/archive/news-archive/3493.html.
32. "UN Estimates 12.6 Million Deaths Each Year Attributable to Unhealthy Environments," *UN News Centre*, March 15, 2016, http://www.un.org/apps/news/story.asp?NewsID=53445#.WKoBxKIrIop.
33. "By the Numbers: World-Wide Deaths," National World War II Museum, http://www.nationalww2museum.org/learn/education/for-students/ww2-history/ww2-by-the-numbers/world-wide-deaths.html, accessed March 17, 2017.
34. Nisha Gaind, "Wildlife in Decline: Earth's Vertebrates Fall 58% in the Past Four Decades," *Nature*, October 28, 2016, http://www.nature.com/news/wildlife-in-decline-earth-s-vertebrates-fall–58-in-past-four-decades–1.20898.
35. "Working for the Few: Political Capture and Economic Inequality," Oxfam briefing paper, January 20, 2014, https://www.oxfam.org/sites/www.oxfam.org/files/file_attachments/bp-working-for-few-political-capture-economic-inequality–200114-en_3.pdf.
36. David Tilman, "The Greening of the Green Revolution," *Nature* 396 (November 19, 1998): 211–212, 211, doi: 10.1038/24254, https://www.nature.com/nature/journal/v396/n6708/full/396211a0.html#a1.
37. Carmelo Ruiz-Marrero, "The Life and Passion of Henry A. Wallace," *Counter Punch*, March 27, 2012, https://www.counterpunch.org/2012/03/27/the-life-and-passion-of-henry-a-wallace/.
38. Juan F. Perea, "The Echoes of Slavery: Recognizing the Racist Origins of the Agricultural and Domestic Worker Exclusion from the National Labor Relations Act," *Ohio State University Law Journal* 72 (2011): 195.
39. Ruiz-Marrero, "The Life and Passion of Henry A. Wallace."
40. Ruiz-Marrero, "The Life and Passion of Henry A. Wallace." Wallace hired Norman Borlaug to carry out corn, wheat, and rice seed hybridization

experiments in Mexico. As a result of this work, Borlaug won the 1970 Nobel Peace Prize for contributions to saving the lives of two billion people. Iowa State University Extension and Outreach, "The Borlaug Chain," January 5, 2012, https://blogs.extension.iastate.edu/seeyouthere/2012/01/05/the-borlaug-chain/.

41. Ruiz-Marrero, "The Life and Passion of Henry A. Wallace."
42. The short-stalk hybrid corn developed by Borlaug in Mexico requires far greater application of nitrogenous fertilizer and has greater water requirements, as well as making it more difficult and less effective to use the corn stubble as fertilizer and animal feed.
43. James C. Scott, *Seeing Like a State: How Certain Schemes to Improve the Human Condition Have Failed* (New Haven, CT: Yale University Press, 1998), 268.
44. Scott, *Seeing Like a State*, 268.
45. Richard Lewontin, "Agricultural Research and the Penetration of Capital," *Science for the People* 14, no. 1 (1982): 12–17, https://www.counterpunch.org/2012/03/27/the-life-and-passion-of-henry-a-wallace/.
46. Vandana Shiva, *Who Really Feeds the World? The Failures of Agribusiness and the Promise of Agroecology* (Berkeley, CA: North Atlantic Books, 2016), Kindle edition, 16.
47. Ruth Davis, "Why Greens Can Build the New Capitalism," *New Statesman*, February 9, 2012, http://www.newstatesman.com/blogs/the-staggers/2012/02/capitalism-market-communities.
48. Davis, "Why Greens Can Build the New Capitalism"; Henry Mintzberg, "Rescuing Capitalism from Itself," *Harvard Business Review*, December 3, 2015, https://hbr.org/2015/12/rescuing-capitalism-from-itself.
49. Michael Winship, "Naomi Klein: 'There Are No Non-radical Options Left Before Us': The Famed Author of 'This Changes Everything' Explains Why Markets Cannot Be Relied on to Solve Global Warming," *Salon*, February 4, 2016, http://www.salon.com/2016/02/04/naomi_klein_there_are_no_non_radical_options_left_before_us_partner/; Naomi Klein, "How Science Is Telling Us All to Revolt," *New Statesman*, October 29, 2013, http://www.newstatesman.com/2013/10/science-says-revolt.
50. "World Bank's 'Green Growth' Approach Denounced," *Bretton Woods Project*, July 3, 2012, http://www.brettonwoodsproject.org/2012/07/art–570790/; "Inclusive Green Growth: The Pathway to Sustainable Development," World Bank Group, 2012, https://openknowledge.worldbank.org/handle/10986/6058; "Inclusive Green Growth: The Pathway to Sustainable Development," World Bank Group, 2012, https://sustainabledevelopment.un.org/index.php?page=view&type=400&nr=69

0&menu=1515; United Nations Development Programme, *A Toolkit of Policy Options to Support Inclusive Green Growth*, http://www.undp.org/content/undp/en/home/librarypage/environment-energy/toolkit-inclusive-green-growth.html, revised July 1, 2013.

51. Paddy Ireland, "Corporations and Citizenship," *Monthly Review* 49, no. 1 (1997): 10–27, 26.
52. Nancy Welch, "La Langue de Coton: How Neoliberal Language Pulls the Wool over Faculty Governance," *Pedagogy* 11, no. 3 (Fall 2011): 545–553, 547–548. French scholar quoted on p. 547.
53. Welch, "La Langue de Coton," 547.
54. Edward Barbier, "A Global Green New Deal," report prepared for the Green Economy Initiative of UNEP," UN Environment Programme, 2009, https://sustainabledevelopment.un.org/index.php?page=view&type=400&nr=670&menu=1515.
55. "Partnerships for an Inclusive Green Economy Are Key to Achieve the SDGS and the 2030 Agenda," UN Environment Programme, May 25, 2016, https://www.unep.org/greeneconomy/news/partnerships-inclusive-green-economy-are-key-achieve-sdgs-and–2030-agenda.
56. "Partnerships for an Inclusive Green Economy are Key to Achieve the SDGS and the 2030 Agenda."
57. Nancy Welch, "La Langue de Coton," 547–548.
58. Welch, "La Langue de Coton," 548.
59. "Climate-Smart Agriculture: Managing Ecosystems for Sustainable Livelihoods," UN Food and Agriculture Organization, 1, http://www.fao.org/3/a-an177e.pdf.
60. "Climate-Smart Agriculture: Managing Ecosystems for Sustainable Livelihoods," 8, 5.
61. https://csa.guide/.
62. Miguel A. Altieri, Clara I. Nicholls, and Rene Motalba, "Technological Approaches to Sustainable Agriculture at a Crossroads," *Sustainability* 9, no. 3 (2017), doi: 10.3390/su9030349.
63. La Via Campesina, "UN-masking Climate Smart Agriculture," press release. September 23, 2014, https://viacampesina.org/en/un-masking-climate-smart-agriculture/; Teresa Anderson, "Why 'Climate Smart Agriculture' Isn't All It's Cracked Up to Be," *Guardian*, October 17, 2014, https://www.theguardian.com/global-development-professionals-network/2014/oct/17/climate-change-agriculture-bad-isnt-good.
64. "[T]he aspirations of citizens are barely heard behind the massive presence of lobbies in the European institutions, in a 'stakeholder' representation system organised in a completely legal way, in which the agri-industry

and industrialized agriculture are represented in an overwhelming and anti-democratic way": Geneviève Savigny, "The Agricultural Policy Must Serve the People," La Via Campesina, March 30, 2017, https://viacampesina.org/en/the-agricultural-policy-must-serve-the-people/; "The Guidelines on the Responsible Governance of Tenure at a Crossroads," La Via Campesina, December 11, 2015, https://viacampesina.org/en/index.php/main-issues-mainmenu–27/agrarian-reform-mainmenu–36/1933-the-guidelines-on-the-responsible-governance-of-tenure-at-a-crossroads; "Climate: Real Problem, False Solutions. No. 4: Climate-Smart Agriculture," La Via Campesina, December 3, 2015, https://viacampesina.org/en/index.php/actions-and-events-mainmenu–26/-climate-change-and-agrofuels-mainmenu–75/1920-climate-real-problem-false-solutions-no–4-climate-smart-agriculture.

65. Brian McKenna, "Great Lakes Not for Sale! Michigan's Odawa Indians Lead Anti-Nestle Fight," *Free Press*, April 22, 2006, http://freepress.org/article/great-lakes-sale-michigans-odawa-indians-lead-anti-nestle-fight.
66. Peter U. Clark et al., "Consequences of Twenty-First-Century Policy for Multi-millennial Climate and Sea-Level Change," *Nature Climate Change* 6 (February 2016): 360–369, doi: 10.1038/nclimate2923, http://www.nature.com/nclimate/journal/v6/n4/full/nclimate2923.html.
67. Clark et al., "Consequences of Twenty-First-Century Policy for Multi-millennial Climate and Sea-Level Change," 360.
68. Tom Bawden, "COP21: Paris Climate Deal 'Our Best Chance to Save the Planet,' Says Obama," *Independent*, December 12, 2015, http://www.independent.co.uk/environment/cop21-ministers-keep-the-world-waiting-for-ratification-of-historic-climate-change-target-a6770821.html; Richard Connor, "World Leaders Hail Paris Climate Pact," Deutsche Welle, December 13, 2015, http://www.dw.com/en/world-leaders-hail-paris-climate-pact/a–18914530; "COP21: Paris Conference Could Be Climate Turning Point, Says Obama," BBC, November 30, 2015, http://www.bbc.com/news/science-environment–34960051.
69. "Paris Agreement Marks 'Turning Point' in History," *Eco-Business*, December 13, 2015, http://www.eco-business.com/news/paris-agreement-marks-turning-point-in-history/; John Authers, "Climate Talks Mark Turning Point for Investors," *Financial Times*, December 16, 2015, https://www.ft.com/content/7f5cbcc4-a36d–11e5-bc70–7ff6d4fd203a; OECD, "Statement by the OECD Secretary-General Angel Gurría on COP21 Agreement," news release, December 12, 2015, http://www.oecd.org/greengrowth/statement-by-oecd-secretary-general-angel-gurria-on-cop21-agreement.htm.

70. Climate Action Network, "Civil Society Responds as Final Paris Climate Agreement Released," news release, December 12, 2015, http://www.climatenetwork.org/press-release/civil-society-responds-final-paris-climate-agreement-released.
71. Grantham Institute, "Nicholas Stern Responds to Publication of the Final Draft of the Paris Agreement on Climate Change," press release, December 12, 2015, http://www.lse.ac.uk/GranthamInstitute/news/nicholas-stern-responds-to-publication-of-the-final-draft-of-the-paris-agreement-on-climate-change/; United Nations, Framework Convention on Climate Change Conference of the Parties, Twenty-First Session, *Adoption of the Paris Agreement Proposal by the President, Draft Decision -/CP.21*, FCCC/CP/2015/L.9 (December 12, 2015), 2, https://unfccc.int/resource/docs/2015/cop21/eng/l09.pdf; Adam Vaughan, "Paris Climate Deal: Key Points at a Glance," *Guardian*, December 12, 2015, http://www.theguardian.com/environment/2015/dec/12/paris-climate-deal-key-points.
72. United Nations, *Report of the Conference of Parties on Its Twenty-First Session, Held in Paris from 30 November to 13 December 2015*, United Nations Framework Convention on Climate Change Report FCCC/CP/2015/10/Add.1, distributed January 29, 2016, http://unfccc.int/resource/docs/2015/cop21/eng/10a01.pdf. (See p. 2 and point 17 on p. 4.)
73. Seth Borenstein, "Clash of Dueling Climate Realities: Science and Politics," Associated Press, December 11, 2015, http://bigstory.ap.org/article/151e68af65e842f78c01c24488e1ebc8/clash-dueling-climate-realities-science-and-politics.
74. "The Road to a Paris Climate Deal," *New York Times*, December 11, 2015, http://www.nytimes.com/interactive/projects/cp/climate/2015-paris-climate-talks/scientists-see-catastrophe-in-latest-draft-of-climate-deal.
75. Kevin Anderson, "Talks in the City of Light Generate More Heat," *Nature* 528 (December 24–31, 2015): 437, http://www.nature.com/polopoly_fs/1.19074!/menu/main/topColumns/topLeftColumn/pdf/528437a.pdf.
76. "The Road to a Paris Climate Deal."
77. Bill Hare, "No Time to Lose: The 1.5°C Limit in the Paris Agreement," *Climate Analytics*, August 10, 2016, http://climateanalytics.org/blog/2016/the–1–5c-limit-in-the-paris-agreement-why-there-is-no-time-to-lose.html.
78. Simon Evans, "Only Three Years to Save 1.5C Climate Target, Says UNEP," Carbon Brief, March 11, 2016, https://www.carbonbrief.org/only-three-years-save–1–5c-climate-target-says-unep.

79. Nicholas Stern, "Poverty and Climate Change—the Two Great Challenges of Our Century," *La Stampa*, July 5, 2009, http://www.lastampa.it/2009/07/05/esteri/poverty-and-climate-change-the-two-great-challenges-of-our-century-Vh9kopC1xkGvUpyZHo2lpM/pagina.html; Vaughan, "Paris Climate Deal"; "Stern: Paris Opened Door on Climate Change," *Bloomberg* video, January 22, 2016, http://www.lse.ac.uk/GranthamInstitute/news/stern-paris-opened-door-on-climate-change/; Greenpeace International, "Kumi Naidoo of Greenpeace Responds to Paris Draft Deal," news release, December 12, 2015, http://www.greenpeace.org/international/en/press/releases/2015/kumi-naidoo-cop21-final-text-paris-climate/.
80. UN News, " 'Dramatic' Action Needed to Cut Emissions, Slow Rise in Global Temperature—UN Environment Report," November 3, 2016, http://www.un.org/apps/news/story.asp?NewsID=55464#.WeYqVxNSxBw.
81. Indigenous Environmental Network, "Carbon Offsets Cause Conflict and Colonialism," *IC Magazine*, May 18, 2016, https://intercontinentalcry.org/carbon-offsets-cause-conflict-colonialism/.
82. Indigenous Environmental Network, "Carbon Offsets Cause Conflict and Colonialism."
83. United Nations, *Report of the Conference of Parties on Its Twenty-First Session, Held in Paris from 30 November to 13 December 2015*.
84. It Takes Roots to Weather the Storm delegation to UNFCCC COP21, "We Are Mother Earth's Red Line: Frontline Communities Lead the Climate Justice Fight Beyond the Paris Agreement," 4, http://ggjalliance.org/sites/default/files/GGJ_COP21_final2_web.pdf.
85. Julia Calderone, "NASA Scientists Are Comparing Climate Change to the Dust Bowl," *Tech Insider*, October 20, 2015, http://www.techinsider.io/nasa-climate-change-dust-bowl-james-beard-conference–2015–10; Joseph Romm, "Desertification: The Next Dust Bowl," *Nature* 478 (October 2011): 450–451, doi: 10.1038/478450a.
86. Romm, "Desertification," 450–451.
87. Indigenous Environmental Network, "Carbon Offsets Cause Conflict and Colonialism."

Seven. No Empires, No Dust Bowls

Epigraph. #It Takes Roots delegation to UNFCCC COP 21, "We Are Mother Earth's Red Line: Frontline Communities Lead the Climate Justice Fight Beyond the Paris Agreement," 29, http://ggjalliance.org/sites/default/files/GGJ_COP21_final2_web.pdf. For more about this alliance of alliances, see the #ItTakesRoots to #GrowtheResistance website: http://ittakesroots.org/about/.

1. The goal of allotment, for example, was assimilation, as were the earlier goals of Christianization and other ideological justifications for colonialism and imperialism. See W. E. B. DuBois, *"The World and Africa" and "Color and Democracy,"* ed. Henry Louis Gates, Jr. (New York: Oxford University Press, 2007).
2. John Steinbeck, *The Grapes of Wrath* (New York: Penguin Books, [1939] 2014), 2.
3. "Working for the Few: Political Capture and Economic Inequality," OXFAM briefing paper, January 20, 2014, https://www.oxfam.org/sites/www.oxfam.org/files/file_attachments/bp-working-for-few-political-capture-economic-inequality–200114-en_3.pdf.
4. Joanna Chiu, "China Has an Irrational Fear of a 'Black Invasion' Bringing Drugs, Crime, and Interracial Marriage," *Quartz*, March 30, 2017, https://qz.com/945053/china-has-an-irrational-fear-of-a-black-invasion-bringing-drugs-crime-and-interracial-marriage/; Brook Larmer, "Is China the World's New Colonial Power?" *New York Times Magazine*, May 2, 2017, https://www.nytimes.com/2017/05/02/magazine/is-china-the-worlds-new-colonial-power.html.
5. Jonathan Watts and John Vidal, "Environmental Defenders Being Killed in Record Numbers Globally, New Research Reveals," *Guardian*, July 13, 2017, https://www.theguardian.com/environment/2017/jul/13/environmental-defenders-being-killed-in-record-numbers-globally-new-research-reveals.
6. Watts and Vidal, "Environmental Defenders Being Killed in Record Numbers Globally, New Research Reveals."
7. Max Weber, "A Letter from Indian Territory," *Free Inquiry in Creative Sociology* 16, no. 2 (November 1988): 133–243, 133.
8. Andrew Rice, "Is There Such a Thing as Agro-Imperialism?" *New York Times*, November 16, 2009, http://www.nytimes.com/2009/11/22/magazine/22land-t.html?mcubz=0.
9. Rice, "Is There Such a Thing as Agro-Imperialism?"
10. Rice, "Is There Such a Thing as Agro-Imperialism?"
11. Rice, "Is There Such a Thing as Agro-Imperialism?"
12. Javier Blas, "UN Warns of Food Neo-colonialism," *Financial Times*, August 19, 2008, https://www.ft.com/content/3d3ede92–6e02–11dd-b5df–0000779fd18c.
13. There have been a number of books written about the new land grabs: Fred Pearce, *The Land Grabbers: The New Fight over Who Owns the Earth*

(Boston: Beacon Press, 2012); Lorenzo Cotula, *The Great African Land Grab? Agricultural Investments and the Global Food System* (New York: Zed Books, 2013); Stefano Liberti, *Land Grabbing: Journeys in the New Colonialism* (New York: Verso, 2013); Alexander Reid Ross, ed., *Grabbing Back: Essays against the Global Land Grab* (Oakland, CA: AK Press, 2014).

14. "The Great Land Rush: Ethiopia: The Billionaire's Farm," Financial Times Investigations, March 1, 2016, https://ig.ft.com/sites/land-rush-investment/ethiopia/.
15. "The Great Land Rush."
16. Worldwatch Institute, "Land 'Grabbing' Grows as Agricultural Resources Dwindle," October 6, 2015, http://www.worldwatch.org/land-%E2%80%9Cgrabbing%E2%80%9D-grows-agricultural-resources-dwindle.
17. Worldwatch Institute, "Land 'Grabbing' Grows as Agricultural Resources Dwindle."
18. Edward Loure and Fred Nelson, "The Global Land Rights Struggle Is Intensifying," *Guardian*, April 27, 2016, https://www.theguardian.com/global-development-professionals-network/2016/apr/27/the-global-land-rights-struggle-is-intensifying.
19. Martin Mowforth, "Indigenous People and the Crisis over Land and Resources," *Guardian*, September 23, 2014, https://www.theguardian.com/global-development/2014/sep/23/indigenous-people-crisis-land-resources; Stephen Corry, "National Parks: America's Best Idea or Con Trick?" *Indian Country Today*, October 7, 2015, https://indiancountrymedianetwork.com/news/opinions/national-parks-americas-best-idea-or-con-trick/; John Vidal, "The Tribes Paying the Brutal Price of Conservation," *Guardian*, August 28, 2016, https://www.theguardian.com/global-development/2016/aug/28/exiles-human-cost-of-conservation-indigenous-peoples-eco-tourism.
20. Jeffrey Gettleman, "Loss of Fertile Land Fuels 'Looming Crisis' across Africa," *New York Times*, July 29, 2017, https://www.nytimes.com/2017/07/29/world/africa/africa-climate-change-kenya-land-disputes.html.
21. Gettleman, "Loss of Fertile Land Fuels 'Looming Crisis' across Africa."
22. Gettleman, "Loss of Fertile Land Fuels 'Looming Crisis' across Africa."
23. Gettleman, "Loss of Fertile Land Fuels 'Looming Crisis' across Africa."
24. Gettleman, "Loss of Fertile Land Fuels 'Looming Crisis' across Africa."
25. Naomi Schaefer Riley, "One Way to Help Native Americans: Property Rights," *Atlantic*, July 30, 2016, https://www.theatlantic.com/politics/archive/2016/07/native-americans-property-rights/492941/; Peter

d'Errico, "Come Over and Help Us: 'New Trail of Tears' Follows Old Script," *Indian Country Today*, August 5, 2016, https://indiancountrymedianetwork.com/news/opinions/come-over-and-help-us-new-trail-of-tears-follows-old-script/.

26. UN Food and Agriculture Organization, *First Meeting of the Global Soil Partnership Plenary Assembly*, GSPPA-I/13/Report (Rome, Italy, June 11–12, 2013), http://www.fao.org/3/a-mi009e.pdf; Global Soil Partnership, *Global Soil Partnership Background Paper*, prepared by the GSP Technical Working Group, http://www.fao.org/3/az889e; UN Food and Agriculture Organization, *World Soils Are under Threat*, by Luca Montanarella et al., Open Access *SOIL* 2, no. 1 (2016), doi: 10.5194/soil–2–79–2016, http://www.soil-journal.net/2/79/2016/soil–2–79–2016.pdf.
27. UN Food and Agriculture Organization, *World Soils Are under Threat*, 80.
28. UN Food and Agriculture Organization, *Status of the World's Soil Resources*, Technical Summary, VIII, http://www.fao.org/3/a-i5228e.pdf.
29. FAO, *World Soils Are under Threat*, 81.
30. FAO and ITPS, *Status of the World's Soil Resources*, Main Report (Rome: FAO and ITPS, 2015), 89.
31. FAO and ITPS, *Status of the World's Soil Resources*, Main Report, 91.
32. FAO and ITPS, *Status of the World's Soil Resources*, Main Report, 374.
33. FAO and ITPS, *Status of the World's Soil Resources*, Main Report, 94.
34. FAO and ITPS, *World Soils Are under Threat*, 81–82.
35. Graham Vernon Jacks and Robert Orr Whyte, *The Rape of the Earth: A World Survey of Soil Erosion* (London: Faber and Faber, 1939), 283.
36. FAO and ITPS, *Status of the World's Soil Resources*, Main Report, 600.
37. Naomi Klein, "Let Them Drown," *London Review of Books* 38, no. 11 (June 2016), https://www.lrb.co.uk/v38/n11/naomi-klein/let-them-drown.
38. Peter Dauvergne, *Environmentalism of the Rich* (Cambridge, MA: MIT Press, 2016); Joan Martinez-Alier, *The Environmentalism of the Poor: A Study of Ecological Conflicts and Valuation* (Cheltenham, UK: Edward Elgar Publishing, 2002); Rob Nixon, *Slow Violence and the Environmentalism of the Poor* (Cambridge, MA: Harvard University Press, 2013).
39. David Naguib Pellow, *Total Liberation: The Power and Promise of Animal Rights and the Radical Earth Movement* (Minneapolis: University of Minnesota Press, 2014).
40. "The State of Diversity in the Mainstream Environmental Sector," Green 2.0, http://www.diversegreen.org/the-challenge/.
41. Pam Wright, "UN Ocean Conference: Plastics Dumped in Oceans Could Outweigh Fish by 2050, Secretary-General Says," Weather Channel, June 6, 2017, https://weather.com/science/environment/news/

united-nations-ocean-conference-antonio-guterres-plastics; Sarah Kaplan, "By 2050, There Will Be More Plastic Than Fish in the World's Oceans, Study Says," *Washington Post*, January 20, 2016, https://www.washingtonpost.com/news/morning-mix/wp/2016/01/20/by–2050-there-will-be-more-plastic-than-fish-in-the-worlds-oceans-study-says/?utm_term=.43dceb5982fc.

42. Richard York and Brett Clark, "Marxism, Positivism, and Scientific Sociology: Social Gravity and Historicity," *Sociological Quarterly* 47, no. 3 (Summer 2006), https://www.jstor.org/stable/4120680?seq=1#page_scan_tab_contents.
43. Herbert Docena, "The Politics of Climate Change," *Global Dialogue* 7, no. 2 (June 2017), http://isa-global-dialogue.net/the-politics-of-climate-change/; "To Change the Heart and Soul: How Elites Contained the Climate Justice Movement," Transnational Institute, January 19, 2016, https://www.tni.org/en/publication/to-change-the-heart-and-soul.
44. Docena, "The Politics of Climate Change."
45. UN Food and Agriculture Organization, *World Soils Are under Threat*, 82.
46. Klein, "Let Them Drown."
47. Dr. Martin Luther King, Jr., "Beyond Vietnam—A Time to Break the Silence." address delivered to the Clergy and Laymen Concerned about Vietnam at Riverside Church, New York City, April 4, 1967; in *A Call to Conscience: The Landmark Speeches of Dr. Martin Luther King, Jr.*, http://kingencyclopedia.stanford.edu/encyclopedia/documentsentry/doc_beyond_vietnam/; Karl Marx, *The 18th Brumaire of Louis Bonaparte* (New York: International Publishers, 1987 [1852]), 15.

INDEX

Printed and bound by CPI Group (UK) Ltd, Croydon, CR0 4YY

16/04/2025

14658399-0001